Teaching Art in a Postmodern World

Teaching Art in a Postmodern World

Theories, Teacher Reflections and Interpretive Frameworks

Edited by
Lee Emery

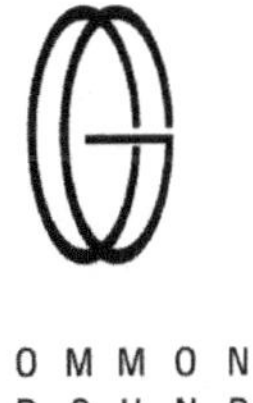

COMMON
GROUND

The editor would like to thank David Williams, Bill Hall, Malcolm Beasley, Anne Carins, Mark Fenech, Michelle Tinta, Nick Wright, Graham Nash, Colin Simpson, Catherine Middleton, Sue Hall, Ross Waterman, and Janis Dunkley for their contributions. Also, many thanks to Autumn Daly-Holt, Catherine Wilson, David Halliday, Felicity Bath, Simon Manley, Michael Salipas, and Scott Gregory for the use of their artworks.

This book is published at theLearner.com
a series imprint of theUniversityPress.com

First published in Australia in 2002
by Common Ground Publishing Pty Ltd
PO Box 463
Altona VIC 3018
ABN 66 074 822 629
www.theLearner.com

National Library of Australia Cataloguing-in-Publication data:

Emery, Lee.
Teaching art in a postmodern world : theories, teacher reflections and interpretive frameworks.

ISBN 1 86335 501 4.

ISBN 1 86335 502 2 (PDF).

1. Art – Study and teaching. I. Title.

707

Cover designed by Diana Kalantzis.
Cover image, 'C.O.D.Y—Come on Die Young', by Sean Layh, Year 12, Billanook College, Melbourne.
Typeset in Australia by Common Ground Publishing.
Printed in Australia by Mercury Printeam on 80gsm White Bond.

Contents

Chapter 1

Teaching Art in a Postmodern World

Theories, Teacher Reflections and Interpretive Frameworks

The postmodern revolution

> (In) the mid-1960s a deep revolution in the history of art took place—so deep, in fact, that it would not have been an exaggeration to say that art, as it had been historically understood, came to an end in that tumultuous decade (Danto, 1990, p.6).

The revolution that Danto describes is also happening quietly in art classrooms within the western world. This book examines the teaching of art in schools at a crucial time of global change. It is hard to know how large global change impacts on life in classrooms, but the microcosm of a classroom is surely affected by the macrocosm of the wider world. Life in the art classroom is attuned to world events and to changes that determine the way students think and live. When students make art, they express values that are implicit in their daily rituals and in the dreams to which they aspire. This publication focuses on a transition time in art education practices in the western world. It centres on the teaching of art in the dawn of postmodernism. The purpose of the book is to examine what this implies in theory, from the perspective of art teachers and in terms of the strategies used to teach art in a postmodern world.

The book is divided into three distinct sections. The first section examines the basic theoretical underpinnings of modernist and postmodernist approaches to art and art education in the first years of the millennium. The second section presents autobiographical accounts by twelve secondary art teachers from England and Australia. These teachers reflect on change, the postmodern world and its impact on attitudes to culture, gender, class and art making in the classroom. The third and final section of the book sets out interpretive frameworks for responding to art in a postmodern world.

There has been a revolution in the history of art and it is not over yet. Modernism has been called to account by a new breed of writers and artists who have dared to challenge the rules of the game. Postmodernists have no quarrel with modernist art itself, but they do challenge the ground rules which define how the game of art is played out in society. Disciplines as diverse as architecture, literature, science and history, as well as the visual arts, have felt the impact of postmodern thought since the 1960s. It would be logical then to presume that teachers of art in schools would have been hotly contesting and debating the arguments put forward by postmodern artists and theorists. After all, postmodernists seem to challenge many of the practices which art educators have seen as fundamental to the teaching of the subject 'art' in schools. However, there have been no wild demonstrations, few wildly contested debates and no radical revolutions. Modernist principles still prevail in most art programs and these have not been challenged to the extent that modernist principles in the wider art world have been challenged. Forty years since the first rumblings of postmodernism appeared in the wider art world art educators are just beginning to feel the impact. While there has been no rupture in school art rooms it seems that postmodern elements are creating ripples which are changing the way art educators carry out their teaching. In my own view these new elements have the potential to change the nature of art teaching significantly in the first decade of the new millennium.

There is a world of difference between the 1905 Fauvist paintings of Matisse and Vlaminck, and the contemporary (and postmodern) works of Damien Hirst, Sarah Lucas and the Chapman Brothers. While the Fauvist works did seem shocking at the time they have gradually been assimilated into the western sensibility and are commonly used for study in art classrooms. In fact the various and diverse styles of modernism are seen as epitomising the sort of free expression and individualism that art teachers wish to develop in their students. However, the postmodern works of Damien Hirst et al are not yet (if in fact they ever will be) viewed as models for student emulation. They still seem shocking and art teachers find it hard to bring such difficult work into the curriculum. These works seem antithetical to all that art education has been about. They challenge notions of creativity, self-expression and individualism and they show blatant disregard for aesthetic considerations which art teachers have seen as defining art itself. While these examples of modernist and postmodernist art may be extremely polarised, they serve to convey the essence of the changes that art teachers are facing as they teach art in a postmodern world.

Postmodern pluralism or curriculum conformity?

Within the last fifteen years the two key influences on the teaching of art seem strangely dichotomous. On the one hand the introduction of outcomes-based curriculum documents and prescribed national and state level curricula have had a significant effect on the way teachers plan, teach and assess art. Nearly all schools in the western world have come under the influence of curriculum initiatives which have made schooling a more accountable process. Art teachers are now very familiar with the need to align their teaching with the broadly stated outcomes prescribed by state or national level curriculum guidelines. While many have tried to resist the imposition of such curriculum initiatives most have had to ultimately comply. However, while complying with curriculum outcomes has become a necessary part of employment practice in the teaching service, most art teachers have ingeniously managed to develop imaginative art programs within the broad curriculum framework. Exciting art programs clearly can and do emerge from a bit of tweaking at the edges of seemingly prescriptive guidelines.

The second influence impacting on the teaching of art has been postmodernism. Postmodern theorists and artists have challenged the fundamentally western patriarchal and elitist tenets of modernism and called into question many of the practices which had become common in art classrooms. On paper this implies that art classrooms should embrace more pluralist practices especially related to cultural, social and gender issues. However while postmodern art practices embrace diversity, curriculum guidelines appear to demand conformity. This is a difficult contradiction for art teachers who on the one hand wish to encourage students to work in diverse ways yet on the other hand have to encourage students to satisfy prescribed learning outcomes (or attainment targets). Plurality and conformity are really binary opposites and it is difficult to see how art teaching can resolve two seemingly different thrusts.

The answer to this dilemma probably resides in the recognition that the postmodern world incorporates both modernist and postmodernist ways of working. For teachers the curriculum is a modernist paradigm. It is a meta-narrative or grand story which describes the nature of learning. And while postmodernists refute and mistrust metanarratives as being reductionist and based on hypothetical norms that do not really exist, it really is impossible to live in contemporary society without them. Societies do live by creeds, belief systems and mission statements and as long as postmodern sceptics continually challenge the limiting nature of metanarratives, many find it easier to live within some guidelines that to live without them.

Modernist and postmodernist art teaching

Fehr suggests that the three most significant differences between modernist and postmodern art education are:

> ...the willingness of the latter to embrace, with comparative comfort, multiple, even contradictory, meanings simultaneously; to accept the tension of perpetual uncertainty as given; and to define truth as specific to time and place (Fehr, 1997, p. 27)

These new attitudes involve a gradual shift away from art education practices based on the fundamental tenets of modernism. Art education programs once based on the basic principles and ideals of the 'western canon' are gradually assuming a more pluralist and diverse nature. In classrooms where once art history was taught in a chronological fashion, starting with the ancient world and gradually moving through movements and styles in western art, critical studies are now taught in diverse ways. In classrooms where copying was once forbidden and seen as antithetical to ideals of creativity and originality, students are now appropriating images from a whole range of sources. In classrooms where all students might have been asked to paint a self-portrait, some students are engaged in designing calligraphic forms because their religion does not permit them to represent figures. In classrooms where once the teacher might have discussed colour theory based on western Bauhaus principles, the teacher now also alludes to traditional notions of colour displayed in Chinese art. Art educators are teaching in a time of change and most seem to have adapted to these changes by gradually introducing more diverse activities, more diverse teaching methodologies and more diverse ways of defining art itself.

As already suggested the term postmodernism signals that there has been a break with modernism; a rupture in the line of art progress. Some refer to this break as the postmodern moment, the moment when we began to rethink modernism. Such rethinking generally involves distancing oneself from something in order to see it for what it really is, or to see it as others might see it. Of course, rethinking in art is not new and the seeds of new thinking have often been sewn by mudslingers using derogatory labels:

> Thus 'Baroque' and 'Rococo' were, before they became descriptive categories, derogatory labels, meant to stop the 'illogical', and excessively decorated forms to which they originally referred ('Baroque' meant a 'misshapen pearl', 'Rococo' meant 'shell like'). 'Impressionism' was thought deficient because it gave only hazy, subjective impressions; 'Romanesque' meant sub-Roman (most 'esque' forms implied degeneracy); 'Gothic' meant 'not yet classic' and also created by the barbarian Goths who sacked Rome, and 'Mannerism' meant overtly mannered. Ironically, these negative epithets did not always work as intended. Indeed reworking the old adage, we might say that 'some paranoid critics create real enemy movements'—fears continuously voiced often establish the very movements they seek to quash (Jencks, 1987, p.13).

However while these labels were initially derogatory the term postmodernism is not really intended to be derogatory. It signals a split with modernism rather than a rejection of it. It also signals the end of the line or the end of historicity as we knew it. While postmodernists call for a rethinking of modernism they still applaud the liberating and extraordinary contributions to art and invention made during the modernist era. As glorious as modernism was though, it had run its course, and for many reasons, which will be explored in following chapters, it was time for a rethink.

The modernist art class

At this point it may be useful to revisit a modernist art room in a hypothetical Australian or English school prior to 1980. At this time computers were unknown in art rooms and students were encouraged to make original and innovative artworks. Common subject matter in secondary art classes involved still life painting, landscape and figurative work. Students were encouraged to be original and to avoid use of derivative styles, although students who worked in the style of Picasso, Matisse, Bacon, Johns, Sutherland or Whitely were rewarded for their understanding of abstraction. Self-expression was encouraged in art classes as long as it avoided popular culture and derivative imagery from other artists. Migrant students were quickly discouraged from using 'stereotypical' cultural elements which seemed at odds with western-style abstraction and 'freedom'. Students were dissuaded from copying or resorting to the media for ideas or styles in art. Kitsch was the enemy of art educators at the time and students who introduced comic-style imagery in their work did so at their own peril. Art teachers drew inspiration from artistic movements such as the impressionists, post–impressionists, cubists, surrealists and abstract expressionists and artists from these movements served as models for students engaging in their own self-expression. The content, styles, processes and life stories of Avant garde modernist artists provided a basis for art programs which led students to be autonomous and individualistic art makers.

In many ways art education was symbiotically aligned with the ideals of modernism. The terms 'creativity', 'originality' and 'self-expression' were closely identified with art room practice and modernist ideals. In the forty year period from WW2 to the 1980s key art education theorists such as Eliott Eisner (1972) in the USA and Robert Witkin (1974) in the UK espoused the significance of art as self-expression and later as cognition. The ideals of art education as self-expression and as embodying creative thought and action aligned so well with the ideals of democracy and freedom. These were uplifting goals and they seemed to offer every child the opportunity to create for him or herself an identity and a release from stifling regimentation. However for students who came from non-western cultures the curriculum served only to marginalise and even denigrate. Theorists and educators at the time failed to realise or acknowledge that the ideals of self-expression, creativity and 'art for art's sake' can, from non-western viewpoints, be seen as elitist, selfish and alienating. Modernism at the time, was assumed to incorporate a universal aesthetic which supposedly crossed cultural barriers.

What is a postmodernist art classroom?

While some theorists see postmodernism as an opportunity to address the elitist and alienating elements of modernist, others see postmodernism as a threat to long-held standards in the arts and education. For theorists such as Ralph Smith postmodernism implies a loss of 'excellence' as a goal in art education. Steeped in the modernist tradition Smith fears that the move to more pluralistic and multicultural practices in art education will bring about irrevocable change in art education. Smith (1992) argues that art teaching standards will be eroded by the inclusion of socially and culturally diverse art curricula:

> Marxism, feminism, and multiculturalism would seem to be fueled largely by political agenda. It is quite clear that a politicized art education will be an art education that differs sharply from the ways it has been conceived since mid-century (Smith, 1992, p. 257).

Smith's fears represent conservative elements in art education which see postmodernism as a threat to the stability and domination of western modernist art curricula. While Smith engages in a form of persuasive politics to argue for the preservation of white middle-class values in art classes, he does not welcome political discussion concerning issues of marginalisation and the notion of critical pedagogy in art classrooms. While some art teachers uphold Smith's views many also acknowledge that art educators cannot hold back the tide. Art education practices may not be able to remain apart from the rest of the world. Furthermore, many art teachers know that their programs are more exciting and relevant when they are culturally and socially diverse. Students in my view like to be challenged and it seems wrong to assume that standards will be eroded by less conservative approaches. In contemporary art practice, politics and art are inseparable. The new curricula will be political and art classes cannot retreat from the reality of political thought related to issues of class, gender and culture.

Howard Gardner has also expressed his fears about education and postmodernism in his 1999 book 'The Disciplined Mind':

> Whatever merits postmodern perspectives may have for the mature student or scholar, I think that they will stir up nothing but trouble for all but the most subtle-minded precollegiate students. As I see it, there may be validity in challenging easy assumptions about truth or beauty or goodness—once these have been consolidated; but to try to undermine the very endeavor to move toward truth (or beauty or goodness) before it has had a chance to take hold seems to me unfair, even deeply disturbing, to the growing mind (Gardner, 1999, p.56).

Gardner acknowledges that he is a traditionalist when it comes to the education of children and his suggestion that postmodernism will cause 'nothing but trouble' if applied to schooling seems to confirm this. However, in my own view the traditional values of 'truth, beauty and goodness' do need to be constantly contested by people of all ages, even young children. If the definitions of these values serve to privilege some while marginalising others, then art educators need to re-think the boundaries which they create. Multicultural schools may be full of students whose futures may not be privileged by certain concepts of 'truth, beauty and goodness' and even Gardner would have to admit that his notion of these three 'virtues' may not match that of an Aboriginal or Muslim student in year 9. Students can experience racism and marginalisation because western stereotypical views are perpetuated through school programs. Truth, beauty and goodness are contestable 'sites for struggle' and students need to be aware of this from an early age. Many people, especially those who have been privileged by modernist theory, do fear postmodernism because it does cause discomfort. However a responsible art teacher cannot avoid 'trouble' in the art program. If art teachers don't challenge definitions of truth, beauty and goodness they run the risk of developing students who are racist and homophobic. While Gardner does want students to understand the horror of the holocaust he must also be aware that elitist western ideologies are a great source of aggravation to some other cultures. One of the tenets of postmodern thought is that westerners must look over their shoulders to understand the sort of hegemonic structures that can lead to the evil abuse of power. My concern about Gardner's view is that he does not see that teachers need to constantly re-examine every aspect of schooling to ensure that western education does not become isolated from the needs and realities of the global village.

Of course, Smith and Gardner may be quite right to question the radical onslaught of postmodern thought in art education. Postmodernism holds no answers to the difficult issues which face teachers in the contemporary world. Postmodernism itself seems to defy definition, it offers no clear direction for anything, let alone education, and it seems to lack any central theory of significance. Its critics dismiss it as yet another movement or as being all hype and theoretical hocus-pocus with no substance in the 'real' world of education, art or anything else. Critics look at the diversity of postmodern art and see a huge range of incoherent and conflicting practices. What is more, postmodern art often seems 'anti-aesthetic'. It is sometimes shockingly confronting but at other times sweetly reminiscent of past practices or even crassly derivative of popular art styles. It is hard to know what postmodern art is about, if indeed it is important to know. With so much unseemly art being produced it is easy to shut the art room door and simply retreat to formalist concerns about colour, line and shape. But will this keep the wolves at bay? How do art teachers open the door to complex issues and still maintain a sense of conviction about the significance of art in the curriculum?

Plurality, shock and censorship in postmodern art rooms

The highly controversial, deliberately shocking and confronting nature of much contemporary art does present art teachers with new and complex decisions for curriculum planning. Contemporary artists defiantly challenge the stance taken by the modernist to key issues such as individuality, race, gender, culture, popular art and history. These issues, largely unexplored by the modernists, have become key issues in the diverse postmodern art world. Writing for the new Tate Modern gallery in London Louise Buck suggests that:

> It is true to say that the most distinctive feature of the artists who are defining British art in the 1990s is the fact that they do not share a common style or medium. They produce figurative and abstract paintings, readymade and handmade sculptures, photography and text, videos, installations and CD ROMs—sometimes simultaneously… What… artists… do share is the desire to use whatever means are at their disposal—paints, celluloid, ballistics, needlework or forensic science—to make work that speaks of what it is to be human and to live in this world (Buck, 2000, p.8).

The loss of 'centre' in the art world provides many complexities for art educators teaching students about contemporary art. There are so many directions, so many artists and so few neat categories for simple study. The issues facing art teachers are complex in this pluralistic and fragmented world and art teachers do not necessarily want their students to emulate the practices of some contemporary artists, however the fundamental issues which concern artists today are the substance of contemporary art.

Art teachers do find it hard to explain why contemporary artists deliberately set out to shock and disgust, and yet students cannot really grasp contemporary art unless they consider some of the issues that trigger artists to work with shock as an artistic device. Politics, religion, gender, culture, oppression and environmental destruction are critical concerns of many contemporary artists and artworks often present these issues in brutally honest and disturbing ways. Of course art of the past has also frequently been disturbing and challenging. However there is a new immediacy and audacity about postmodern art which makes work by Bosch, Breughel and Goya seem acceptable and even tame. The atrocities, banalities and genetic mishaps displayed in the work of Jake and Dinos Chapman, Sarah Lucas and Tracey Emin are confronting for most adults, let alone adolescents. Postmodernism does present art teachers with new challenge. It does take art teaching to new dimensions outside the boundaries of art history, art criticism, aesthetics and art practice. It looks sideways at the links between art and other areas of knowledge. However Smith and Gardner are still right to forewarn that art education is a practice which may need to be removed in some way from some aspects of art in the wider politicised world. The dilemma for art teachers is to find a satisfactory way of fusing modernist and postmodern politics within their art classes.

The co-existence of modernist and postmodernist approaches in art classrooms

In acknowledging that modernism and postmodernism co-exist in art classrooms this book takes quite a different stance to that advocated by more radical education postmodernists such as Giroux & McLaren (1995, p.32), Stuart Parker (1997, p.145) and Carr & Kemmis (1986). All of these theorists advocate the rejection of rationality in favour of a critical pedagogy which urges teachers to become hard-hitting political activists. Arguing that oppressive curricula and bureaucratic structures simply reproduce the values and privileges of existing elites, radical postmodern educators press for teaching practices which would simply be impossible for most art teachers to implement. Using the sort of emotive language (which they actually criticise rational bureaucrats for using) they suggest that teachers must work to subvert the education system. Stuart Parker even implies that teachers are duped by realist, technical-rationalist language and thus are compelled to comply with oppressive systems which manipulate them:

> Many teachers are like Catholics whose apotheosis of the biblical text compels them to swallow a man-made dogma under a naturalistic disguise. Given a realist, technical-rationalist basis for their traditionally humanitarian, liberal view, teachers are vulnerable to a rhetoric which preserves and employs that rational base while utilizing it to contort and subvert teachers' value commitments (Parker, 1997, p.146).

In suggesting that teachers are subject to oppressive forms of coercion Parker over generalises the situation in my view. It is true that many art teachers find the introduction of national and state level curricula imposing. However, it is also true that many art teachers respect working to broadly based learning outcomes. What art teachers seem to have found out is that they can work within broad guidelines and still develop their own unique teaching programs. Art teachers, it seems, may not be proactive at the wide political level, but within their own schools they can turn the system to suit themselves. Art teachers who do feel overly oppressed by the bureaucracy are possibly those that cannot for various reasons work creatively within limitations, and some teachers have already left the system because of this. However, those that work effectively within given school constraints are those who see imaginative potential in the cracks of the system. Such teachers do find ways to teach critical pedagogy even in the strictest confines of a conservative institution. The solution is not to get rid of the curriculum as Parker suggests (p.151) but to develop curricula that allow for plurality and which facilitate deconstruction of dominant discourses.

In my own view, postmodernism offers art educators a new opportunity to rethink the role of art education in a new millennium. It offers opportunity to ask many questions about the way students engage in and experience visual culture in a changing world. Postmodern visual artists provide diverse directions for art educators as they explore new technologies, challenge boundaries between areas of knowledge, explore issues of culture and identity, and question the construction of gender and power. When art teachers address these issues in the art program they clearly move art from the confines of the remote studio into a wider more socially and culturally aware world. Modernism still frames much of the way art teachers structure art programs however postmodernism seems to be impacting on the way students view the art world and the construction of art values. I do not wish to imply in this publication that postmodernism, as the newer body of art theory, will replace modernism in art rooms. Rather it is understood that they are both present in most art teaching programs. As Hassan (1996 p. 390) says, 'Modernism does not suddenly cease so that Postmodernism may begin: they both *co-exist'*.

Consideration of art education in terms of modern and postmodern practice has been apparent in many recent art education publications but within schools art teachers do not seem to use the terms modernism and postmodernism to describe their teaching. In gathering together a set of chapters authored by British art lecturers on recent changes in art education Richard Hickman (2000) notes:

> The authors argue that art education today must contend with new intellectual developments in philosophy, the social sciences, education and the visual arts. These developments, widely heralded as the change from a 'modern' to 'postmodern' sensibility, reflect a widespread rejection of a system of intellectual presuppositions and prejudices inherited from the eighteenth-century Enlightenment (p. xiii).

While Hickman acknowledges the change from 'modernism' to 'postmodernism' in art education he does not suggest that art teachers would use this language to define changes in their practice. However as art teachers do try to develop more inclusive art programs they are moving away from Enlightenment 'presuppositions and prejudices' even though it is not conceived in this way. Art teachers today do reject many art education practices that were common twenty years ago even though they may not directly attribute these changes to postmodern theory. When, for example, art teachers explain that they never teach art appreciation these days from a chronological perspective, favouring instead more eclectic and pluralistic approaches, their practice does however, begin to take on a more 'postmodern' approach. In other words the language used by art teachers is linked to the realities of school organisation whereas the language used by theoreticians is linked to the more esoteric world of academia.

One thing that seems clear is that no two people define postmodernism in the same way. Depending on a host of factors, including which writers and artists have been studied, individuals construct different definitions of postmodernism. This book then presents stories of difference. It begins with my own reflections on the theoretical issues that emanate from the two fields of modernist and postmodernist theory. However, as a lecturer in art education rather than a teacher of art in a secondary school my own views may bear little resemblance to the following views of the thirteen art teachers. There has always been a schism between theory and practice in art education and this book may serve to highlight that difference. While my discussion is intended to set a context for the issues discussed by the teachers, the introductory chapters are not intended to set a precise frame for the ensuing accounts. The teachers' accounts are presented as spoken in teacher-talk whereas the introductory chapters are written. This makes for some difference in style within the sections of the book. However the thing that links us all is our profession. We are all art educators responsible for teaching the subject art to secondary students, or in my case, teaching art education method to tertiary students in teacher preparation courses. As such we are all immersed in a period of change which sees the introduction of postmodern practices impacting on our 'tried and true' modernist programs.

Section one of this book outlines nine orientations which form the crux, as I see it, of change in contemporary art education. On any one of these orientations art teachers can adopt either a modern or postmodern stance (or both). Chapter two sets out nine key orientations which characterise modernist art and art education. These characteristics have formed the basis of much art teaching in art classrooms between World War Two and the 1980s as art teachers focussed on the teaching of art as a vehicle for self-expression inspired by the Avant garde artists of the modernist era. Chapter three sets out the same nine orientations from a postmodern perspective. These orientations reveal key differences between modernist and postmodern theory with the purpose of highlighting the wider social and cultural possibilities of teaching art in a postmodern world.

The second section of the book presents the views of thirteen secondary art teachers as they discuss changes in their teaching practice. The focus in this study is upon secondary schooling because it is in the adolescent years that teachers involve students in more critical discussion about contemporary art. However, the issues are also relevant for primary art teachers and it is considered that the introduction of students to a socially and culturally diverse art program can begin very early in a child's art education. This study draws together the views of teachers who are concerned with artistic development in the secondary school through the general curriculum up to ages of 14 and 15 and then through the senior syllabus in the final two years of schooling. Nine art teachers have been selected from three eastern States in Australia and four teachers have been selected from the south of England. Each of these teachers is responsible for the teaching of the subject 'art' at the senior secondary level and is thus involved with introducing students to both past and contemporary visual art practices. The autobiographical accounts are the direct transcripts of one hour interviews generally held in the classroom (or in one case, the home) of the teacher. The interviews have only been slightly edited for length. In general, the teachers were recommended by other art teachers, as being art teachers with an interest in contemporary issues in art education.

The final section of this book outlines key interpretive frameworks that may be used by students when interpreting artworks. The frameworks suggest that there are many ways in which to view art. Each one is based on one of the main theoretical orientations outlined in chapters two and three. The formalist framework is well known and commonly used in art classrooms, however the remaining six frameworks encourage students to examine artworks from wider social and cultural positions and adopt a deconstructionist stance to interpretation.

The Interpretive Frameworks offer students key strategies for looking beneath the formalist qualities of artworks to reveal layers of meaning.

Section 1

Modernist and Postmodernist Theories

A summary of key differences between modernist and postmodernist art and art education

Chapter 2

Modernism and Art Education

Defining modernist art, as all art teachers know, is difficult. It was (or is) not a single movement but rather a collection of successive movements and styles. Most theorists (e.g., Foucault, 1970) suggest that modernist thought started in the 18th century with the Enlightenment. However, the height of modernism was reached in the late nineteenth century as artists, led by the Avant garde, explored new approaches to art production. The succession of styles, including the realists, impressionists, post-impressionists, cubists, expressionists, minimalists, surrealists, etc., are key movements which embodied the modernist drive for free expression and liberation from orthodoxy in art. And while some movements such as the dada and pop artists (especially Warhol) challenged the notion of originality in art, the general thrust of progressive individualism continued. Progressive individualism then can be seen to be the key characteristic of modernist thinking.

Prior to WW2 art teaching in schools adopted a mimetic approach to art production. Students drew from plaster models or from given drawings and they may have made specific craft objects in wood or textiles. However since WW2 art teaching has aligned with the basic tenets of modernism. In art education Viktor Lowenfeld (1950), Herbert Read (1943), Robert Witkin (1974) and many others have presented theories which espouse self-expression, the development of sensate intelligence and individual autonomy as goals for art education programs. In the wider world of art, theorists and critics such as Clement Greenberg (1961) espoused the notion that recognition of art required understanding of the aesthetic principles fundamental to all art

Although schools in the western world have generally followed modernist principles there have still been many changes within that scenario. At various times art education has focussed on the following; the exploration of materials, design and problem solving approaches, the exploration of new techniques, the development of installation and environmental work and related arts experiences. However in my own view these approaches to art teaching have been closely aligned with each other and are in general sympathy with a modernist paradigm. In my own mind I envisage that the two forces of postmodernism and technology will bring about greater changes to art teaching than any other movement or theoretical stance advocated in the last fifty years. For this reason I have set out a dual set of orientations which outline the key characteristics of modernist and postmodernist art education. While this presupposes that postmodernism does herald some breaks with past practices in art education it also implies that both modernism and postmodernism will probably play dual roles in art classrooms for some time. If any significant break with modernism occurs it is technology, in my view, that will facilitate the break to occur. At this point in time I do not have a clear picture of the art class of 2020 but I envisage a global classroom in which students interact in culturally and socially diverse ways within a predominantly visually world. This alone would describe a postmodern rather than modern approach to art teaching.

Some say that it is not possible to understand postmodern theory until modernist theory is understood. In other words, if one knows nothing about modernism it would be difficult to conceive of postmodernism, as it is clearly a reaction to the fundamental premises of modernism. It certainly seems true that we cannot react to something until we have experienced it. For this reason it is appropriate that I set out my own views of modernism even though I think that there have been changes in teaching within this modernist paradigm. Modernist art education never was a static approach. Many changes will always occur in modernist classrooms due to the fact that modernism is concerned with progress and with creativity. However, while postmodernists do respect creativity they see other issues as deserving attention in a contemporary world.

Nine orientations of modernist art education

The following nine orientations, in my own view, summarise the key issues that divide modernist and postmodern thought in both art and art education. As already stated, this is not a definitive list and there are obviously many other issues that could be listed. However these nine serve to highlight the fundamental drives which propel modernist artists, (from the late 19th century through to the 1960s, and possibly to the present) to search for newer and newer forms of self-expression. They also align with significant principles in art teaching and form the basis of curriculum planning in modernist art education. Art teachers will decide how they align themselves in relation to each issue and they will select art experiences according to their own views and the needs of their students. In most cases art teachers have some modernist and some postmodernist orientations. The discussions in each orientation offer a broad summary of the modernist orientation to art and then offer a suggestion about how that orientation is evidenced in art classrooms.

1. Artists as heroes: the significance of self-expression

The key quality of modernism is the belief that individuals can attain autonomy and freedom through self-expression and creativity. New and original ideas are highly valued by modernists and individual artists who can create daring and innovative new techniques and imagery are most highly regarded. The modernist 'Avant garde' artists were those who strove to break with the past by inventing new and more progressive art styles. In doing so, they showed a disdain for the past and great optimism that a more modern approach would reveal the essence of aesthetic experience. Aligned with notions of democracy and independence from the constraints of past styles, modernism celebrated individualism and aesthetic freedom.

For art teachers, immersed in the modernist tradition, student art making focuses on the development of individual self-expression. Students are encouraged to gradually develop into autonomous art makers by drawing on personal experience, ideas, feelings and observation. For example a frequent classroom process involves the refining of ideas from personal observation (eg. of objects, people or the natural world) through progressive phases of refinement through to some sort of abstraction (often based on one of the modernist art movements such as cubism, impressionism, surrealism or Fauvism).

The modernist approach to art history involves introducing students to recognised individual modernist artists who demonstrate the psychological link between personal intention and art. The aim is to provide students with a kind of connoisseurship that will enable them to recognise certain aesthetic qualities that have become understood as great breakthroughs or creative inventions in the progressive search for new forms of 'aesthetic' experience. The uplifting narrative accounts of the often tragic but glorious lives of individual Avant garde artists daringly breaking with tradition are the focus of the modernist story. Through the study of the lives of modernist artists students could come to understand how art could be used as a vehicle for the expression of an inner sensibility. This personal sensibility was encouraged in art rooms as students worked their way toward the development of a personal style which demonstrates their own emergence from constraint and the attainment of identity.

Individualism, attained through self-expression and creativity is seen to be the key drive in modernist art. The individual student of art is viewed as being capable of finding autonomy, identity and 'selfhood' through art making.

2. The role of the Avant garde

At the heart of modernism is also the drive for progress; progress in art, music, literature, science and of course, industry. In art and art education, progress means a fascination with originality and the search for new approaches to aesthetic experience. Driven by Avant garde artists who break with convention, modern art is one of successive change as new and more daring images and forms appear and are subsequently accepted. As Clark says:

> Metaphorically speaking, modernism can be considered a parade of visual styles, each passing by the reviewing stand for a brief moment of critical acclaim. Each new style follows the same route—setting out briskly at the periphery of obscurity, reaching full-stride at the centre of recognition, and fading inexorably at the edge of imitation (Clark, 1996, p.3).

For art educators during and after WW2 child art offered hope for a better world untainted by the evils of war and the sophistication of modern life. In the eyes of the English art educator Herbert Read (1943), art was the means of attaining personal integration and social harmony. Both Read and Viktor Lowenfeld (1950) expressed the notion that free expression would lead to the growth of healthy and creative children. In Lowenfeld's view the imposition of adult ideas would thwart the child's spontaneous and natural creative development. Based on his own experience of the 1938 German invasion of Austria, Lowenfeld's theories reflected his personal experience of the horrific destruction wreaked on society through totalitarianism. In Lowenfeld's view adult discipline of an authoritarian kind had an extremely negative effect on the child's development. For this reason Lowenfeld advocated that children be sheltered from social corruption and allowed to make art freed from adult interference. This meant that art teachers should actively discourage students from copying other images, resorting instead to observation of the natural world and their own imagination. In line with these theories the modernist Avant garde artists were seen as role models, creating daring new images which demonstrated their own freedom from oppression or tradition.

Modernist art teachers have a positive belief that art will engage students in a search for a personal aesthetic freedom and sensibility. Emerging from the devastating effect of two world wars, art education after the 1940s offered a panacea for the world's evils; a retreat to another world which lay within the mind. In modernist art rooms, students work with materials, draw from observation, use imagination and gain inspiration from the sensuous artworks of the modernist Avant garde. Art classrooms focus on western notions of style, subject matter and technique with little regard for other societies which observe and revere different traditions. In fact, for many other societies the notion of an Avant garde intent on breaking with tradition, is antithetical to the very basis of cultural preservation and identity. The Avant garde artists are by definition anti-authoritarian iconoclasts who would not be tolerated in most traditional non-western societies. Art and art education associated with the Avant garde is fundamentally western in style and ideology. Adherence to a modernist set of principles in art education primarily comes to mean marginalisation of other aesthetic canons. Within modernist art classrooms certain aesthetic principles prevail. Undoubtedly western aesthetic principles are dominant within modernist art classrooms.

In art classrooms 'originality' is seen as highly valued in modernist terms. Students are advised not to copy images from other sources but to look around them for new ideas based on their own unique experience. Young children are discouraged from using colouring books and copying adult art or images from popular culture. Senior students are also discouraged from copying the works of other artists and encouraged to take an autonomous stance to find their own art style or content. Avant garde artists are seen as role models who daringly demonstrated new ways of art making.

3. 'Art for art's sake'

In rejecting the values of the official salon in Paris the impressionist painters focused on the visual world as they saw it rather than as previous fashion had dictated it should be seen. Focus on the world of vision led to examination of the notion that painting was a process of translating the 3 dimensional world onto a 2 dimensional surface and thus modern painters became absorbed with the nature of flatness. Now that the camera was able to record the visual world faithfully it was up to artists to record the world of impressions, experience, structure, sensation and dreams. The picture surface in modern art becomes a space for discovering new approaches to visual experience—free from the constraints of social concern or the need to faithfully record visual phenomena. A type of disinterested aesthetic prevails as artists explored abstraction and became immersed in the aesthetic possibilities of the surface and the form.

As modernist art progressed it became increasingly recognised for its own aesthetic qualities, separated from any need to serve other ends. 'Art for art's sake' means that art takes on a disinterested function removed from its previous representational or narrative roles. Removed from the mundane need to tell stories or depict anything at all, art becomes progressively alienated from social function or need. While key artworks such as Picasso's 'Guernica' depicted human horror and Van Gogh's 'Potato Eaters' depicted poverty, they still contained a generalised quality which removed them from the viewer's concern. As viewers we do see the plight of the people depicted but we tend to focus on the aesthetic compositional structure of the work rather than the social issues at stake. The surface manipulation of paint in modernist art tends to create a barrier between the viewer and the deep issues potentially within the work.

Modernist artists also choose to disassociate themselves from the business and commercial world. They have tended to work in isolated studios away from the crass world of finances and social concerns. While they may have had their own private concerns about money they always distanced themselves from the financial side of their art. In general, their role was to make art for others' contemplation. Art served no other purpose than this.

In modernist art classes students are encouraged to explore visual imagery without the need to depict narrative content. Students are advised that they need not seek realism and that art need not mirror the natural world, nor need it tell stories or provide illustration to other ideas. Students are given license to work on the surface and eliminate unnecessary literal references. Art is seen to be legitimate as an activity in itself. It is seen as having a role in society separate from other areas of knowledge and as serving no purpose other than that of 'self-expression'.

4. Fine art

Because modernist art is removed from ordinary or mundane forms of visual experience it is elevated to assume a special role in society. Modernist artists disassociate themselves from art with commercial or popular appeal. Popular art styles associated with film, journalism, fashion and television are seen as second rate in relation to 'fine art'. Art that draws upon popular stereotypes is often seen as kitsch and is regarded as the antithesis of 'real' art. In the modernist tradition up until the 1980s popular art was often not welcomed in art schools. Modernist tertiary art schools at that same time taught the principles of art through life drawing, and through classes in composition but then expected students to develop their own style of modernism from there. Students in modernist art schools were encouraged to draw from life but were not encouraged to copy the work of other artists. Derivative styles were generally viewed negatively. However while copying the work of other artists was considered as an inappropriate activity in 'serious' modernist art circles, modernist artists did 'borrow' 'motifs' from other cultures eg. African and Japanese. These 'references' were seen as demonstrating a fascination with a more exotic form of aesthetic, and thus were not really seen as copying per se.

In modernist art classrooms students were, and still are, steered away from too much reliance upon stereotypical images. Cartoon characters and superheroes are frequently not allowed in art classrooms. Modernist art teachers make a distinct separation between 'fine art' and other art. Topics which are legitimate in modernist art rooms frequently focus around figure drawing, still life and landscape with reference to the styles of abstract expressionism, surrealism, fauvism and cubism. Within the school curriculum subjects such as 'design' or 'visual communication' have assumed responsibility for teaching students about commercial art. Activities such as package design, fashion, and product design have been removed from 'art' so that the dual roles of 'fine art' and 'commercial art' can be separated.

This separation of art and design (or fine art and popular art) has led to the notion that modernist art is elitist and only able to be understood by a privileged few. Modernist art did create a hegemony of art styles and art forms which saw 'fine art' at the top of the scale and other art forms descending in importance down the scale. Modernist art forms (at the top of the scale) were 'tasteful' and were not to be confused with art of the 'tasteless' masses (at the lower end of the scale). However, as some theorists point out, even modernists were really very concerned about selling their work and even if they did not handle sales themselves they were involved in the commercial business of art. As Meecham and Sheldon suggest:

> ...by and large, under modernism artworks often disguised the economic activities of capitalist society (Meecham and Sheldon, 2000, p. 35).

However modernist artists did not want to think of themselves as being involved in the commercial world and in that sense their art was elitist. It was not until late modernism that Andy Warhol challenged the 'removed' status of art from society by using multiple images of packaged commercial objects to critique the 'purist' aesthetic of modernism. Pop art and Dada were therefore quite different to other modernist styles and may be seen as forerunners to postmodern thought.

In the modernist art room students are encouraged to work in abstract ways. They are discouraged from working with kitsch ideas which are seen to be of a lower order in the art world. Teachers remind students of the difference between serious art and the less serious art of commercial graphics (cartoons), television and media. In art history students are encouraged to study the work of accepted artists rather than unknown artists of lesser importance.

5. The assumption of western universality

Modern art primarily focussed on European and later upon American art. Even though reference to the art of other cultures was frequently made and artists often borrowed motifs and forms from Asian and African cultures, these art 'motifs' were generally accommodated into the western style. Many modernist artists were fascinated by art from other 'exotic' cultures and many modernist artists infuse their work with elements inspired by non-western cultures and art. However, the embeddedness and even sacredness of art from other cultures went unacknowledged and modernist artists felt at liberty to plunder works from 'exotic' cultures to be assimilated in the visual aesthetic of western sensibility.

The disinterested, abstract quality of modern art actually tended to suggest a universality that transcended culture or boundaries. It was assumed, by modernist theorists, that abstraction, focusing as it did on the elements of art rather than on content, offered a universal art, able to transcend time and place. It was even assumed that when artists appropriated imagery from non-western cultures this made modern art even more universal in outlook. (Exploitation was not considered as a possibility at the time). In art schools the study of theories of colour and the exploration of art elements (based on Bauhaus principles) were seen to be universal theories. Colour theories were studied and by implication were put forward as universal concepts. Art lecturers rarely (if ever) acknowledged that in China, Japan or Chile such colour theories were irrelevant and not applicable. Nor was it generally acknowledged that other cultures have different views and beliefs about colour that may even be antithetical to the western canon.

In art education Graham Chalmers suggests that the dominance of the western canon has excluded the study of many art forms which matter to many students. According to Chalmers:

> Prejudiced notions concerning race and gender—for example, that great art has almost exclusively been produced by European males—have conditioned our understanding of art... There can be little doubt that art curricula in North American schools, and some art education scholarship, have been (and continue to be in some areas) dominated by particular notions of good art. Some art educators have charged that these notions are Eurocentric, culture-bound, elitist, and even racist... Others have also seen them as sexist... (Chalmers, 1996, p.14).

Within western art classrooms art teaching is western in orientation simply because classes are conducted in a western language and it is seen as desirable to teach students about art in their own country. However, as school populations become more multi-cultural and as global awareness increases it is clearly inappropriate to suggest that western art is superior to non-western art. Racism is fed through biased curriculum selection and art teachers are now aware that all theories about art, including colour theories and theories of composition in painting, are culturally embedded. No theory is universal and no theory is automatically transferable from one culture to another.

Modernism did privilege western art and it did serve to marginalise those groups whose art forms did not conform to the aesthetic principles of modernist thought. The traditional folk art forms and indigenous artworks, for example, of many countries (such as New Zealand, Taiwan, Australia and New Guinea) were relegated to the bottom of the modernist art pyramid by being labelled as 'artefacts' or 'craft'. Modernist art was, and still is, extraordinarily loved in many countries, but it is not a universal movement.

In art rooms modernism is studied as though skills and content are universally accepted and understood. The fundamental study of art elements and visual composition, for example, are considered as universal basic principles of art, transferable to all cultures. In art classes the study of images is predominantly western in nature. Students from all cultures are taught about key 'masters' of western art and the views of 'known' critics' and 'historians' are quoted and respected. Students born into non-western cultures however have considerable difficulty satisfying the assessment criteria as their practical work seems derivative and stereotypical to the eyes of western teachers.

6. The role of art critics

In describing the style of language used by modernist art critics Meechan and Sheldon suggest that:

> Art critics used colourful language (poetic equivalence) to recreate in words the thrill when looking at works of art they held in high regard… Underlying the central tenets of 'art appreciation' lay a sincere belief in the power of art to enhance, uplift and improve human life (Meecham and Sheldon, 2000, p.xx–xxi).

Modernist critics, such as Clement Greenberg (1961) believed that beauty resided in the art object and that 'taste' lay in 'the viewer's capacity for appreciating beauty. As modern art became less concerned with notions of representation, the role of critics assumed greater prominence as they were required to interpret and define the work's quality for those who could not discern these things. So while artworks were supposed to speak for themselves, they really only 'spoke' to certain people who had acquired a certain type of art understanding to 'see' and appreciate them. The vast mass of the population may have only been able to see blotches in abstract art, but the critics (usually white males) possessed the required sensibility or 'taste' which enabled them to interpret art for others.

Greenberg's approach to art criticism was a formalist one in which emphasis was placed on the uses of art elements such as line, colour, tone and mass at the expense of the meaning or subject matter of the work. Formalist approaches give minimal or no attention to the social context of artworks relying instead on the visual sensibility of the viewer. This implies that in art classes students should give a 'personal response' to artworks by using a formalist model devised by Edmund Feldman (1970). In this model students focussed on the composition of the work and followed a four stage plan involving describing, analysing and interpreting and finally judging artworks. In other words, a painting is conceived firstly and primarily as a surface manipulated by the artist and covered with colours and shapes; the subject matter and meaning are of secondary concern.

In art classes the art criticism model devised by Edmund Feldman provides a useful way of looking at the formalist properties of artworks. Students are encouraged to offer a personal response to artworks by offering a *description* of what they see, an *analysis* of the use of art elements and compositional devices, an *interpretation* of the meaning of the work and finally a *judgement* offering their opinion of the work. Key sources from the writings of critics and historians are used as a basis for art knowledge and student research about the work.

7. Art history as linear progression

Gombrich's book 'A Story of Art' (1950) was for many years (up until the 1980s) the bible for art history courses in schools. Supplemented by other texts such as Janson's 'History of Art' (1962) and in Australia Graham Hopwood's ' A Handbook of art' (1955) these texts offered epic stories of art written in the grand narrative modernist style. Using these texts art teachers passed on the language of these authors and others to many young school students who regurgitated huge passages from them in art history exams. These texts are inspiring, extremely optimistic and 'informative' for young people. They also portray the history of art as a series of progressive linear movements from the beginning of civilisation to modernism. In a similar way, until recently, art galleries displayed art in historical progression with art from the same periods of time grouped together. While this approach to teaching art history has the advantage of introducing students to a logically organised art 'meta-narrative' it has been seen as just one particular way of presenting knowledge about world art. These texts represent only certain histories and have since been recognised as highly selective and particularly biased.

A further reason that the chronological approach to the teaching of art appreciation disappeared from art rooms was that the approach was simply seen as tedious and formulaic. When art history programs began with Egyptian art, it took a long while to reach contemporary art. By the 1980s art teachers were developing other ways of presenting artworks to students for study to break the monotony. Thematic approaches which group artworks together around ideas, issues, themes or technique have been developed in recent years so that a more lively approach can connect students with their own art practice.

By 1980 also many art teachers began to recognise the limiting western and patriarchal focus of many art textbooks. Most texts were limited to the study of the 'holy trinity' of art mediums; painting, sculpture and architecture. Few texts contained images by women artists and most texts excluded reference to art forms in which women dominated. The history of art seemed to be recorded by males but it also seemed to be only about male artists. Once art teachers recognised this the search for new texts about women artists began. Recent texts which include women histories (her stories) have become highly sought after in art rooms. Simply getting sufficient resources has become a concern for teachers who want to include both male and female artists in their art theory programs.

It is also recognised that history itself is a western construct which has been challenged by recent theorists. Australian Aboriginal people do not recognise the notion of history as such. The Dreamtime concept is linked to spirituality and the preservation of culture in a way that is antithetical to western notions of recorded history. In recognition of the fact that many non-western cultures view the past differently it seems appropriate to convey this notion in art programs. While a chronologically organised history of world art provided a logical structure for presenting art theory to students it also presented students with a biased, limited and possibly (by implication) racist understanding of world art. By the 1980s the unfolding story of art as told by Gombrich had become a self-perpetuating, closed circuit for students of art in schools. Students simply learned how to see art through Gombrich's eyes and this was being increasingly seen as an inadequate and narrow-minded form of art education for young students. By the end of the 1980s the chronological approach to teaching art history had disappeared from art classrooms.

In modernist art classes teachers feel that an understanding of the past is necessary in order to understand the present. Art teachers want to show students an unfolding sequence of art movements and styles so that they can gain a sense of the factors that determine change. They also want students to be able to identify the antecedents of present day art. In studying the art of the past in this way the focus was often upon certain art forms at the exclusion of others. Western painting, sculpture and architecture were well documented but other art forms and other cultures were allotted minimal space or left out entirely.

8. Gender and modernism

School students prior to the 1980s were rarely shown art by women. Not only were women marginalised as artists but their works were excluded from written art history books. Whitney Chadwick suggests that modernist art, centred as it was on the notion of the Avant garde spearheading new progressive developments, 'marginaliz(ed) the woman artist as surely as did the guilds in the fifteenth century, and the academics in the seventeenth and eighteenth' (Chadwick, 1992, p. 265). Art textbooks written in modernist times paid no attention to women artists. Furthermore, by focussing on the three art forms of painting, sculpture and architecture, modernist art texts gave no space to the field of textile arts (or crafts) which had been dominated by women.

In modernist art women do however feature prominently as the subjects of painting. While the male nude was the revered subject of classical art (the Greeks and subsequently Michelangelo in the Renaissance) the female nude is the revered subject of modernist artists. Women are portrayed in the art of male artists as passive and subservient; the object of the male gaze. The female nude features significantly in modern art and is a favoured subject embodying the disinterested aesthetic notions of abstraction and modernism. Female models are depicted in an objective way and regarded as fascinating subject matter because of their visual qualities rather than their human or social qualities. There is little attempt to look beneath the surface at 'real' female thought. As Chadwick writes of Gauguin:

> Gauguin's many paintings of Tahitian women replay the unequal relationships of the male artist and the female model in the inequities of the white male artist's relationship to native women in a colonised society. His paintings bind women to nature through repetitions of colors, patterns, and contours;

> crouching female figures are placed in a submissive relationship to the downward gaze of the male artist and the women's blank gazes offer little insight into the specifics of their lives ((Chadwick, 1992, p. 271).

Until the 1960s the female nude was a focus of art study in western art schools as well as in artworks. All tertiary students of art were compelled to do life drawing and the model was invariably, although with some exceptions, female. In fact, the ability to draw from the female nude model became the yardstick for determining drawing ability, even when young artists may have never actually wanted to use figures in their work. For modernist painters the female form became subject to many gross distortions in the name of abstraction. Picasso's nude figures, for example, became a visual playing field for constructing cubist compositions causing feminist writers to suggest that the image of the violated female body became a dominant theme. By way of contrast the male nude or male genitalia never featured in modernist artworks, and images of the male nude by women artists never appeared in modernist art texts.

In modern art it seems that the artist is conceived as 'the thinker' and the female nude is seen as 'what the artist thinks about'. The female nude is the most recognisable iconic subject matter of modernist art. This issue has, of course, given rise to the feminist revolution by women of the western world in the post-modern period.

In art classes up until the 1980s students rarely looked at artworks by women. Modernist art teachers accept that the female nude is a common theme in modernist art and that modernist artists are predominantly male. Art history focuses on the lives and works of the 'great masters' and centres on the study of painting, sculpture and, to a lesser extent, architecture. Gender issues as such, are not discussed as an area of study.

9. Optimism

> To be modern is to find ourselves in an environment that promises us adventure, power, joy, growth, transformation of ourselves and the world (Taylor, 1987, p. 34).

Taylor suggests that modernist artists seem to pursue a type of dream which is inspired by reality. The artwork is conceived as a subjective version of reality. Artists explore techniques as an expression of inner subjectivity. Taylor (1987, p. 34) suggests that for many modernist artists (e.g. Picasso, Kandinsky, Kirchner, de Chirico) there is an assumed notion of a 'recoverable aesthetic'. In other words, the notion that neither visual phenomena nor the human self are obvious in the real world, rather they lie hidden waiting to be investigated by artists who reveal their hidden structures. Modernist art is optimistic because it is based on the premise that life can be changed; that a pure aesthetic world lies waiting for us, if only we can learn to see it. The outside world may be disgusting and brutal but modernist artists look within themselves to find a more suitable place to dwell. Even in moments when artists did dwell on 'unseemly' subjects (e.g. Picasso's 'Guernica') the aesthetic unity of the whole provides a distance from which to speculate on the ghastliness of the event.

Modernism gives rise to the notion that art is a projection of the inner image. The purpose of art is not to emulate actual vision but rather the felt sensation of the 'virtual' world (Langer, 1953). Art is about the sensate life, and is nearer to the senses than to the physical appearance of the visible world. Art is not concerned with replicating what the eye can see, but it is concerned with revealing the fusion between inner life and external reality. As Suzanne Langer suggests, art in modernist terms is concerned with finding the link between feeling (the sensate experience) and form (the medium).

The optimistic tone of modernism offers art teachers considerable inspiration. Creativity and self-expression are laudable goals for students' personal development. In modernist art classes students can be inspired by stories about great artists which seem to suggest that liberation can be achieved through creativity. Modernist art education is built on the notion that through innovation in art students can achieve personal autonomy and freedom from oppressive traditions. Ironically however, the liberating ideals of modernism have been challenged by postmodernists who see that liberation of one culture or group often comes at the expense of another.

In art classrooms the optimistic notion that life can be improved if only we keep searching for a pure aesthetic provided an energetic foundation for teaching art to young people. The modernist-style optimist enthuses about the formalist properties of the artwork but often avoids discussing concomitant views of culture and meaning. Modernists look ahead to a bright future and see the past as a stepping stone to the present. Modernism brings forth a celebratory ethos in art education as art is seen to offer students a means of self-expression and a way of finding identity and autonomy.

Summary

By and large art education practices in schools since WW2 have been based upon modernist values of 'seriousness, purity and individuality' (Best and Kellner, 1991, p.11). Essentially art teaching has been based on the powerful and fundamental theory that art experiences will lead to personal autonomy. This 'personal' theory has been modelled through the teaching of art history which has been told as a series of stories outlining the personal successes of individuals who have so often risen from obscurity to acclaim. This model has served as the basis for classroom practice in which student success is also measured by the output of individually developed 'original' and 'self expressive' folios of work. Originality and self-expression have been seen as ways in which students define themselves as unique and different from others. Art teachers have steered students away from the use of derivative, stereotypical, kitsch or 'commercial' images and ideas and directed them towards direct observation from life and use of imagination.

Modernism provides an inspiring set of ideals for art teaching. Art is freed of the need to serve any other purpose than itself. In art classrooms students make art to express their own life and interests. Art is not conceived as a political arena and issues such as gender, culture and race are issues to be dealt with in other areas of the curriculum. Even though individual students may tackle such issues in their artwork, these matters are not developed as key curriculum issues. Modernist art celebrates western democracy; the great successes of white male artists who have developed new ways of fusing the visual world and the sensate life. Art education theory focuses on the development of the senses (Langer, 1953) and the cognitive aspects involved when art is conceived as a symbol system (Gardner, 1983) but rarely do theorists acknowledge that modernist art is western, insular and patriarchal. Such suggestions only surfaced with the postmodernists and feminists who began to see that modernism was an inward-looking series of art movements whose practitioners had become myopic and whose theories had become self-fulfilling prophesies. The new theorists looked sideways at those who seemed to be marginalised by modernist views. Modernism provided, and still provides, art educators with a vigorous and inspiring set of ideals for young minds. Through creativity and self-expression students are seen to find autonomy and a sense of self. Modernism celebrates the ideals of democratic freedom and the right of the individual to carve out a life for him or herself.

In the next chapter it will be seen that postmodernists look at life through different eyes. For postmodernists the world is not so rosy. Instead of optimistically looking forward to a brighter future postmodernists tend to look sideways and backwards in search of the sources and origins which frame values, tastes and attitudes. In terms of the nine orientations outlined in this chapter it will be seen that postmodern thinkers see many issues quite differently. While postmodern art teachers may still see their students as individuals they may do so in a wider cultural and societal framework. It is this wider social and cultural view that frames the basis of postmodern thinking.

Summary of key modernist orientations in art education

1. Artists as heroes: the significance of self expression

Individualism, attained through self expression and creativity is seen to be the key drive in modernist art. The individual student of art is viewed as being capable of finding autonomy, identity and 'selfhood' through art making.

2. The role of the Avant garde

In art classrooms 'originality' is seen as highly valued in modernist terms. Students are advised not to copy images from other sources but to look around them for new ideas based on their own unique experience. Young children are discouraged from using colouring books and copying adult art or images from popular culture. Senior students are also discouraged from copying the works of other artists and encouraged to take an autonomous stance to find their own art style or content. Avant garde artists are seen as role models who daringly demonstrated new ways of art making.

3. 'Art for art's sake'

In modernist art classes students are encouraged to explore visual imagery without the need to depict narrative content. Students are advised that they need not seek realism and that art need not mirror the natural world, nor need it tell stories or provide illustration to other ideas. Students are given license to work on the surface and eliminate unnecessary literal references. Art is seen to be legitimate as an activity in itself. It is seen as having a role in society separate from other areas of knowledge and as serving no purpose other than that of 'self expression'.

4. Fine art

In the modernist art room students are encouraged to work in abstract ways. They are discouraged from working with kitsch ideas which are seen to be of a lower order in the art world. Teachers remind students of the difference between serious art and the less serious art of commercial graphics (cartoons), television and media. In art history students are encouraged to study the work of accepted artists rather than unknown artists of lesser importance.

5. The assumption of western universality

In art rooms modernism is studied as though skills and content are universally accepted and understood. The fundamental study of art elements and visual composition, for example, are considered as universal basic principles of art, transferable to all cultures. In art classes the study of images is predominantly western in nature. Students from all cultures are taught about key 'masters' of western art and the views of 'known' critics' and 'historians' are quoted and respected. Students born into non-western cultures however have considerable difficulty satisfying the assessment criteria as their practical work seems derivative and stereotypical to the eyes of western teachers.

6.The role of art critics

In art classes the art criticism model devised by Edmund Feldman provides a useful way of looking at the formalist properties of artworks. Students are encouraged to offer a personal response to artworks by offering a *description* of what they see, an *analysis* of the use of art elements and compositional devices, an *interpretation* of the meaning of the work and finally a *judgement* offering their opinion of the work. Key sources from the writings of critics and historians are used as a basis for art knowledge and student research about the work.

7. Art history as linear progression

Art teachers want to show students an unfolding sequence of art movements and styles so that they can gain a sense of the factors that determine change. They also want students to be able to identify the antecedents of present day art. In studying the art of the past in this way the focus was often upon certain art forms at the exclusion of others. Western painting, sculpture and architecture were well documented but other art forms and other cultures were allotted minimal space or left out entirely.

8. Gender

In art classes up until the 1980s students rarely looked at artworks by women. Modernist art teachers accept that the female nude is a common theme in modernist art and that modernist artists are predominantly male. Art history focuses on the lives and works of the 'great masters' and centers on the study of painting, sculpture and, to a lesser extent, architecture. Gender issues as such, are not discussed as an area of study.

9. Optimism

In art classrooms the optimistic notion that life can be improved if only we keep searching for a pure aesthetic provided an energetic foundation for teaching art to young people. The modernist-style optimist enthuses about the formalist properties of the artwork but often avoids discussing concomitant views of culture and meaning. Modernists look ahead to a bright future and see the past as a stepping stone to the present. Modernism brings forth a celebratory ethos in art education as art is seen to offer students a means of self expression and a way of finding identity and autonomy.

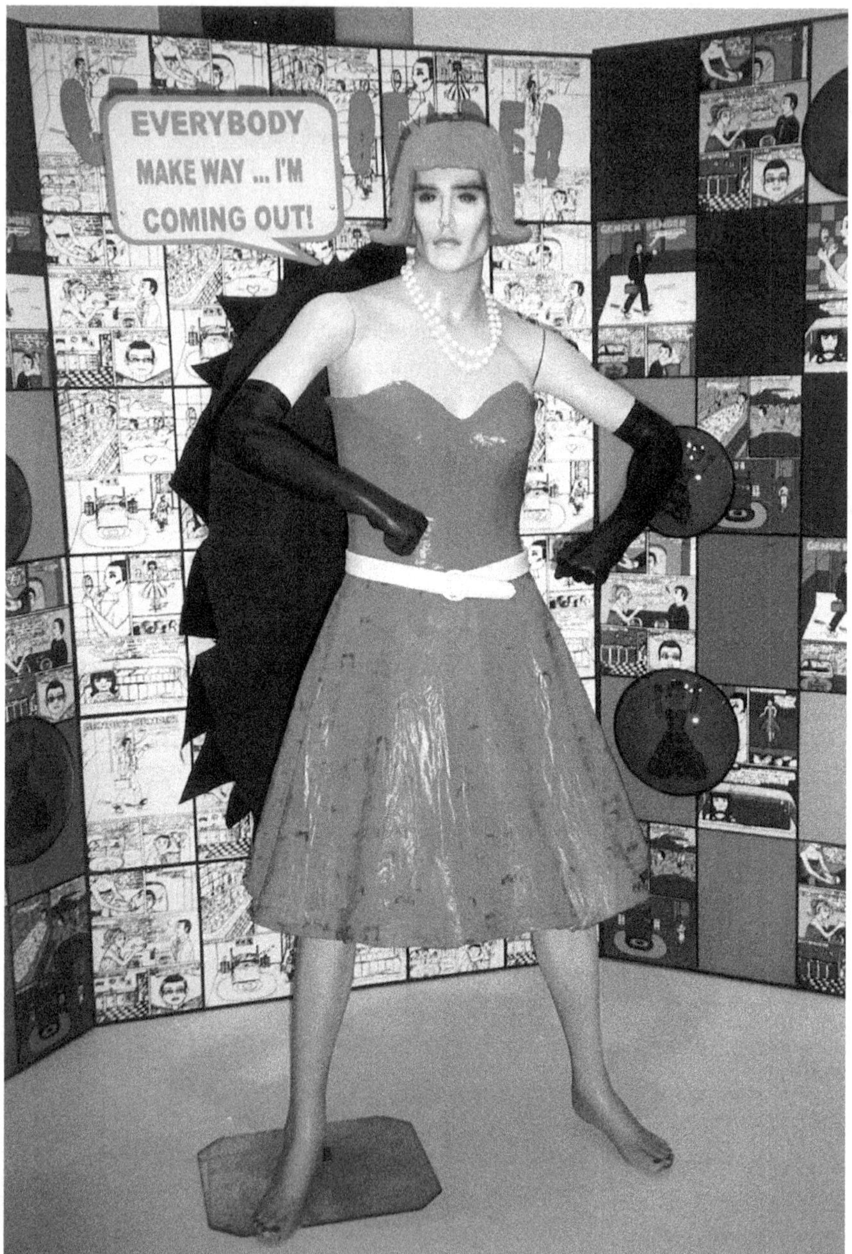

Figure 1:
'Gender Bender', Autumn Daly-Holt, Year 12, McKinnon Secondary College, Melbourne.

Chapter 3
Postmodernism and Art Education

Open any art magazine, journal or recent book and postmodern voices can be heard. These voices are often conflicting voices which define postmodernism in very different ways. At one end of the scale there are extreme and radical postmodernists who refute all aspects of modernism and see the totalising power of modernism being replaced by some sort of multi-dimensional pluralism which defies definition. At the other end of the scale there are more conciliatory theorists who would see postmodernism as a break from modernism, but at the same time embrace the more positive aspects of modernism. Between these extremes there are many others. Some deny that postmodernism is a break with modernism and suggest that postmodernism is just a continuation of modernism. Others suggest that postmodernism is just an esoteric theoretical debate which has no substance in the real world of art. Within the field of art education it seems that a 'soft' style of postmodernism offers a constructive force which if effectively built into art programs, will make art education practice more equitable, more relevant to students and more meaningful in the wider context.

While postmodernism does come after modernism it is not a term which refers to a 'style' or movement after modernism. Postmodernism is more a split with modernism, a stated break with all, most, or some (depending on how radical the view), modernist theories. Within schools and art rooms the break may have hardly been discernable, yet changes are occurring and schools are finding it difficult to remain locked in a modernist framework while the rest of the world is grappling with the impact of postmodernity. As Jencks suggested in 1986:

> The modern age, which sounds as if it would last forever, is fast becoming a thing of the past. Industrialisation is quickly giving way to post-Industrialisation, factory labour to home and office work and, in the arts, the Tradition of the New is leading to the combination of many traditions. Even those who still call themselves Modern artists and architects are looking

> backwards and sideways to decide which styles and values they will continue (Jencks, 1986, p.7).

Nine orientations of postmodernist art education

Postmodernism is a political force which, because of changes in the global arena and in the world of technology, is impacting significantly on schools and art programs. Art teachers recognise that there are many changes within art and education which are political in nature and which influence the content of art program. While art students have always dealt with issues in their artwork, contemporary issues and contemporary art practice is often very confrontational and 'hard hitting'. Contemporary artists and art theorists are less concerned with aesthetic issues and increasingly concerned with issues which are socially and culturally based. These issues are complex and pose many new possibilities for art educators. While modernism provided an optimistic and coherent vision for the future, postmodernism simply opens up countless more possibilities. The key problem faced by postmodern art teachers is that of choice. Without a central force guiding aesthetic issues, the art teacher is responsible for choosing art experiences from the vast plethora of available possibilities. And choice is always a political act because selection is always based on some sort of reason or theory. Choosing art experiences which have a postmodern orientation *will* be contentious. While modernist approaches to art teaching have become acceptable and expected in western art rooms, postmodern practices present students with increasingly complex issues. Postmodern art teachers will have to live with uncertainty and will have to find ways of accepting that there are multiple viewpoints about many, if not most, issues. This plurality of possibility can seem overwhelming for art teachers faced with limited hours in which to present very complex ideas to students.

However, art teachers will continue to draw on both modernist and postmodernist theories in art programs. Modernism provides a basis for personal art making and it provides a basic structure for teaching certain skills and planning art experiences. Postmodernism however makes us aware that art concepts are contestable and unstable and because of this art educators need to vigilantly examine and re-examine what is meant by, to use Gardner's terms (1999), 'truth, beauty and goodness'.

While postmodernists generally disagree on a definition of postmodernism, there are some broad issues which differentiate modernism from postmodernism. Using the same nine orientations set out in the previous chapter to define modernist thought, this chapter presents some key aspects of postmodernism. The following views are my own and I must state that the twelve art teachers in this book may see postmodernism in quite different ways. However these orientations frame the sort of issues which are broadly presented as questions to the twelve art teachers for discussion.

1. The individual in context

One of the key differences between modernism and postmodernism is the way the individual is defined within the two theoretical frames. While modernists celebrate the right of the individual to free expression postmodernists have taken a critical look at the notion of what it actually means to be an individual. In the 1860s, impressionist artists defiantly sought freedom from the stifling constraints imposed by the official art academies in Paris. In successive modernist movements artists have been lauded for their ability to break with the establishment and invent new defiant techniques and imagery which celebrate their individuality and their capacity to break free from dogma. However postmodern theorists, such as Pierre Bourdieu (1994), claim that in fact artists are not separate, free individuals but rather they are always products of their time and place. Bourdieu suggests that without the structure of art institutions, galleries, critics, historians, auction houses, schools and art journals, artists would go unnoticed. The implication of this notion is that individuals (such as artists) are not the free autonomous beings that modernist theory suggests. Rather, artists are each shaped by and accountable to the wider culture, and they are workers in a field of 'cultural production'.

In defining 'The field of cultural production' Bourdieu (1994) describes art education as being one of the fields which shape the way people value and perceive art (Bourdieu, 1994, p. 51). Bourdieu's contention is that the field of art cannot be understood by looking at artworks or artists alone. Rather, he suggests that these works and artists must be seen as products of the whole art field which has supported them. Art teachers, for example, are seen by Bourdieu as significant players in the field of cultural production because they have the responsibility of defining 'art' for young people who will then become viewers, consumers and artists. Teachers therefore are active agents in shaping and defining the field of art in society. Bourdieu claims that:

> The work of art is an object which exists only by virtue of the (collective) belief which knows and acknowledges it as a work of art (Bourdieu, 1994, p.56).

Artistic understanding then requires us to:

> ...consider as contributing to production not only the direct producers of the work in its materiality (artist, writer etc) but also the producers of the meaning of the value of the work—critics, publishers, gallery directors and the whole set of agents whose combined efforts produce consumers capable of knowing and recognizing the work of art as such, in particular teachers... (Bourdieu, 1994, p.58).

As a participant in the wider 'field of cultural production' the art teacher plays a significant role in creating the culture in which art is valued and invested with meaning. The type of art experiences selected for study by art teachers matter a great deal as these selected experiences are seen to 'represent' the wider field of art. By selecting materials and experiences in which students will make and study art, teachers help students define art. Conversely, by deleting other experiences from the curriculum art teachers simultaneously define what is <u>not</u> art. The division between what gets studied and what doesn't, defines the boundary around the field of art education.

Whereas modernists view the individual as an autonomous, free being whose goal in life is to seek liberation through progress and 'creativity', postmodernists claim that individuals do not operate freely, rather they are embedded within society and are the active participants in it. Each individual plays a role in shaping and reshaping the 'thing' that we collectively call 'art'. Furthermore postmodernists believe that we are all basically human and that we cannot escape the fundamental human qualities which bind us. For art teachers this reconception of the individual means a shift in thinking away from the notion that the child should be autonomous to one which conceives of the child being a product of his or her context. Instead of looking inward for meaning the student is encouraged to explore the world around for signs that signify personal, social and cultural meaning. Postmodern art students are urged to consider 'otherness' and through art are encouraged to focus both inwardly and outwardly in their art making.

This shift in orientation of the individual leads art educators to reconceive basic notions such as the emphasis on 'originality' in art. If artists are seen as products of their context then the ideas that they use in their art are also derived from that context. Ideas are not seen to simply arise from individuals in isolation. Furthermore, it is probably not coincidental that postmodernism has developed alongside the rise of the digital age. With both the proliferation of computers in classrooms and the influence of postmodern art, most art teachers have had to re-define the term 'originality' in relation to student artwork. While deliberate copying from other sources was once discouraged in art rooms, copying or appropriating from other sources is now rampant in student art. It seems that personal autonomy can now be achieved by openly assimilating ideas from multifarious sources. Not only have art teachers had to redefine notions of 'originality' they have also had to rethink what is meant by personal autonomy. Personal autonomy is seemingly not so 'personal' when students deliberately appropriate and rework art by others. In postmodern classrooms art is often now made from other art; images from other images. Although many art teachers may not directly see this change as a consequence of postmodern theory, these changes are consistent with a general changing notion about the role of the individual in relation to society and the newer notion that original ideas always derive from some source.

It may no longer be taken for granted that teachers should aim to lead a student to 'personal autonomy' if it is not possible to be free, or apart from, the society which shaped the student in the first place. Students are not really separate from their world, they are participants, consumers, viewers and social agents in it. While art teachers will always be concerned to develop students as individual makers, a postmodern orientation will lead toward considerations of 'social reconstruction' through art. The postmodernist is as fascinated by the individual as the modernist, however the fascination takes on different forms. Whereas the modernist focuses on the visual world and its aesthetic qualities, the postmodernist looks at what it means to be human. Some controversial postmodern artists have become fascinated with how the human body functions and have used bodily fluids and excretions in their art, others are absorbed by the way the human body is dissected and analysed in a post-mortem. Artists such as Damien Hirst present dead animals and question the way we eat meat and value living creatures. His bisected cow and calf forms present the viewer with many contradictions about human life and contemporary society. Other artists have suggested that we in fact have many selves and these artists reinvent themselves through their art in many guises. This is particularly evident in computer art where users can invent new identities on the internet or by digitally changing their body image.

It is not that postmodernists have lost faith in the individual but rather that they see the need for individuals to recognise each other. In many societies the individual is never seen as separate from the community. As Dissanayake notes:

> Emphasis on the self at the expense of the larger family or group, or as an entity whose expression and satisfaction is considered to be a desirable goal or virtue, is unknown to members of traditional societies. There men and women generally find satisfaction in performing well the role that custom and authority assign to them (Dissanayake, 1990, p. 187).

Some contemporary artists have worked collaboratively to subvert the modernist tendency to focus on individualism. Gilbert and George for example, work together to create photo pieces and performance art. Other artists work together to create large installations or group pieces such as Judy Chicago's 'Dinner Party' of 1973–'79. Individualism has become only one approach in postmodern art. Within schools collaborative art practice has been seen in classrooms for some time especially in projects such as murals or group ceramic works requiring, for example, each student contributing a tile or section of a piece. However, collaborative practice involving two or more students working together is not common practice at senior levels in the visual arts. One of the problems is that assessment is based on individual performance and art teachers are uncertain how to assess collaborative practice where the respective roles of each student are blurred. In this sense it is hard for art teachers to implement postmodern practice when assessment practices are based on modernist conceptions of art practice. Art educators could actually learn a great deal from current assessment strategies used in the performing arts areas of dance, drama and music where group performance is assessed and processes have been constructed to consider both individual input and collaborative product.

In summary then, the notion of art focusing on personal free expression, has been challenged by postmodern theorists. Contemporary artists are viewed as co-players in a large field. This field comprises many agencies, institutions, patrons and educators who co-exist to create 'art'. The field of cultural production (Bourdieu, 1994) comprises many 'players' who all contribute to the way art is valued, viewed and recorded. While artists make artworks they also rely on many other individuals and institutions to support them and to provide the structural framework in which to work and exhibit. In acknowledgement of this, some recent art books look at the views of dealers, patrons, commentators, art schools, funders, exhibition organisers, and magazine editors, alongside the works of artists (e.g. Buck, 2000). In other words, postmodernists seek a more equitable world where the separate and privileged status of autonomous artists is challenged.

In postmodern art rooms art teachers understand that individualism is a western concept which may not apply to students of some cultures. Postmodern art teachers conceive of students as participants in the culture/s around them. Students are therefore not seen as autonomous and apart from society but as participants in it. Postmodern art teachers develop in students a sense of the 'other' so that students develop an awareness of different cultures and different ways in which identity can be defined.

2. Aesthetic pluralism

Throughout the modernist art era, the Avant garde took risks to present the art world with progressive and new aesthetic experiences. Avant garde artists invented new techniques and approaches in daring and shocking new ways. However, these new ways were eventually accepted until they themselves became establishment. What began as shocking was eventually assimilated until the very concept of art changed to accommodate it:

> The gradual assimilation of oppositional art into institutional orthodoxy represents one of the failed utopias of the modern world (Meechan and Sheldon, 2000, p.15).

The notion of an Avant garde could probably only develop in liberal societies which encourage individualism and 'free' thinking. Artistic innovation requires that artists be allowed to take risks and openly present radical new forms of art in public. However, as already indicated, there are many cultures in which individualism is not valued and where other values such as collectivism, nationhood, community and religion bind people together. While western cultures celebrate freethinking and self-expression, there are many cultures in which self-expression is viewed negatively. It may be seen by some as self-serving, hedonistic, irresponsible and alienating. It may also be seen as leading to the destruction of family and social values. In cultures where people come together because of common identity and for the continual renewal of traditional beliefs, self-expression may be viewed as sinful and as anti-social. Seen from these cultures, modernism may also be seen simply as an assertion of white, western and male supremacy.

Therefore while modernism began as a series of art movements which celebrated freedom and individuality, it later became an elitist movement which in fact marginalised and excluded many art forms which did not align with the modernist ethos. The dominant aesthetic of modernism was not understood or relevant to most indigenous cultures, most women artists, most craft artists and many non-western cultures. It was a western series of art movements which had increasingly become 'politically incorrect' in contemporary society.

The contemporary world is increasingly being described as a global village. As such it is seen as a multi-cultural world in which western domination is challenged by 'others' who have been marginalised by the powerful spread of modernist theory. Some postmodern theorists suggest that there must be other ways of working artistically. Gablik, for example, suggests that unless people work together they run the risk of destroying the planet as it is known:

> Today, remaining aloof has dangerous implications. We are all together in the same global amphitheater. There are no longer any sidelines. The psychic and social structures in which we live have become too profoundly antiecological, unhealthy and destructive. There is a need for new forms emphasizing our essential interconnectedness rather than our separateness, forms evoking the feeling of belonging to a larger whole rather than expressing the isolated, alienated self (Gablik, 1991, p. 5–6).

As Gablik points out, to highly successful artists, the very idea that art might be directed at cultural global concerns rather than self-expression requires an enormous change of heart. In Gablik's view it is not longer acceptable for artists to separate and divorce themselves from the key issues which will impact on the future of humanity. In her view art today must have a social responsibility. This is a key issue for art teachers in schools to consider. On the one hand art teachers can adopt the modernist view that art education develops autonomous free thinkers who make art for the sake of it. But on the other hand, there is also some responsibility to demonstrate that art helps develop socially responsible students who care about the world they live in.

For many groups postmodern thinking provides a platform for challenging dominant aesthetic values which have marginalised their interests. Postmodern theorists challenge the way certain discourses attain power over others. Graham Chalmers (1996) suggests that art educators cannot achieve more pluralistic practices in art education unless they teach students that art is made for varied reasons and purposes in different cultures. In essence this means adopting a more open and fluid definition of art itself. In this way students are introduced to the notion that people make art to serve many roles. This will require that students become, at least a little, immersed in other social and cultural systems so that they can begin to respect how and why people make things in other times, places and situations. Multiculturalism teaches students to tolerate 'otherness' and to respect difference. And while it is acknowledged that some cultural groups seek a separatist rather than a multicultural approach in education, within a western context where art classes comprise students from mixed cultures, a multicultural approach seems to be the less racist approach.

A more postmodern approach in the art room means a more pluralistic approach to art making as well as art theory. This may mean tolerance for a wider range of art mediums and styles in art classes as well as inclusion of a wider range of social and cultural studies. It may mean depiction of subject matter previously thought inappropriate or it may mean acceptance of mediums previously considered stereotypical or kitsch. Pluralism may also lead students to consider how values about art are constructed and reinforced. And this may then lead to discussion about why different people hold views about art that are incompatible with each other. Students in the class can discuss their own incompatible values and how they formulated these values. When it comes to differences of opinion modernist and postmodern teachers generally adopt different approaches to deal with this. Whereas a modernist art educator would seek to find a resolution through reason to bring the issues together, the postmodernist is prepared to live with uncertainty and tolerate the fact that there are multiple viewpoints about many issues. In other words, while the modernist uses logical theory to conceptualise an art program, the postmodern art teacher may allow many reasoned arguments and belief systems to co-exist. Already most art teachers recognise that there is greater diversity in the sorts of artworks produced in their art classes than ever before. Modernism is not rejected in many pluralist views and in fact many postmodern art teachers may embrace the modernist approach as one possibility among many.

Aesthetic pluralism in postmodern art classes may mean that students study art made for diverse purposes eg as religious icons, as used in costume, as used for propaganda or as domestic decoration. Students may also work collaboratively to explore issues of global, environmental or political concern. This does not mean that all art must take on these forms but that more diverse approaches to art making are tolerated and encouraged to reflect the nature of art in diverse cultural and social contexts. Postmodern art denies any dominant aesthetic style, medium or movement, however collage becomes more prominent than painting and art is often made from other art. In postmodern classes students study how art values are constructed and reinforced within cultural groups.

3. Art for meaning

Modernists view art as having a role separate from the rest of society. Modernist art need serve no other 'master' than itself. Removed from the need to mirror life (pre-modern) or to embellish buildings (Gothic and Renaissance) modernist art is art, and nothing else. Modernist artists see their role as providing uplifting and disinterested aesthetic experience. Abstract art does not have to mean anything, it is to be contemplated and viewed; art exists for art's sake. Postmodernists however suggest that rather than being removed from life, art is actually about life and is part of life. Postmodernists therefore challenge the notion that art should speak only to the art cognisant (those who have learned how to 'read' it). They scrutinise and challenge institutions, systems and individuals who serve to alienate art from the majority by using esoteric language, treating art as highly 'precious' and generally upholding an elitist attitude to art knowledge.

The postmodern theorist claims that much modernist art generally had little meaning for most people. Modernist art usually meant nothing to those who came from non-western cultures or whose interests were not served by modernist aesthetics. Many people do not identify with the images and forms represented in modernist art. Nor do many people identify with the colours, techniques and styles used in modernist composition. While, to some eyes, a fauvist painting by Matisse may be described as sensuous and vibrant, to others it may be seen as a lurid painting of a bourgeois 'chick'. Furthermore to others the whole work may be described as sacrilege. The modernist credo 'Art for art's sake' implied that art could be divorced from meaning. Art could simply be art without other reference points. In terms of modernist sensibility impressionist art, for example, was simply a visual feast for those who loved to look at the world in this way. For others, impressionist paintings could simply be meaningless marks.

The postmodernist disputes the notion that art can be divorced of meaning. The postmodernist suggests that all art contains signs that signify its origins and meaning/s. Meaning is therefore culturally and socially defined. Postmodernists in fact suggest that no art is original and that ideas are always derived from other ideas and can always be traced to previous sources. As Clark suggests:

> ...the modernist concepts of originality-as-process and originality-as-product have been swept aside. Postmodernists deny the existence of singular founding references or points-of-departure; instead they speak of signifiers and deconstructed meanings which produce an infinite array of interrelated and circular interpretations. There are no original ideas in art; images can always be deconstructed to reveal antecedent constructs and concepts (Clark, 1996, Virginia: NAEA).

The modernist notion of 'art for art's sake' has been seen by postmodern theorists as self-indulgent elitism far removed from the social concerns of the populace. As Taylor writes:

> Mondrian's squares which stand for 'pure universal relations' of humanity obviously offered no solace to the victims of Dachau and Auschwitz... on the one hand, modernism's subjectivity—however impressive and beguiling in certain cases—was ultimately too exclusive and too limited to be of value beyond the confines of the artist himself and the intellectuals who were able to understand its workings. The very lifestyle of the modernist artist, after all—committed to the solitude of the studio and a restricted social group—was probably too unworldly to provide the real tests by which the 'self' could be truly developed (Taylor, 1987, p.125).

The modern art 'masters' such as Manet, Cezanne, Hockney, Warhol, Picasso, Dali, McCubbin and Nolan may have had some concerns about social justice issues, but they were much more concerned with aesthetic issues and their commitment to 'art for art's sake'. Their artworks explored issues of aesthetics more than issues of social or cultural concern. Modernist artists celebrated the attainment of liberty and freedom from institutional constraint. They were not seen as having concern for marginalised groups or others with views different from their own. By contrast many postmodernist artists explore issues within groups that have been marginalised and many are deeply involved in issues related to culture, gender, power and class.

Another key element that postmodernists find meaningful is the past. To the modernist the past had little meaning. While past motifs were sometimes used in modernist art the tendency was to look inward and forward for new and more innovative imagery. In general, modernists were not nostalgic for the past and the past was usually discarded to make way for the new. Each successive style was seen to offer a more advanced and insightful way of viewing the world. Modernists didn't look back. By contrast postmodernists look backwards and sideways rather than forward. The postmodernist is interested in the past and seeks to re-examine past styles and motifs to re-invest it with new meaning and to see how meaning/s were constructed. For this reason postmodern artists appropriate art from the past and juxtapose it in new contexts. They look for signifiers of meaning in past and present contexts and often see meaning as more important than aesthetic sensibility in their art.

For this reason art criticism assumes a different focus for modernist and postmodern art. When discussing modernist art it is appropriate for the critic to focus on the aesthetic qualities of the composition and form because this is what modernist art involved. However it is often not appropriate to apply the same process to postmodern art in which meaning may take precedence over aesthetic considerations. To analyse an unmade bed by Sarah Lucas in terms of its composition alone would be ludicrous. New methods of art history and criticism offer new interpretive frameworks appropriate for postmodern works where the meaning rather than aesthetic composition becomes the more significant element. Feminism, masculinism, semiotics, post-colonial theory and Marxism provide interpretive stances for discussion of artworks whose intent is other than modernist in orientation.

It may be said that modernist artists were viewed as unique individuals whose role was to make art with a form of 'disinterested aesthetic'. The purpose of art was to simply make something to be contemplated, freed of all other references to life. Modernist artists believed in freedom from the constraints of repressive institutions. However, in seeking freedom from these repressive forces modernists became self-absorbed and blinded to their own lack of social awareness and their disregard for others who were unlike themselves.

Seeing this limitation in modernist art postmodern artists seek ways to connect art with the meaningful lives of people. Sometimes this brings viewers to confront shocking and sensational images. Postmodern artists suggest however, that life itself *is* shocking and that art can be about both the beauty and the horrors of life. When Damien Hirst suggests that 'Art is about life, and it can't be about anything else' (Buck, 2000, p.28) he suggests that art can be about all aspects of life. When Hirst exhibited an oversized ashtray and filled it with thousands of cigarette butts at the Saachi Gallery (Ant Noises 11 exhibition, 2000) viewers were repelled and disgusted by the stench. However, they could not avoid a response to the work and it was not a meaningless work. Its meaning was simply a blatant 'in your face' statement.

In summary and to coin a phrase, 'meaning takes on new meanings in postmodern art'. Meanings are multi-layered and fluid. Boundaries are blurred, new (and old) territory is explored (and re-explored), and the meaning of human experience is pushed further and further. Writing about the exhibition entitled 'Apocalypse: Beauty and horror in Contemporary Art' (Royal Academy of Arts, 2000) Max Wigram suggests:

> The idea of extremity in art is not a new one. For personal and political reasons artists have consistently produced challenging images to explore questions of religion, disillusionment, dissatisfaction and death. These areas have interested artists because they are a permanent part of our experience of the world... Each artist's work explores a different aspect of the apocalyptic. Issues of genocide, religious belief, violence and sexuality are tackled using beauty and horror to engage the visitor in a dialogue.

The tendency of modernism was to ignore negative concepts altogether by simply focussing on the preferred so-called 'normal' concept. Postmodernists point out however, that 'normality' only has meaning in relation to concepts of abnormality. As Parker suggests:

> The fantasy of realism, and traditional theorizing in general, is that language and reason would be purer if in the conceptual oppositions of rational thought the negative concept could be eliminated altogether, if it could be forgotten or if it never had existed. But this can only be a dream; for the negative must, of necessity, exist since it is part of the meaning of the preferred 'normal' concept. The preferred concept only has a meaning insofar as it is capable of enabling distinctions to be drawn between those cases to which it applies and those to which it does not (Parker, 1997, p 79).

Postmodern art teachers understand that deconstruction is a tool for examining texts and images to reveal the meaning systems upon which the work is based. For postmodern art teachers the challenge is to provide students with the cultural and social understanding that equips them to think critically when responding to artworks. It also requires teachers to introduce students to appropriate methodologies so that they can interpret postmodern art in various ways.

Postmodern artists are concerned with meaning rather than with formalist composition or technique. Postmodern art teachers discuss how meaning is constructed and explore multiple readings of artworks through irony, parody and pastiche. Art students may be introduced to artworks through semiotics by focussing on signs and signifiers in artworks that convey meanings through visual means.

4. High and low art

Modernist art was not art for the populace. It was art for those who had certain understanding about aesthetics and who had learned to value the formalist concerns of modern artists. Those artists and viewers who were not immersed in these concerns were excluded from the very definition of art. A hierarchical and elitist set of values thus developed which saw popular art such as graphic illustration, devalued in relation to 'fine art'. Fine art was considered as more serious and cerebral, involving higher order thinking. Popular or commercial art from film, graphics, fashion, book illustration, television and advertising art were considered as less serious and often described as 'kitsch'. A strict division existed between design as practised in tertiary graphics courses and art as it was taught in tertiary schools of art. While these courses are still taught separately the strict division between high and low art is now more blurred. Within schools of art the influence of postmodern theory has created a more pluralistic approach to art making and students seem to draw upon both popular and more traditional sources within their art making.

Within art classrooms in schools modernist art teachers have often been reluctant to allow students to copy art from popular culture. However since the early 1980s this has been a source of contention. While Lowenfeld (1950) discouraged students from copying adult imagery, Brent and Marjorie Wilson (1982) suggested that it was only natural for students to absorb the imagery they saw around them in the media. Art 'purists' of the modernist school believe that students should observe the natural world and look within themselves for ideas uncontaminated by external influences. However, the postmodern view (more aligned to the Wilson's theories) would suggest that the world comprises many potential influences and students are the products of that world. The postmodern approach would be to adopt a pluralist approach and tolerate both ways of art making; seeing that each plays a role and that each approach can be appropriate and legitimate.

However, the separation between the serious art of modernism and the 'not so serious' world of commercial art may not be as great as it appeared. While modernist artists showed great disdain for art that was produced for the commercial market, they were ostensibly in the commercial market themselves. The hypocritical way in which modernists declared their art to be above commercialism yet were clearly intent on selling their work, has not gone unnoticed by postmodern theorists. While modernist artists probably left their business affairs to their dealers they clearly relied heavily on their dealers and upon gallery directors to display and sell their work. However, this commercial side of modernist art, was concealed and seen as apart from the artist's real role of producing original art. Artists retreated from any association with the 'seamy' notion of art as commodification. Postmodern theorists have challenged the pretence in this modernist 'hidden-style marketing' and openly recognise the interdependency of art and commercial activity. Postmodern artists also deliberately fuse high art and commercial art images in their work using a range of devices involving, for example, irony, parody and pastiche.

Although Andy Warhol was probably not a postmodern artist, his works heralded postmodernism by refuting much of the fundamental principles of originality and 'purity' upon which modernism was based:

> Pop art of the 1960s traded-in the unique signature style of abstract expressionism for an unabashed impersonal and reproducible collaborative and commercial art. By using commercial techniques like silk-screen printing and drawing on imagery from advertising and by paying scant attention to 'finish', the artistic 'purity' of abstract expressionism's serious endeavour was mocked (Meecham and Sheldon, 2000, p.137).

For some postmodern contemporary artists the crass commercial world is fascinating and instead of rejecting it they revel in it. Jeff Koons, for example, sees himself as a product of consumer culture. However, his objects are not the disinterested objects and forms of modernism. His huge bunny and puppy figures are familiar icons which most people recognise as toys. The connection that viewers have with Koons' work is firstly through the familiarity with the representation and only secondly through the aesthetic design of the figures. It is this that separates the work of Jeff Koons from a modernist sensibility. He is more concerned with meaning than he is with the aesthetic, even though he is fastidious about presentation.

The division between 'fine art' and 'popular art' in modernist thought was symptomatic of the many hegemonies that developed in the modernist art world. Hierarchical ordering is established when one pole of opposition is seen as 'normal' and its opposite is by implication, seen as a negative. Key concepts then become binary oppositions where one is seen as the norm and the other is viewed as a distortion or perversion of it. In the following list then the first concept is seen favourably while the second is seen less favourably:

- Fine art/popular art
- Teaching/indoctrination
- Art/craft
- Male/female
- Knowledge/belief
- Design/kitsch

Such terms form the bulk of most discourse and when the favoured term is present in art language the biases of the writer can be revealed by the use of favoured and non-favoured terms. The postmodern art teacher can help students identify bias in art language by pointing out how writers use opposing terms to suggest particular viewpoints in their discourse. Such viewpoints can, of course, be seen to be racist, ethnocentric, sexist etc.

One of the key tasks which postmodern theorists have set themselves is to 'unpack' the discourse that surround such dichotomous views to see how elitist notions become entrenched in society. Caputo (1987) suggests that for Derrida, 'deconstruction' is a means of 'unmasking pretension' to ensure a fair playing field:

> The task of deconstruction is to keep the ruling discourse in question, to expose its vulnerability and the tensions by which it is torn (Caputo, 1987, p.195).

In Derrida's view (according to Caputo) the aim of 'deconstruction' is not to end up with confusion and anarchy but to ensure free and open debate:

> A good deal of Derrida's goal is to make the debate fair by exposing the dismissive and exclusionary gestures that tend to characterize the ruling discourse. Students, women, blacks, gays, the retarded, minorities of all sorts, 'amateurs'... nonprofessionals nonexperts, Jews, Catholics, atheists,

> scientists—all have in various ways and at various times been simply deprived of participation in 'normalised' discourse (Caputo, 1987, p.197).

Postmodern artists also deconstruct modernist art to re-examine the assumptions on which it was based. Deconstruction however must not be confused with the process of analysis of art used in modernist art criticism. As Stuart Parker explains the two processes have quite different strategies and purposes:

> Another myth is that deconstruction is synonymous with 'close reading' or 'analysis' and consequently nothing more mysterious than or additional to those notions: we take apart the text, therefore we are deconstructing! This is a mistake. Deconstruction does involve close reading and textual analysis; but it is a particular strategy of close reading and analysis. This strategy may be compared with gamesmanship. It does not just read the rules of the text closely but applies them beyond the normal limits which an etiquette of reading would require (Parker, 1997, p. 69).

Deconstruction provides a potent tool for both art teachers and students. Used in art criticism deconstruction can be used to unpack the ideologies of power, gender, class or race upon which artworks are constructed. However deconstruction can be done in many ways. Instead of simply offering criticism deconstruction actually subverts or challenges by out witting the opposition. Using irony, satire, parody or false reading deconstruction undermines an idea, image or text with tactical manoeuvres that emphasise unexpected aspects etc. When Jeff Koons makes huge stainless steel sculptures of balloon animals the image is ironic. By using 'serious' art materials to make images of 'non serious' and impermanent toys, Koons deconstructs the serious and traditional concept of a sculptor and his/her conventional subject matter. He fuses the roles of toy maker and sculptor leaving the viewer to ponder why someone would bother.

In summary, the postmodern art teacher understands that students will draw upon many sources in their art making. Postmodern art often pushes the boundaries between traditional and popular worlds and fuses them to create new worlds. Art is also seen as deriving from previous art and images are eclectically drawn from contrasting sources. As Parker says the 'trace' of other presences can be seen in all texts:

> Texts cannot be self-contained with regard to their meanings and the significance of, for example, their movements of characterization and emplotment. They are neither self-contained nor self-coherent but bear the *trace* of various readings—prior readings and possible readings—and other texts which might influence their interpretation. A text is therefore always

already a *palimpsest* of multi-layered writings and interpretations (Parker, 1997, p.80).

Postmodern artists challenge the modernist division between fine art and popular art by deliberately fusing these together in their work. Postmodern art teachers explore contemporary artists who use double-coding and parody to lampoon convention, stereotypes and 'serious' (taken for granted) values.

5. Multiculturalism

As modernist theories were associated with seemingly democratic and uplifting notions of emancipation, progress, originality and personal freedom it was assumed that these were value free, neutral, objective and universal principles. However postmodern theorists have taken a stance of hostile opposition to such assumptions and pointed out that modernist art, theorists and institutions were in fact instruments of power, suppression and marginalisation. The very success of modernism came at the expense of other art forms, artists and institutions which were excluded from modernist theory. Theorists such as Foucault have analysed modernist institutions to reveal ways in which they masked social difference by favouring conformity and homogeneity. Foucault suggested that institutions which establish totalised systems tend to be reductionist and coercive in their practices. Institutions such as art galleries and schools are powerful institutions which have until recent years often adopted modernist principles in their curricula and operational charters. Moves toward more pluralistic practices in these institutions are occurring, but in some areas these moves are undertaken slowly and reluctantly.

Modern art was a western art movement which gave only token acknowledgement to art from other cultures. Even though many modernist artists admired, for example, Japanese, African and Pacific Islander art, they appropriated (or exploited) from these art forms with little consideration for the intended cultural purpose or spiritual value of them. Modern artists westernised art from other cultures and this tended to simply reinforce western notions of domination and superiority. In focussing on western values and western aesthetics, modern art marginalised 'other' values and 'other' cultures, The arts of women, indigenous cultures and non-western cultures were excluded from dominant modernist discourses thus creating a sense of 'otherness', or the notion that there are two groups in the art world 'us' being the art cognoscenti and the 'others' being everyone else.

The western art canon formed the underlying rationale for modernist art and even though modernist artists admired and appropriated art from minority cultural groups they basically viewed them as less 'artistic'. Similarly in art education, the arts from minority cultural groups have been 'added on' in tokenistic fashion to primarily western-based curricula; a practice which simply reinforces the superiority of western art and the marginalisation of non-western arts forms. Rachel Mason points out that:

> The existence of bicultural national curricula withstanding, (eg. New Zealand and Japan—[ed.]) the Western art canon is the dominant force in the majority of the world's formal art education systems (as evidenced in the predominance of Western instructional approaches to drawing, the emphasis on 'creativity' in syllabuses, textbooks, examination systems etc.). For the new multiculturalists, this is problematic for all sorts of reasons (Boughton and Mason, 1999, p. 5).

According to Mason there are four key reasons why this is problematic. The first is that the western canon is Eurocentric and, as Chalmers points out, this falsely privileges fine art such as oil painting, sculpture and monumental architecture above art made for different purposes (Chalmers, 1996). Secondly Mason suggests that the western canon is racist and that western art history books 'transmit racist messages of exclusion' (p.5). Thirdly she suggests that it is imperialist as it has a colonising effect on smaller marginalised cultures which become dependent upon dominant western theory rather than teaching about their own cultures. Finally Mason suggests that the western canon is inappropriate in a globalised world where the previously stable categories of aesthetics are being challenged by changing conceptions of identity and culture as well as the growth of the digital revolution.

For these reasons alone it seems that art education is currently in a melting pot. Given that, as a consequence of shifting migrations of people to countries like Australian and Britain, many art teachers are teaching classes of students born in many diverse parts of the world, this is a compelling reason for art teachers to rethink the direction of western dominated art programs. However new directions are complex and there are currently many competing theories about how to construct art programs in a cultural melting pot. One way is to simply add on the study of many other cultures to the curriculum. However, without helping students to examine how values are created in art through dominant discourses the add-on approach becomes simply one of proliferation rather than real understanding. Teachers it seems, need to help students stand in the shoes of others to see that the world is experienced differently when one is born in a non-western culture. Multiculturalism in art education is diverse and requires the crossing of boundaries. It also requires us, as art educators, to imagine and respect life as it is lived in non-western shoes. Viewing the role of art through Aboriginal eyes or Islamic eyes means that art teachers need to learn about the spiritual and cultural meanings attached to imagery within other cultural groups, but this is very complex.

Richard Hickman's research of students from Muslim backgrounds is relevant here as it focuses on issues relating to religious laws and the use of imagery in the art classroom. Hickman's studies of Muslim students in Singapore and England indicate that:

> Muslim learners have no real problem in producing two-dimensional figurative work, if it is in an educational context and for educational purposes. There is however some reluctance to produce three-dimensional figurative work. The principal reasons for this are related to the belief that those who have created figures 'out of clay' are attempting to imitate God and will therefore be asked to breathe life into them on the day of judgment (Hickman in Boughton and Mason, 1999, p. 298).

Hickman does suggest that there are also great variations also within differing Islamic traditions and thus art teachers have to be careful to avoid cultural stereotyping. He warns that teachers need to be informed about the various attitudes that different students from the same culture may have. In other words, he suggests that while it is a commonly held view that Muslim students are not allowed to represent figures and animals in art classes, this is not entirely the case. Students are able to draw partial figures and they are allowed to make some figures in certain contexts. However most will avoid representing a whole figure and they may not have figurative representations in their homes.

Theories about multiculturalism also need to be carefully reworked in relation to indigenous cultures. Research by Rita Irwin and Tony Rogers indicates that current theories about multiculturalism are inappropriate to indigenous cultures as they simply seem to reinforce western domination once again, without offering Aboriginal people rights that are theirs. For example, multicultural polices based on notions of equity and individual freedom are irrelevant to Aboriginal cultures which focus on shared ownership and the responsibility of individuals to the society and the land. Such policies are also seen as undesirable in countries with bi-cultural policies where indigenous groups insist on a division between the indigenous group and the non-indigenous group (with non-indigenous groups being lumped together in one amorphous group). The notion of multi-culturalism is therefore complex and needs to be carefully developed with sensitivity to the teaching context.

Most art curricula in Australia include some study of traditional and contemporary Aboriginal art. In senior secondary art programs most art teachers direct students to artists such as Karen Casey, Lin Onus, Tracey Moffatt and Trevor Nickolls to point out how art can be used to make political statements about issues such as identity, colonisation, land rights and power. These works are very powerful and feature in most large gallery collections in Australia. However the difficult task for many Australian art teachers is to investigate other aspects of the art program to see how the western canon defines traditional Aboriginal art such as bark and rock painting. If text books and art programs continue to suggest that there is a different purpose between 'fine art' and 'craft' then traditional Aboriginal art is pushed to the margins. However, if art teachers redefine art, as Chalmers suggests, to indicate that art is made for many purposes in many cultures, then Aboriginal art may be valued for its own purposes and roles within that culture. In other words art teachers may need to find inclusive language so that the concept 'art' may include objects and images that are made for varying purposes in different contexts.

In modernist terms, as Freedman points out, the word culture often referred to 'high culture' (Freedman, 1996, p. 77). However, postmodernism has meant a total revision of the ways in which we see the nature of cultures and related issues of power, class and race. And as has already been indicated cultures are now more 'porous' than they have ever been. For many the domination of western culture is seen against the global issues of economies, world debt and human issues of poverty. As the world reels in the aftermath of terrorist attacks on the World Trade Centre in New York western communities have come face to face with global issues relating to poverty, mass migration and anti-western hatred. As a journalist in a Melbourne newspaper wrote:

> According to the International Labour Office, there are now 120 million migrants in the world... as long as the global inequalities that now exist remain, illegal immigration will not be controlled. Terrible poverty persists in many Third World countries (Pamela Bone, The Age, Melbourne, June 2000).

Essentially the rally call made by postmodern theorists has been for equity and a more level playing field. It is no longer possible to deny the existence and significance of non-western cultures in a global village. Classrooms in most western countries are not mono-cultural. Students from all countries sit side by side in most big cities and in regional country towns. As Bookchin suggests, in the postmodern world educators may need to look towards the 'periphery' and the 'margins' to find the 'core' (Bookchin, 1986).

Previously marginalised cultures and groups are given voice by postmodernists. Indigenous art and art from non-western cultures are legitimated through new journals, exhibitions and study. Issues of identity, nationalism and heritage are examined as the world becomes a global village and cultures become more porous. Postmodern art teachers acknowledge that modernist art is western and that the 'western canon' makes presumptions of universality. Postcolonial ideas are discussed and the arts of non-western cultures are studied alongside issues related to power, colonisation, land rights etc.

6. Viewers as critics

There are possibly three main reasons why art criticism has assumed a new role in postmodernism. The first is seen to relate to the recognition that the artist is not the only one responsible for creating meaning in an artwork. The second is the challenge to the notion of artistic self and the third relates to the postmodern view of language and its role in constructing meaning.

In modernist art the critic held a privileged role as the person who held exclusive knowledge about art. 'His' role was to interpret art for those who simply did not have access to the kind of exclusive knowledge about art that was required in order to 'appreciate' it. Postmodern theorists however question this privileged status and suggest that viewers actually construct the work in their own way and that in doing this they actually participate in the making process by constructing new meaning. Art is therefore said to have multiple meanings rather than a fixed and stable meaning, previously thought to be determined by the artist's intention. In fact, in postmodern theory artists and viewers are both key players in art meaning-making. In his now famous article 'Death of the Author' Barthes (1977) suggested that it is not only the artist that makes the work but also the viewers who bring to the work their own way of 'reading' it. This theory places a very different emphasis on the intentionality of the artist in the construction of artistic meaning. From a postmodern perspective, knowing what the artist intended may not help viewers construct meaning from a work at all. Furthermore, there is no way that an artist can transfer his or her sense of meaning to a mass of unknown viewers. Viewers many not see the world as the artist does at all. So transfer of meaning via statements of intentionality may be misleading, impossible or useless. In postmodern terms the viewer assumes new status as a credible critic of artworks. The 'Death of the Author' it is said, has given rise to the 'Birth of the Reader'. Pluralist voices offer pluralist ways of reading meaning in art and the postmodernist recognises that each 'reading' is only one among a host of others.

In modernist art criticism it was assumed that the artwork was a true reflection of the artist. This assumed that artists were stable beings who were capable of transferring their 'true' selves in their artwork. Postmodernists however, suggest that the individual is more complex than this. Their challenge is based on their different view of the self. In modernist terms the self and the artwork were seen as one. The artwork was seen as the personal vision of its maker and therefore it was extremely important for historians and critics to examine the biographical details of an artist's life as it was thought that the two were inseparable. The notion here suggested that to know the person was to know the work. However, postmodern theorists have suggested that in fact artists and authors can invent selves in their works and that artists can assume and invent many selves, both fictional and real. Artworks are not necessarily vehicles for conveying autobiographical records of artists' 'real' selves. For one thing, artists may not begin with a definitive notion of what they mean and may seek meaning in the actual making of the work. The work may be, and often is, the means used by the artist to seek meaning. The artist may not have a clear notion of intentionality at all. For this reason contemporary art writing may give little credence to statements written by some artists relying instead on the way viewers respond to and interpret artworks.

A further issue relating to changing perspectives in art criticism relates to the new focus on the role of language in creating meaning about art. For modernists the fixed role of language was assumed. Words, such as beauty, harmony and sensuality were assumed to be commonly understood. However postmodern theorists suggest that words and experience are inseparable; that experience is known in words (see p. 52). Several theorists (Derrida 1976, Foucault 1970, Barthes 1977, Lyotard, 1992) suggest that language (the signifier) is more important than the artwork (the signified) and that meaning is constructed from words not objects. Derrida (1976) also claims that language constructs a hierarchy of values about art which serves to privilege so-called 'fine art' but to exclude other forms of art making. Words used by critics to describe art set up a hierarchy of values which elevate the status of some art while denigrating others. He argues that language can be deconstructed into binary oppositions which determine polarised sets of values. For example, the following sets of terms set out modernist high and low art: art/craft, civilised/primitive, art/kitsch, art/artefact. By using certain terms modernist art critics established hierarchical values about art which then created a set of assumed values in the art world. Postmodernists deliberately deconstruct art language to reveal the way binary opposition and other devices are used to create hegemony in art. The term 'political correctness' has been adopted as a term referring to the need to use language which does not privilege one group at the expense of another. Thus, it is now considered politically incorrect to use language that has gender, race or cultural bias.

In the last thirty years art writing of all types has assumed greater significance in the art world. As early as 1970 in America a group of radical art historians and critics who called themselves the New Age Association declared in one of their newsletters that modernism was no longer relevant to them:

> We are against the neutrality of art.
>
> We deny that aesthetic experiences flow only into further aesthetic experiences, for we believe there is a firm tie between the artistic imagination and social imagination.
>
> We object to the study of art as an activity separated from other human concerns...
>
> We are against the reduction of art to an object of speculation and an ornament for exploiters...
>
> We are against the artificial segregation of the study of art from other disciplines-anthropology, history, etc.—and its careful protection from social issues. We are against the fragmentation of knowledge which suppresses the real implication of our cultural heritage by providing an ideology which upholds the racist, patriarchal and class structures of our society (New Age Art Association newsletter, Sept. 1970, in 'Politics', Artforum, Nov, 1970, p. 39).

While this manifesto-like statement began as a piece of political activism it ended up becoming the agenda that would dominate academic discourse for the next 30 years. The authority of the expert has been challenged. And although art critics still have a role in contemporary art many more people are writing about art. The digital age has made it easier for many more to access art and to write about it. For art teachers in schools, art writing now forms a part of all art curricula. Knowledge about art is seen to emanate from writing about art as well as from art making. In school curricula students make artworks but they also discuss artworks; their own and those of others. Artistic meaning is viewed as something to be constructed rather than given through statements of artists' intent. Meaning instead seems to emanate from many sources and to be multi-layered and interwoven. Making and discourse are seen as co-dependent ways to construct meaning in the art program. For this reason students engage in these two processes and come to understand that artistic meaning in a postmodern world comes from both what is made and what is said about it.

Postmodern art teachers encourage students to read diverse art criticism and to write with their own voice acknowledging their own cultural perspective. The privileged role of critics (especially white, male western ones) is challenged. Each viewer is seen as a constructivist, able to construct his/her own meaning in relation to a work of art.

7. Art knowledge as non-linear

As stated in the previous chapter, history of art books such as those by Gombrich 1950, Janson 1962 and Hopwood 1955 (Australia) described, from patriarchal points of view, a succession of art movements focussing on western civilisation. Each successive movement was described as an advance on previous movements. New ways of exploring the expressive potential of media and imagery were described in inspiring and romantic terms as though the story of art was leading to some modern aesthetic utopia. Art teachers up until the eighties generally taught art history in a chronological fashion as it was felt that the present could only be understood by understanding the past. Postmodern theorists however see the past differently and many question the modernist tendency to discard the past. They question whether in fact the present is better than the past and they suggest that in fact, many good things are sacrificed in the name of progress. Progress, some say, is leading to self-destruction. They suggest that we cannot presume that resources are limitless so we must save our past by revisiting and revaluing past ideas, objects and imagery. Progess may be futile if it leads to a sterile aesthetic desert.

Another postmodern view relating to progress is the notion that we live in a digital world which is so different from the past anyhow. Baudrillard (1994) suggests that the mass media in contemporary society has had a significant impact on the way we see and understand reality. Baudrillard uses the word 'simulacra' to show how the notion of 'reality' has changed in the contemporary world. The 'simulacra' is a copy which has no original. For example a film comprises many copies but it seems useless to refer to the original. Baudrillard suggests that there is no longer any distinction between the original and the copy and this makes it impossible therefore to maintain a fixed set of values in contemporary society about such things as 'truth', 'originality' or 'reality'. Everything is a copy of everything else and there can be no hierarchy of values relating to 'creative' products. This is a radical view and many refute Baudrillard's theories and their implications. In his examination of American Disneyland culture, for example, Baudrillard sees a fusion of fantasy and reality. As Meecham and Sheldon explain:

> Disneyworld, with its sanitised environment and its lack of urban detritus (vagrants and litter), simulates an American utopia. Baudrillard claims that Disneyland is presented as imaginary so that we can believe in the 'real' America. And this, he argues, is not real either. It is not a question of false representation of reality, but an 'act of concealment'. The real is no longer real, we are constantly told: in fact, it is simulated, and so we need an act of fiction (Disney) to convince us of our reality (Meecham and Sheldon, 2000, p.59).

Baudrillard's virtual world is a world of paradox and hyper-reality. It is a world in which there is no linear progression and in which there is a total collapse of certainty. Critics of Baudrillard suggest that this is a nihilistic and futile view which simply leads to chaos and anarchy. However, art teachers who use multi-media with their students will know the non-linear way in which digital programs function and they will recognise students' willingness to suspend logical thinking in order to appreciate digitally produced films such as The Matrix. Contemporary image making is frequently non-linear and fragmentation has become a tool of trade for the postmodern 'bricoleur'. The story line is often replaced by a collection of fragmented images which are juxtaposed in seemingly random fashion. Collage has replaced painting as the medium of the moment and artists revisit existing imagery as a source for ideas. However, if art educators were to relentlessly pursue Baudrillard's nihilistic approach, they may deny the future role of art teachers completely. If Baudrillard's theories were pushed to the limit there would be no need for formal education at all as the student of the future may simply draw upon the resources of computers and the community without the need of a structured schooling. In this sense most art teachers will need to cling to modernist principles of essentialism (i.e. there are some essential ideas that art teachers have in common) while they concurrently draw on more moderate and constructive postmodern theory.

Other theorists refute notions of progress in art because they think that it is no longer possible to explain phenomena with one single meta-narrative. Lyotard (in Brooker, 1992, pp. 139–150) suggests that in a postmodern era: 'The grammar and vocabulary of literary language are no longer accepted as given' (p.149) and thus there are no stable definitions which enable all people to share meaning. Lyotard suggests therefore that there is no consensus of taste which makes it possible for all people to draw similar meanings from objects. Rather than there being a stable set of rules which enable meaning to be determined, he suggests that it is actually *through* the artwork that the artist *seeks* rules. Similarly for the writer, it is *through* writing (eg art criticism and history) that the writer *seeks* rules. The rules then are not fixed and given a priori:

> A postmodern artist or writer is in the position of a philosopher: the text he writes, the work he produces are not in principle governed by preestablished rules, and they cannot be judged according to a determining judgment, by applying familiar categories to the text or to the work. Those rules and categories are what the work of art itself is looking for. The artists and the writer then, are working without rules in order to formulate the rules of what will have been done (Lyotard in Brooker, 1992, pp. 149).

The rejection of meta-narratives in art history and in education as a whole, has profound implications for educators if taken to extreme. It is difficult to imagine how teaching can occur without theories (meta-narratives). However, it is recognised that overarching, reductionist theories need to be carefully deconstructed to reveal hidden biases. In the field of art history it may be more useful for students to understand art in terms of mini-narratives. Through mini-narratives students may take a deep penetrating look at an artist and the process of art making. They may also examine the artist in context and offer critical examination of the notion of self, a notion that seemed to be taken for granted in modernist thought. Postmodern artists also explore the notion of personal signature and the nature of identity. 'Who, am I?' and 'Why am I?' become central issues in the postmodern search for self where the artwork is not so much a product of self-expression but rather a vehicle for discovering self. Mini-narratives then become quite personal allowing individuals to construct idiosyncratic versions of art knowledge; a step far removed from the metanarrative style of art history texts.

Finally the greatest challenge to the meta-narrative historical view of the history of art has come from all of the groups left out of the story. Single history of art texts, written by white western males, served to privilege other white males while simultaneously marginalising and devaluing art by all other groups. Postmodern theory calls for the rewriting or the new writing of art histories and art stories from diverse cultures and social groups. For the art teacher inclusivity becomes a new challenge as art programs take on board the study of art from a wide range of contexts. Gathering resources and information about art from diverse social and cultural contexts becomes a key issue for art teachers wanting to help students see that there are many histories of art that have been written and there are also many more to write.

Most contemporary art teachers use a range of art text books which bring together art from diverse cultures and which are designed to have students explore art from different viewpoints. By focussing on diverse issues, themes, and approaches to art many student texts now lead art teachers to approach art curricula in non-linear ways. Furthermore with access to the internet students can access information in a non-linear fashion tailored to their own interests and directions.

Students write about all types of artists. In art classes students question the way knowledge is constructed and reinforced especially when systems of knowledge are seen to privilege certain groups above others. Meta-narratives are replaced by mini-narratives and so postmodern art teachers direct students to art by lesser known as well as well known artists. Students examine why some artists become known and others not.

8. Gender

> In the early 1970s, feminist artists, critics and historians began to question the assumptions which lay behind the masculinist claim for the universal values of a history of heroic art which happened to be produced by men and which had so systematically, it appeared, excluded women's productions from its mainstream, and so powerfully transformed the image of woman into one of possession and consumption (Chadwick, 1992, p.8).

While many feminists at first sought recognition in modernist art and were therefore modernist in their attitudes to art, other feminists have rejected many modernist principles and supported postmodern notions of pluralism and equity. Clark (1996, p.35) defines two distinct waves of feminist theory. First generation scholarship he suggests was concerned to establish the superiority of women and to reclaim a place in the world that rightfully belonged to women. This first wave feminism contained three strands. The first 'social analysis' involved women examining the social conditions which served to exclude women, the second involved political activism and the third involved the development of alternatives to existing patriarchal systems in society. First generation scholarship in the art world, often adopted an aggressive stance in order to simply be heard. However second generation scholarship has tended to focus on equity aspects and address related issues. The first of these related issues asks whether disciplines such as art and education can be reconstructed to support equality for men and women. A second issue has been the examination of gender construction to determine whether 'femaleness' is biologically or sociologically created. A third area of examination has focussed on the implications of feminist theory for educators.

It is the last issue that is of concern for art teachers. One reason why gender has become a key issue for consideration in art rooms is that it is so bound up with the whole way in which art has been constructed to privilege male artists. And the solution is not to simply add studies of women artists to the male dominated curriculum. The issue is more complex than this because postmodern art teachers take students further by having students examine *how* gender differences can be constructed and reinforced through art. In postmodern art classes students not only study art by women but they deconstruct past images of people to see that males and females have been portrayed in certain ways which define them as having certain qualities. They also see that contemporary artists can portray males and females in ways which challenge stereotypical views of gender. In other words, the postmodern art teacher plays a key role in shaping societal values. How we learn about gender relationships, roles and expectations is very much bound up with how we have seen these portrayed in images, be they film, photographs or paintings.

Modernist artists were usually male and the female nude became the most common subject matter of modernist art. The woman became the object of the male gaze. Male artists looked upon women as beautiful subjects (or objects) for depiction within modernist painting and sculpture. It was never the other way around. Few female artists in the modernist era obtained recognition for their art. It was these issues that fuelled the feminist movement and gave rise to two main groups of feminist artists; the first a modernist group hoping for recognition within modernism and the latter rejecting modernism for postmodernist principles. Early feminist artists challenged the domination of male artists by trying to gain acceptance within the modernist paradigm. More recent postmodern women artists however rejected the modernist paradigm and tried to establish recognition on their own terms. Many now deliberately parody the treatment of women in modernist art in order to reveal the gender bias within specific artworks. Postmodern artists such as the Japanese photographer Morimura re-examine the subject of the male gaze by putting himself as the reclining figure in a re-make on Manet's 'Olympia'. By swapping the male and female figures in modernist works teachers and students can begin to see the way gendered conventions have been established and taken for granted.

Within the profession of art education teachers have had to re-examine art history texts to expose the elimination of women artists from them. Teachers now seek more recent texts which provide rediscovered information about the forgotten women artists of modern and pre-modern times. A further task has been to examine the profession of art education to see whether classroom practice equitably serves the interests of both boys and girls. On a broader scale art teachers have had to consider whether both males and females are assuming equal responsibility at the top of the profession, in administrative and leadership positions. In the art room itself the exploration of gender issues is extremely popular for adolescent students. Issues related to gender and all aspects of life including sport, culture, the media and fashion are frequently explored in student artwork. The key difference between a modernist and postmodern approach however, rests upon whether teachers accept traditional gender roles in art or whether they encourage students to become critical thinkers who question how art shapes and reinforces gender roles. The latter is a more political role and many teachers may find this more difficult.

Postmodern art teachers know that representations of people are always statements of positioning. Students study new feminist histories and art by women, especially art which explores identity and issues of gender. Masculinist art teachers and students also examine the impact of feminism on them and explore the construction of masculinity.

9. Scepticism and postmodern doubt

Postmodern discourse is sceptical: it is about dissidence. It *does* require that students and teachers adopt a different attitude to 'art' than modernist discourse. As Taylor writes:

> One the one hand, post-modernism in most of its forms is undoubtedly a vigorous and even critical manifestation. It takes a hard look at some of the doubtful assumptions of modernism and attempts variously to undermine them. To that extent it may seem to be at least a vigorous critical art. In other ways, however, it seems a disconnected even alienated art form (Taylor, 1987, p.8).

Modernism has been described as the embodiment of optimism. Great theories, great inventions and great art provided a buoyant foundation for art education. Lowenfelds' description of the natural unfolding of children's drawing symbolised the great progressive path that modern art pursued. Lowenfeld's theory was one of optimism; faith in the natural ability of children to grow and draw spontaneously untainted by the evils of commercialism, adult corruption and societal clichés. Unfettered the child would be a healthier, more pure and more innocent being as 'he' moved through the various drawing stages. Yet the same optimism which sought a more modern, more rational, more progressive and more perfect world, also gave birth to the Nazi regime and the holocaust. Reason and grand visions may sometimes serve to mask other attitudes which have been suppressed and marginalised in the quest for recognition. It is hard to see any sinister side to Lowenfeld's joyous visions of childhood (although Lowenfeld himself knew well the sinister side of Nazi Germany and fled Vienna for America at the onset of WW2). The other side of Lowenfeld's theory however lies possibly in his exclusive focus on western children (and art) at the exclusion of non-western cultures.

When everything seems to be going well the postmodernist always looks at the flip side. This is seemingly a pessimistic sceptical way of viewing reality, but it a realistic way of cautioning us to be aware and to consider phenomena from more than one perspective. Art educators may see this as a 'downer' and as against the spirit of art which, in modernist terms, is meant to inspire. However, it also cautions teachers to direct students to think about art in community and cultural context. It encourages consideration of the 'other' and it decentres focus from the reckless freedom of the individual to the responsibilities of global care and cultural tolerance. Globalisation in art education may be considered in many ways and issues relating to politics, economics and religion cannot be ignored and separated from the study of contemporary art. Postmodern art is complex and it fuses art with the complex problems being faced in all spheres of life as well as across disciplines. Art and science have never been closer and language and art are being seen as inextricably interwoven. Postmodernists are not pessimists but postmodern doubt serves as a reminder that contemporary art is pluralist and multi-faceted.

For some postmodern artists the use of world resources is a key issue. Art teachers may have to concede that there may not be an endless supply of bleached cartridge paper in the storeroom. Students do know that the world's forests are not limitless. They recognise that issues of conservation cannot always be someone else's problem. While art teachers may examine these issues with students, when it comes to changing practice not many really want to make art from scrap just to use to use up the world's waste resources. Suzi Gablik suggests that 'In modern times, the basic metaphor of human presence on the earth is the bulldozer' (Gablik, 1991, 77). Many postmodern artists focus on the destructive use of the earth's resources while others deliberately use nature unobtrusively and respectfully. Andy Goldsworthy for example works in sympathy with nature and imposes no extraneous materials on it. His leaves joined with thistles, arrangements of stones, constructions of sticks or icicles are gentle human structures which convey human presence in harmony with the environment. Saving the environment however, is only one issue among many for student exploration.

Postmodern doubt takes many forms. Postmodernists question the use of words and language and how these convey meaning and values. They question taken for granted values about self, identity, originality and power. They also question progress and the impact of it on the earth's resources. They question western domination as a given, in a world composed of many cultures all living together in a cultural melting pot.

Students and teachers challenge many 'taken for granted assumptions'. Hierarchical values are questioned and borders are redefined. Postmodernists deconstruct meaning to see how values are constructed. Postmodern art teachers lead students to 'sites for struggle in art': art knowledge is not seen as fixed and stable. Critical pedagogy is however introduced in safe and supportive contexts which facilitate debate in constructive ways.

Summary

Postmodern art education offers new challenges for art teachers. Instead of focusing on the teaching of aesthetic sensibility from a predominantly western canon, students in a postmodern world can be made aware that there are many art canons which have been developed in different cultures and societal groups. Using varied forms of critical pedagogy postmodern art teachers can help students see signs that indicate how, where and why particular artworks have been constructed. Through strategies of deconstruction students can understand how power impacts on the way images are represented in art. In relation to gender, class, culture and even age, students can investigate artworks to reveal the values and meaning systems that underpin them. In their own artwork postmodern students feel comfortable with the notion that their personal aesthetic sensibility is derived from other sources and that making meaning in art can be an eclectic practice which draws on many disparate origins. Postmodern students will not necessarily seek a unified aesthetic in art making but will live with the notion that through pastiche and collage art may have multiple meanings and be deliberately double-coded to suggest layers of interpretation. Postmodern art rooms will be places where real and often difficult issues are examined and interrogated. Art will not remain apart from other domains of understanding in a postmodern world. Students will begin to examine links between their studies in science, history, English, media studies and mathematics. Postmodern art education will break down boundaries between high art and popular art and students will have great fun fusing the serious with the 'crass'; the sacred with the profane. Boundary breaking is the crux of postmodern art and the boundaries around modernism will be moved, although not entirely destroyed.

Summary of key postmodernist orientations in art education

1.The individual in context

In postmodern art rooms art teachers understand that individualism is a western concept which may not apply to students of some cultures. Postmodern art teachers conceive of students as participants in the culture/s around them. Students are therefore not seen as autonomous and apart from society but as participants in it. Postmodern art teachers develop in students a sense of the 'other' so that students develop an awareness of different cultures and different ways in which identity can be defined.

2. Pluralism

Aesthetic pluralism in postmodern art classes may mean that students study art made for diverse purposes eg as religious icons, as used in costume, as used for propaganda or as domestic decoration. Students may also work collaboratively to explore issues of global, environmental or political concern. This does not mean that all art must take on these forms but that more diverse approaches to art making are tolerated and encouraged to reflect the nature of art in diverse cultural and social contexts. Postmodern art denies any dominant aesthetic style, medium or movement, however collage becomes more prominent than painting and art is often made from other art. In postmodern classes students study how art values are constructed and reinforced within cultural groups.

3. Art for meaning

Postmodern artists are concerned with meaning rather than with formalist composition or technique. Postmodern art teachers discuss how meaning is constructed and explore multiple readings of artworks through irony, parody and pastiche. Art students may be introduced to artworks through semiotics by focussing on signs and signifiers in artworks which convey meanings through visual means.

4. High art and low art

Postmodern artists challenge the modernist division between fine art and popular art by deliberately fusing these together in their work. Postmodern art teachers explore contemporary artists who use double-coding and parody to lampoon convention, stereotypes and 'serious' (taken for granted) values.

5. Multiculturalism

Previously marginalised cultures and groups are given voice by postmodernists. Indigenous art and art from non-western cultures are legitimated through new journals, exhibitions and study. Issues of identity, nationalism and heritage are examined as the world becomes a global village and cultures become more porous. Postmodern art teachers acknowledge that modernist art is western and that the 'western canon' makes presumptions of universality. Postcolonial ideas are discussed and the arts of non-western cultures are studied alongside issues related to power, colonisation, land rights etc.

6. Viewers as critics

Postmodern art teachers encourage students to read diverse art criticism and to write with their own voice acknowledging their own cultural perspective. The privileged role of critics (especially white, male western ones) is challenged. Each viewer is seen as a constructivist, able to construct his/her own meaning in relation to a work of art. The death of the author has meant the birth of the viewer.

7. Art knowledge as non-linear

Students write about all types of artists. In art classes students question the way knowledge is constructed and reinforced especially when systems of knowledge are seen to privilege certain groups above others. Meta-narratives are replaced by mini-narratives and so postmodern art teachers direct students to art by lesser known as well as well known artists. Students examine why some artists become known and others not.

8. Gender

Postmodern art teachers know that representations of people are always statements of positioning. Students study new feminist histories and art by women, especially art which explores identity and issues of gender. Masculinist art teachers and students also examine the impact of feminism on them and explore the construction of masculinity through art.

9. Scepticism and postmodern doubt

Students and teachers challenge many 'taken for granted assumptions'. Hierarchical values are questioned and borders are redefined. Postmodernists deconstruct meaning to see how values are constructed. Postmodern art teachers lead students to 'sites for struggle' in art: art knowledge is not seen as fixed and stable. Critical pedagogy is however introduced in safe and supportive contexts which facilitate debate in constructive ways.

Section 2

Teachers Reflect on Teaching Art in a Postmodern World

Thirteen secondary art teachers from Australia and England reflect on teaching practice in a postmodern world.

Each teacher responds to key questions related to recent changes in their art curricula and methodology. Focus is upon the teaching of postmodern ideas related to gender, class, culture and social issues. The use of technology is discussed as it relates to postmodern practice.

Chapter 4

David Williams

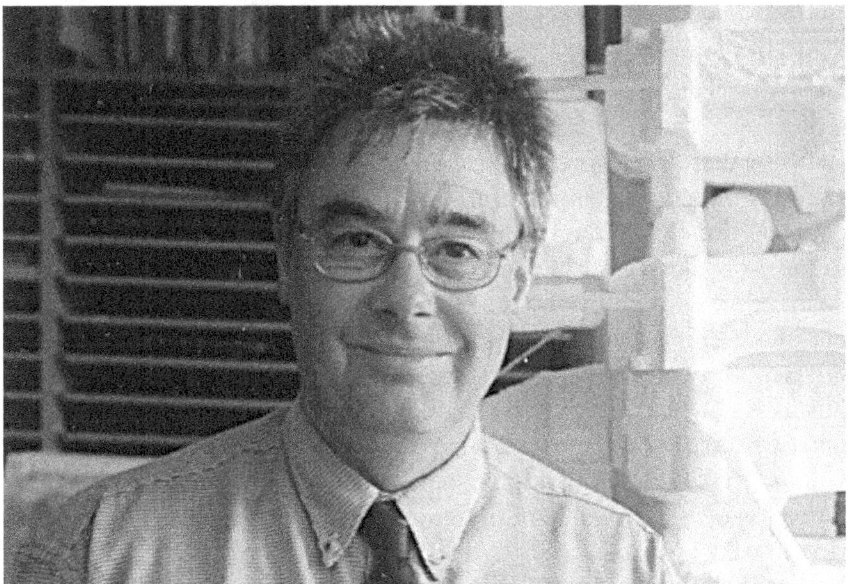

David Williams is head art teacher at Camberwell Boys' Grammar School in Melbourne. The school is set in a leafy eastern suburb and the art and graphics rooms are relatively new, bright and well equipped. The school has a growing population of Asian students and the school ethos is generally one of discipline and structure, in the modernist sense. The primary school has a lively art program and the secondary school offers ceramics, graphics and art. David has been teaching for 25 years. He has established a strong artists in residence program in the art department and runs annual senior art exhibitions and art camps. In rejecting prescriptive approaches to art making David encourages students to search for art and identity in the process of making. In doing this David offers students a world in which risks are taken, alternatives explored and multiple viewpoints celebrated. (ed.)

I realise that there are certain aesthetic principles underlying my teaching and one of the reasons that I have never liked the current Victorian Certificate of Education (VCE) model, although I have to teach it and have taught it for some years, is that it is very prescriptive. It presupposes that there is a certain way of working and a certain way of making art and this is definitely not the way I would do it. In fact I hate having to impose this on my students because I don't think it is the way artists necessarily work, I think it is the way people like to tidy it up and pretend that it works this way. I was speaking to our current artist in residence, David Porter today and he was saying the same thing. He never does preliminary drawings. He never pre-plans his work. He just launches himself onto the canvas and does it from there. He just makes it up and anything that needs altering or correcting he does on the canvas. This is the way I go about it too.

In thinking about the philosophies underlying my own teaching I knew that there certainly were some there and when I thought about it a bit longer I realised that in fact they are paramount in my mind. In my view there are two ways of going about art making. One way is to see something and then illustrate it, which I think is what most people do, but I think this is only one way of going about it. And the other is to have no idea at all but to make art anyway. It is a matter of just being brave enough to start and I have always said that the ideas come out of the doing. But to do this I think you have got to have a culture in a school which is very, very safe because it allows and encourages mistakes. I actually call them triumphs in the sense that if you don't make mistakes you are not moving anywhere. If you are to go through your art making without any mistakes you are in fact marking time, as far as I can see. You are simply going up and down on the same spot. If you make a mistake and if you recognise it as such you are actually moving forward because you are wanting to go beyond what you are already doing. So I encourage students to experiment enormously and to make what they call mistakes, although I don't really see them as mistakes, I just see them as part of the ongoing process. In order for that to happen the studio space, the teacher and the class have to be very comfortable with the idea that things might not work out as planned. I believe that if you don't have a plan to start with everything works out alright. I think that is the better way to work and I also think that it is the harder way. You only have a very loose idea of what you want; a very small idea but it builds with the doing of it, rather than having a very clear and very planned idea and then illustrating it. I think that is a 'cop out' because it is not far removed from colouring-in books where you have a tight outline and you just apply colour to it.

I have collected a lot of statements about these things which have impacted on my teaching. For example, Brett Whiteley said in 1990: 'The moment you know what you are doing it is just illustration, not art'. That encapsulates what I am trying to say. I don't like planned art to the point where there are no further decisions to be made, where it is just a matter of carrying it out. Just looking through this list of quotations which I have always had pinned on my board (you can see all the pin holes which show I have used it a lot) I like Alechinsky's statement (1961) that 'One does not choose the content one submits to it'. It's nice when you start off with a portrait and all of a sudden it starts to look like a landscape. In the video about Brett Whiteley he does this very thing. He turns the painting on its side. It is a portrait of Patrick White and he turns it into a landscape. So one doesn't choose the content. The painting speaks to you as much as you speak to it. I think you have to be alive to messages you are getting back from the artwork, not just to what you are trying to impose on to it.

I also love this statement by Philip Guston in 1978. He says 'I enjoy having a subject to paint. But it's not very controllable, in fact totally uncontrollable because meaning keeps shifting and so does the structure'. I think this is what students find a lot. They start off their work and they get to a certain point and they say 'Oh, it's wrecked' or 'Damn, it hasn't worked out'. At that point you have to save the work from being thrown in the bin because they want to. However, if they throw it in the bin, they will start again and they will get to exactly that point and it still won't work. And then they will start again and so on. But when they realise, or when you can encourage them to go beyond that point to recognise that, in fact, it isn't wrecked it has just changed, that is the point at which artistic learning really starts.

'In every real experiment there is a moment of zero predicability'. I love that statement by Asger Jorn (1964). When you don't know how it is going to turn out, that is when I think art works best. But it is all very well for experienced artists to understand these things but for students to employ these things the art room has to be a very safe environment. Students have to know that they can actually startwork without knowing how it is going to turn out. I encourage students by reassuring them all the time. I tell them that it's great to not know where it's going or leading. A good teacher can see when they know or see what they are doing. It is not perplexing any more and they can see the point of it. This is terrific. Jasper Johns (1959) says 'Sometimes I see it and then I paint it. Other times I paint it and then I see it'. There are two ways of going about it. I think drawing an outline or planning and drawing it very tightly and colouring it in, is the least creative way of going about art. I think it should evolve and grow on the canvas like an organism. It should just evolve. I think it should change as thinking changes and I think students shouldn't be afraid. I encourage students doing paintings to hold them up to the mirror to have a look at them. The mirror is a nice useful tool because it reverses the image. Sometimes I get them to turn their work upside down and I say well does it look better this way? They say they have never seen it this way so I suggest that it could be seen this way, it doesn't really make any difference. So something that starts off in one way might end up in another. I think these ideas do permeate my teaching.

I have taught students to draw something like a face and then told them to turn it into a landscape and then just when they think that is the end of the exercise I tell them to turn it into an interior. So it's a little bit like that piece in Hamlet where they're looking at the clouds and Polonius says 'Me thinks it looks like a weasel' and this other person says 'Me thinks it looks like a whale'. So you can see things differently and I have been interested in that sort of approach for a long time.

The other thing tied to this idea is that instead of starting with an idea in art, you can start with the materials and you work with them until an idea comes out. It doesn't matter what the materials are. It could be oil paint on canvas, coloured pencils on paper, vegemite on tissue paper, glue and sand, or sticks, string, masking tape and rubber bands. I think an artist is just somebody who works creatively with stuff; with anything; just with things. They can work with found objects, manufactured objects or colours, cut paper or even coffee grounds. I read somewhere that Braque used to mix coffee grounds with paint. It doesn't matter what you are working with. I think artists in the Arctic circle or the Kalahari desert work with the materials that are at hand whether it's walrus tusk or elephant dung.

Today when our artist in residence David Porter came in here he remarked on how many materials we had in our art storeroom. He asked if it made better art. I said that I don't think that it does. You can make very good art with a ballpoint pen on paper. Of course it makes things easier when you have a range of materials for a range of experiences, but this doesn't necessarily make better art. In fact, when I have been in other schools and I haven't had all of these things, it didn't make any difference because one can work just as well with a pair of scissors, some black and white paper and some newspaper. I will never forget visiting a large school in France which had over 2000 students. I asked the art teacher whether the school gave him a budget. The teacher said yes and he told me in French francs. I calculated the amount and it came to about $200. I asked if I could have a look in the storeroom and there were all these shelves with not a thing on them. I asked him if he had any paper. 'Oh no', he said, 'we can't afford that'. 'Pencils?' I said. 'Oh no', he said, 'we can't afford them either'. 'Well what do you do?' I asked. Well they have to bring their own. And then when I looked around I noticed that the students were doing some very interesting work with cardboard cartons from the supermarket, advertising material, cutting and pasting material, drawing on it with textas, making masks and figures, all with these recycled materials. And I thought well that's right, all you need is a pair of scissors and a bit of imagination and you can make wonderful things.

I was showing a video to my students the other day about Rauschenberg. He says he used to go for a walk around the block in New York every morning in any direction, and would pick up enough material to work with for the rest of the day. He said if he didn't find enough stuff he would allow himself one other block in any direction. I don't think you need to have expensive materials to make good art. You probably need some things but things can be found or attained in ways other than through a chequebook. You can ask people to donate things or you can find off-cuts that you can use very creatively. I don't think expensive materials are the answer. I think that what you do with stuff is more important than what you actually work with.

Although my initial training was in painting and drawing I think that is far too narrow a way of working for students. I encourage them to work with all sorts of found objects and things they might come across. I am looking now at a box of feathers which I have been offering students but we still have not found a way of using them. However last week one student discovered the new laminating machine in the library and we have been looking at the possibility of laminating the feathers between sheets of plastic and hanging them from the ceiling. So this could be quite interesting. We also found a collection of small boxes which are like little frames and a student has commandeered those to exhibit small photographs. So he is going to put photos in these and arrange them all over a wall, maybe at random.

Actually, 'at random' is a concept I like very much because utilising chance is as logical as using a logical structure. You can use 'chance' as a logical system for working. Duchamp used chance many times. He would throw pieces of string in the air and would draw lines where they landed. It always seems to me that chance is as good a way of working as any. I remember Rauschenberg buying tins of paint at the local hardware store that had all lost their labels. He had no idea what colours there were, but in a sense it didn't matter because he could work creatively with what colours he had. If you spend a lot of time choosing colours you are employing a discriminatory system that is logical maybe, but it is just as logical to do this in reverse. So I quite like that idea. Often if a student says to me 'Have we got any more green paint?' I would most likely say 'Well why don't you use blue?' It is a bit like the old question 'Which ice cream is best, chocolate or strawberry?' Who cares? They are both OK. So, if there's no green paint there, why not use blue. It might be better anyway.

I do encourage students to use foreign materials. I don't think anything is beyond being useful. If you want interesting things to work with, looking through the local garbage skip you find all sorts of wonderful things. In fact I have a student at the moment doing Expressionist-Fauve-type portraits. He found some of that packing stuff which comes inside boxes. It looks like egg cartons and it is in a particular sort of shape. He was able to paint on that and create a sort of head out of it by putting some eyes and mouth on it. And when you think about it a blank piece of white paper is about the most boring surface you can imagine if you want to do something interesting on it.

In terms of art appreciation I remember that when I was at school the textbook we used was Graham Hopwood's 'Art Students Handbook'. It was the first art text I had read. We progressed from that to E.H. Gombrich's 'A Story of Art' in which I discovered that not one female artist was mentioned. It had a profound impact on me when I discovered that half the population of the world was not represented. I think we have come a long way to addressing those sorts of imbalances. In those times when I taught matriculation and Higher School Certificate (HSC) the focus was very much upon traditional western art from the Renaissance and Baroque periods. Or, if you were fairly progressive you might have taught about late 18thC or early 19thC art. In fact this was the very popular period in the HSC course in which people would teach about Turner or Constable or maybe David, Gericault or Delacroix. This was the period of art that 50% of the students in the state were studying. But I think teachers have progressivley moved forward from that point and I think most teachers are now teaching about 20th century and even contemporary art. The VCE tried to address this by saying that teachers had to address art since 1945 and then since 1960 and the revised study says since 1970. So there has been a considerable shift in the sorts of things teachers are presenting to their students. I think most of it is now focussed on the 20th century rather than the 19th century, which was the case 20 years ago.

I have been running the artist in residence program at this school successfully since 1981 and we have had 80 or 90 artists through here with as many as six a year. This has been very interesting for me because when I came to this school 20 years ago I thought I would set up my easel alongside the students and I thought I would teach by example. I thought this would be a good way to go. So I tried it but I very quickly realised that the more I concentrated on my own work the less I was concentrating on my class. And the more I concentrated on the teaching the less I was able to do my own work. It wasn't working for me at all. It came to a point when I realised that I would have to do something about it. So I chose the teaching. I would do the teaching and someone else would do the painting. I got a friend of mine to set up his easel and he started painting and then I was able to focus all my attention on the students. Then when he finished his time here I got somebody else and then when I ran out of friends I had to look around and see where I could get some more artists. I thought of my old art school, the Victorian College of the Arts, and so I sent them a letter to them asking them if any of their postgraduate students would like to come and work here. They work on their course work so we are not asking them to do anything different. It is just a change of studio. We provide them with lunch, travelling expenses and all the materials they need to work with, and at the end of their time here we usually purchase a work from them directly or from their end of year exhibition at the VCA.

Another initiative of which I am quite proud because it has worked very well, is the annual art camp that I run in conjunction with a couple of other schools. We started it 12 years ago and it has gone from strength to strength. It has something to do with networking. Each year in the term one holidays we take a group of about 70 year 12 students from three schools which are geographically very close, to a camp at the beach called the Lord Somers camp. We have an intensive experience for five days. I tell the students that they can achieve as much in those five days as they can in a term at school, because the way days are structured at school are not very conducive to art making. Also there is a social agenda there. The three schools just happen to be single sex schools but we strike a balance between boys and girls so it is valuable to have this as well. It is a very highly structured camp. It is very intensive. When everyone around you is working so hard you just feel that you want to be part of it. I think that is what is so valuable for us as art teachers. We are so committed to it that we are totally prepared to do it even though it might be holiday time. We couldn't possibly do it in term time and we look forward to it every year.

We are standing in front of a very large student painting which is very much influenced by Rauschenberg, I guess. This was done by a boy who was lucky enough to go to America at Christmas time and he saw a lot of art in New York including Rauschenberg's work. I like the rectilinear structure in this work. It is a large canvas of about a couple of metres square and it is basically primary colours, red, blue and yellow on a white ground. But what he knows is that you don't have to put down areas of red or blue or yellow paint. He has gone out and found pieces of tin, pieces of cloth and a discarded raincoat and he has started gluing all these things down. Then when he started hanging pieces of cloth off the front, just to see whether he wanted another blue square or white square etc. There is a nappy up there. He had a white nappy but he realised it was too white so he got some spray paint out and has painted it blue. What he was doing was looking to see if it needed a blue square in the top part of the painting but as he was pinning the blue cloth in the top part of the painting he began to realise that the pieces of cloth would do the job anyhow. He didn't actually need to put paint. It doesn't really matter whether there are areas of paint or areas of cloth or areas of tin in this work. When he was looking to put something in the bottom right hand part of the canvas he found an old discarded painting apron which he thought would do the job adequately. So he just hung it there. He then found a coat hook which he screwed into the stretcher of the canvas and hung the apron on it which does the job. I think there are still some areas he wants to work on. He wants to stencil some areas and put something over some areas, but essentially all the elements are there now. So this is terrific development for this student and he will go beyond this in other subsequent works.

This next work is a sculpture of a bandaged leg. It is done by a boy who on the first day of school this year, came on crutches. I said 'My goodness, what have you done to your leg?' and he said 'Oh it's all right now but I had an operation on it during the holidays'. And I said 'Well it looks wonderful. You should do drawings and paintings and take photographs of that' because with all the metal of the crutches either side of this leg and with all the white bandages around it, it looked terrific. I said there is a lot of stuff to work with. Anyhow he found a shop mannequin's leg which he thought looked too feminine. He got a bucket full of hair from the barbers which he put on with brown varnish, and this makes the leg look more masculine. He has put a shoe and a sock on it and added a plaster bandage on the knee and the whole thing is suspended with these huge G-clamps attached to a metal frame. It looks like an amputated leg suspended in space, held together with these pieces of metal very cruelly screwed into the side of the leg. It's quite an evocative piece and its good in the sense that it comes from his own experience and from the operation. He is actually using what he went through in the summer holidays as the material for his art making.

I want to now describe a work that was done last year. This student wanted to do a painting that was related to him without it being illustrative or representational. He has some large trays with various medical instruments in them. Then he started sticking all these trays and medical paraphernalia onto a large board. He then attached plastic bags containing various objects which related to his own person, such as scabby old used bandaids, hair that he had cut off his body, toenails, fingernails, used tissues and other things. It was almost like a set of exhibits at a coroner's inquest, however it was all put up on a wall and called 'art'. It was quite provocative but it was also very liberating for him because he could see how one could make a work that went beyond the expected boundaries of 'school art'. It actually propelled him into another way of thinking which was very liberating for him but also very meaningful. These very good students work very hard on the meaning in their work. It is not just decoration. It goes far beyond that. It becomes a means of communication. It becomes a dialogue. It is meaningful rather than meaningless.

In thinking about postmodernism I can remember quite distinctly hearing the word postmodern for the first time and I was shocked because I thought that modern art was art of the current time. And then I heard Robert Hughes say that modern art was finished and it was now an historical style. It makes a lot of sense to me now. Modern art grew up some time in the second half of the nineteenth century and the great period of modernism was the first half of the 20th century and the last gasp was probably in the sixties or seventies or sometime like that. And as impressionism was replaced by post-impressionism I think at the end of a century there is always a summing up and a looking back and revisiting certain sites. I think this is what postmodernism is doing. It is looking to see what has been achieved, where we've come from, how we can reuse the information or use it differently. When I talk to my students about this they can see all that. I say to them that artists in the nineteenth century used to paint nature. They would go out into the countryside and they would paint hills and trees and nature would be their inspiration.

Well for artists today there is a different sort of nature which is the media. We are bombarded with images and information from so many places. When I see Andy Warhol's paintings of Campbell soup tins they are in a sense a new nature. That is as real an experience and a much more everyday experience than the hills and trees that one associates with traditional nineteenth century paintings. And when one realises that a lot of our information is gleaned from television and pre-packaged images, edited and given to us in another format, we see how incredibly true they are. In the same way a painter like Rauschenberg paints disparate images that seem to have no obvious link, and in fact they don't. It's like when you turn the sound off television and you see people running and moving and weeping and car accidents and you see advertisements being flashed at you and you see somebody else talking. It is life and that's how life looks and that's the way it is presented to us. And an artist like Rauschenberg is very real in the sense that his paintings are just like the way we experience life. And so I think that he is postmodern, in the sense that he is dealing with life in a new way.

Chapter 5

Bill Hall

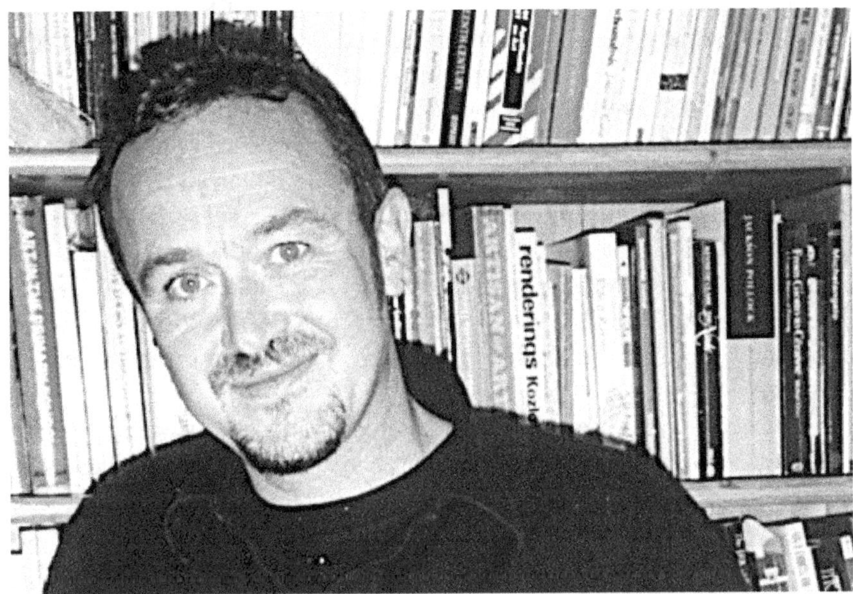

Bill Hall is Head of Art & Design at Mascalls School at Paddock Wood, south east of London in Kent. He has been teaching for 24 years. In 1992 he completed his Master of Arts (in Art & Design Education) thesis at Manchester Metropolitan University. His thesis was entitled 'Modernism to Postmodernism: An examination of change in secondary art and design education in England'. He has been active in Art & Design Education both regionally and nationally through his involvement with the National Society for Education in Art & Design (NSEAD) and work with practising and trainee art teachers. He is also an active artist. (ed.)

My school is between Maidstone and Tunbridge Wells. It is semi-rural and the school population is almost 100% white. It has a varied population with people from very middle class backgrounds, including some from parents commuting to London each day, as well as many working class families. We have a small number of settled traveller families (gypsies) in the school which reflects the Kent heritage of itinerate rural labourers. There are also some families who are second generation East End Londoners who, years ago, moved out of the smoke of the city and stayed on after their summer jobs of harvesting apples and hops. Our pupils represent the full range of academic ability but the majority are in the average to below average bracket because we lose many 'high flyers' to the grammar schools. However, having said that, we actually do very well by our students and have an active sixth form. Many go on to university courses and every year there are students who get three As at A levels.

My M.A. thesis was stimulated by my work with NSEAD (National Society for Education in Art and Design) in about 1987/'88 at a local level. In 1988 I found out about the M.A. in Art Education course at Manchester. It was in the second year of the course that we were introduced to postmodernism. I had never heard of this before. I began to hear that artists like Rauschenberg and Warhol didn't fit into the modernist paradigm. Critics like Clement Greenberg didn't go for it. I began to see that, for example, Lichtenstein and Warhol, didn't fit into it. Their work was so anti the high modernist ideal of abstract art. Then we started looking at other artists like Jeff Koons who were doing new things, and these didn't fit anywhere into the modernist paradigm.

I started to pick up on that. It interested me because I had never felt that I fitted into modernism anyway. I never really liked the dogma of it. Something didn't quite click. The thinking wasn't free enough for me. So when I saw postmodern architecture it seemed so much more interesting than all that right angled glass and steel stuff. Postmodernism could be quirky and eclectic. It had all kinds of new possibilities. I started to read work by Charles Jencks and thought 'this is great'. That's when I started to ask whether art education was going postmodern. I started to think about the idea of 'Critical Studies', and how the growth of this reflected aspects of postmodernist thinking. I discussed this with my course leader and she supported it as the basis of my thesis. I then started researching it in more depth and reading Lyotard and Baudrillard etc. It was fantastic. I skipped all the deconstructionist and post-structuralist stuff because it seemed to be an interim stage and I thought, 'Why go through all of this seventies theory when I can go straight to the present'. It was Harvey's book 'The Condition of Postmodernity' that I really found helpful at the time.

Harvey was a geographer but he pulled in all sorts of material from film, art film, economics and every aspect of contemporary life. His case for a paradigm shift struck a chord with my ideas. Some of the changes he described could be seen as negative, in relation to the ideals of the modernist thinkers which had preceded it. I didn't necessarily approve of everything labelled as postmodern. It then struck me that even now the word 'modern' is usually seen as very positive. But try a phrase like 'modern warfare' and see how positive that sounds. Similarly I realised that postmodern can be both positive and negative and every era has its positive and negative side—like two sides of the same coin. This idea also got me going—the sort of 'Zen duality'. It all tied in with things I had read back in the early eighties; people like Fritjof Capra who had fascinated me at the time. This was the most exciting set of concepts I had come across in years and years.

I began by trying to establish what modernist was. I had done an essay in art history comparing modernism and postmodernism and I realised that what I had to do was expand it, define the terms and then survey the development 20th century art & design education. The aim was first to establish if there had been such a thing as 'Modernist Art Education' and had there been a shift towards a more 'postmodern' approach towards the end of the century. I started by looking at Cisek, Lowenfeld and Richardson to see how they broke the ground for modernist art education. Then I looked at the' Basic Design' approach of Kurt Rowland, Saumarez and others whose ideas were still current in the 1970s when I first came into teaching.

It soon became clear to me that all these theorists were influenced by the interpretation of the contemporary art of their own time. These approaches were taken up by teachers who found theories echoed their own ideals of art and produced results which looked (superficially at least) like 'real art'. In the sixties art students came out with a grounding in abstract art and Basic Design (the latter forming the core of art 'foundation' courses based on the philosophies of the Bauhaus) and supported modernist ideals. For those who went into teaching in schools it really suited them to introduce Basic Design to their pupils. It was the newest thing. It was logical and it made sense. Students experimented with colour; they drew lines of boxes with different textures; they cut out little shapes and arranged them in different compositions in pursuit of a visual vocabulary. The resulting images had the look of abstracts by Victor Passmore or Jean Arp. The Kurt Rowland books laid down a whole course which did much not only to develop aesthetic awareness but in particular promoted the values and clean lines of modern design and architecture. The stated aim was allow the students to develop their own vocabulary which they could then use to 'express themselves' more fully. Students were supposed to have a fresh vision, uninhibited by the art practices of the past and so were never introduced to the work of actual artists. However, by the end of year 9, when you had done all of this, and students started exam courses and were given the opportunity to do their own thing, they just went off and copied record album covers. They didn't connect because basic design was a 'hands off' thing. The notion was that students should learn the skills first, then they would have the vocabulary to express themselves. But what did they have to express? They didn't know what ART looked like or what it was trying to do. The only artwork they had come in to contact with were cartoons and the latest album covers of their favourite band. They didn't really know what was possible.

In the seventies I remember introducing students to the idea of Pop Art. Naturally, at that time I didn't show them examples of the real article. Exposing the students to artists' work was still frowned upon; it would prevent them from developing their own ideas. Students made giant electrical plugs and matchboxes and they looked like fun. But what were they actually doing? It wasn't really Claes Oldenberg, they had never heard of him or seen his sculptures, let alone tried to appreciate the point of his work. It's not really 'self-expression' either, since I had set the brief to make these huge objects. There were many other projects of this kind such as teachers encouraging their students to do copies of cartoons, aping the work of Lichtenstien without ever having seen it. Of course it was popular with the students; kids love copying cartoons, but was it art? Art & design education needed some sort of 'shot in the arm' to prevent it from being either teacher-directed 'how to make it' exercises or copying from magazine photos and album covers. We knew how to show children how to do things, what we couldn't get to grips with was 'why do we do art?'

In my view art teachers at the tail end of Modernism were a bit lost. They didn't know where to go. In the seventies and early eighties we were teaching bits of traditional practice for the O level course where students had to paint 'proper' pictures. They had to do a three-hour observation drawing exam and a 'composition' exam. We all knew that images could be stylised a little bit but it had to be representational and demonstrate a sound grasp of conventional perspective, light and shade etc. However, while some students took this traditional course, less able students were doing CSE and this was quite a different exam. It was internally assessed and externally moderated and it was marked on site. So we could do all sorts of fun things for that. And that started to get more interesting. Not many people were doing abstract art from my knowledge. They were doing a ragbag of different things for example op art, pop art, surrealism etc. While surrealism was popular only a few students could actually handle it technically. Since they had never seen a Magritte, starting points such as 'All in the mind' resulted in lots of daggers and skulls, the products of morbid adolescent imaginations fed only on comics and tattoos. Modernism at that time was going nowhere as far as art education was concerned.

The difference between modernism and postmodernism in the art room lies in the way you approach it. We were already doing a lot of these things. But with postmodernism you haven't got an overarching philosophy that says 'Look we are doing Kurt Rowland's books 1, 2 and 3 in that order'. Nor would we do some Lowenfeldian-style drawing course. Those approaches had all been worked out scientifically and were very logical. But with postmodernism, what we can do is mix and match. We can do whatever is appropriate. It is very pragmatic in its view. So we use sketchbooks. We draw. We do observation drawing but we can move from there to abstract work or pop art. We can dip into anything we like. We can dip into other cultures. You could do quite crazy things if you wanted to.

I did a project with year 8, which I later wrote up in a conference paper. It involved looking at Ancient Greek 'Red-Figure' vases. We used papier-maché over balloons for a base and then added handles and tops and bottoms to make vases. They looked great. We sketched Greek vases showing everyday life, myths and legends and famous sports personalities throwing discuss and javelin etc. We asked 'What would a 1990s version of a Greek vase look like?' So we ended up with footballers, pop stars, super heroes as myths and legends etc. And we did these in Greek red-figure style using felt-tipped pens for outlines and filled in the backgrounds in black paint. We did modern day logos around them and anything they wanted to put on as decoration and we produced contemporary versions of red-figure vases. In my view this was an ideal form of critical studies because the students learned as much as 12 year olds can, about Ancient Greek art. They became aware of Greek art and by working through it they actually knew more about it than if you had just told them about it. They appreciated what real red-figure vases were because they had produced one themselves; one that related to their everyday life as opposed to Ancient Greek everyday life.

We used the craft skills of papier-maché and there was real satisfaction in doing that. We produced a nice display which the Head likes to have in the foyer, but at the same time we had also done this in a very postmodern way. We had not treated these replica vases as sacrosanct. In modernist terms to do a modern version of a Greek vase would have been heresy. Postmodernism gives you license to do these things.

I remember a workshop at Chester College where we were given photocopies of Henry Moore's work and we were working with clay. We had previously done some drawing of figures. Anyhow, we were asked to draw and paint over the Moore photocopies. My initial reaction was 'you can't draw and paint over a Henry Moore'. This was taboo. But of course you can. It is only a bit of paper. You are not defacing the original. So you can take that and then move on. I think that is something that students now are much easier about. They are freer about it because they are from a culture which allows them to do that. You only have to listen to the radio to hear parts of well-known rock songs from the past mixed to synthesise with other elements. It's OK. But we weren't allowed to do this in my school days. It had to be original and it had to come straight from the artist's experience. We couldn't synthesise from what's already out there, which if you think about it is total nonsense. Picasso did precisely that. Maybe he was postmodern.

Modernism, as a movement, was still concerned with the history of 'dead white male artists'. There was a canon there. Modernism upholds that canon although it says it doesn't. You only have to go to the Tate Gallery and count the number of female artists there. They are now trying very hard and are pulling out all their women artists to put on display. But if you looked at the total sum of women's work in the Tate it is perhaps going to amount to 5%. However, postmodernism allows you to treat women's art the same way that you treat everything else. It takes that kind of restriction off. The biggest problem we have in addressing issues like gender in school is resources. A book on Paula Rego may cost between 25 and 40 pounds. But if you want a book on Monet you just have to go down to the cheap bookshops and there are loads of them. For five pounds you can have a whole set of illustrations for a class. If you laminate some prints you can have as many haystacks and waterlilies as you could possibly want. Resources are a problem so you end up doing fairly mainstream artists. Hence we try to fit in female artists who are easy and cheap to resource. In GCSE for example, we look at Georgia O'Keeffe because there is plenty of material on her.

In terms of gender there are a lot of artists out there to choose from but we have to cover Picasso because you can't understand 20th century art unless you have looked at him. So we consider cubism and although it sounds clichéd, all the students should know about Picasso after GCSE. The discovery of cubism is a liberating experience for most students. But then in order to balance that we look at Georgia O'Keeffe. The students are not told that Georgia O'Keeffe is not as famous as Picasso. As far as they are concerned Georgia O'Keeffe is just as important as Picasso because they did a whole term's project on her—drawing skulls and flowers and making prints and paintings. She is presented in exactly the same way, with work that is accessible to fifteen year-olds. I could sit down and talk with them about Judy Chicago's 'Dinner Party' but it is not really going to lead them anywhere unless we actually did a project around her. Or we could take a look at Cindy Sherman or Barbara Kruger but we have to think how they could do that as a GCSE project. As a teacher you have to get them to produce the practical course work for assessment. With Georgia O'Keeffe they have access to books, they also have access to things like bones and flowers. And the students do begin to appreciate these objects and the art which can be developed from them.

In terms of more controversial contemporary female artists we have had a number of sixth form students doing work on Jenny Saville for example. But you can't really do a whole-class project on Jenny Saville with fifteen year-olds by getting in some big female life models to paint from. Also, many of Jenny Saville's paintings are about her. She uses herself as a model. You don't really want adolescent girls using themselves as life models in the art class. You are into all kinds of issues there.

We do address these issues with our older students. For example, we took the sixth form to the Sensation exhibition two or three years ago and they really did relate to it. We did a whole project on Shock. In particular Jenny Saville's work did make an impression. However, it is a sensitive issue to discuss with a 16 year-old girl who happens to be a bit larger than the average size. I ask myself 'How far can I go down this line before I am crossing over a serious boundary?' Recently, for instance, we discovered the 'Body Shop' web site, which is quite interesting because it uses images of women who are larger than the usual size one usually sees in advertisements. I have had one or two students who have followed that line. I think it was quite a revelation for them, especially the notion that there is nothing wrong with being this size. After all, Jenny Saville's works are wonderful paintings in their own right.

I suppose that we have followed some very 'dodgy issues' at times. The sixth form students have to present a written project of 4000 to 5000 words for assessment at A level. We have had some interesting studies over the last few years, several dealing with pretty serious contemporary issues.

For example, one followed the work of Sally Mann, the American photographer whose candid images of her own children presented challenging views of childhood, and in several cases the children were naked. There were a lot of problems with her exhibitions in the United States for obvious reasons. My student also looked at the photographic work of the Victorian writer Louis Carrol. His images of young girls (including Alice, the heroine of his books) were seen as visions of innocence in his own time but are now regarded with suspicion. As part of her research, my student also started taking black and white photographs of her young sisters. Although, in this case, they kept their clothes on, these children were staring at the camera in a knowing adult way, quite unlike society's preferred childlike smiles. It didn't look like 'happy families'. These sidelong and serious looks at the camera by children can be quite disturbing. The girl entitled her finished written study 'Art or Pornography', and considered in detail the contemporary issues surrounding photographic images of children. Also, as a result of her research, her own practical work became centred on photography, proving the value of 'critical studies' research. The problem in dealing with this kind of subject matter in a school situation is that it is very, very easy to suddenly find yourself on the wrong side of a line.

There is art that I would not show students. There would have to be. Some of the Chapman brothers' work for example, is already censored in exhibitions and you have to be 18 to see it. If it is censored then, as their teacher, I cannot allow the students to see it. I have to follow the law of the land. When we went to the Sensation exhibition the Chapman brothers' work was screened off in a separate gallery. Some of our students were old enough to go in and I didn't prevent them, even though I don't particularly like the work myself (it consisted of a very disturbing series of distorted mannequins of children). So where do you stand as a teacher introducing younger students to that type of work? I wouldn't do it. I couldn't lay myself that open. It would only take one child to say something to a parent and the parent could then check it up etc. That's the sort of thing that ends up reported on the front page of the Sunday papers.

High Modernism was safe in comparison. That was a key issue in the acceptance of abstract art. In the late forties and fifties much of the art which was receiving critical acclaim had no real content or at least it didn't seem to have content. With the students though I don't really get into controversial issues until sixth form although we have one or two of the students in year 11 who are going that way. In the days when art advisers called in to schools regularly (when it was free of charge) I remember Rod Taylor asking at what age should you teach perspective. I suggested that it would be about year 9. But he said 'No, you teach it when they're ready for it'. And in a sense he is absolutely right because if you try and take a student through perspective before they are ready for it, it is like showing a dog a card trick. They can follow the actions but the point may not actually register. In my B.Ed. work we did a lot of work with Piaget and I am a firm believer that there are kinds of stages. Maybe they are not as ordered and rigid as Piaget defined. But there are points where kids can understand. There are points when babies can be potty trained, and points when they can't. You have to just wait for it and you are just wasting your time trying to do it before they are ready. And so it is a matter of being there ready at the right time. So at that time you can say 'Oh, have you noticed that all the lines go together when you look down the road?'. And they see it for the first time. The penny drops and the lights go on. And some of these issues are like that. If you take students there too quickly you are pulling the ground from under their feet.

If you are showing a student how to draw you may show them how to use the 6B pencil and then drag a rubber through it to get a certain effect. The students react with 'Wow that's great'. But you then say 'That's enough for now. Just play around with that technique'. Then later you give them another idea. You need to build slowly. Students need something solid under their feet. It's like open-ended 'integrated arts' courses. They are OK for Fine Art students who have a solid foundation in their own area but if you do that with younger students who haven't got that foundation, it disturbs them. I believe that adolescents actually do want to be able to represent the world using perspective and tone. They want to have a go at that. Once they've got the hang of perspective then you say 'OK. You've got that. Now let's look at cubism'. You don't want to tell some seven year old about cubism because it is just too much. It is just confusing. I am not excluding twentieth century art from 7 year olds. You could look at certain aspects of painters like Matisse and they would love it. But they don't really understand Matisse fully; they just think 'These are nice colours'. There are some concepts which are actually too difficult for them to grasp. You can't tackle the Theory of Relativity unless you can understand Newton's Laws of Motion in the first place. So why should we starting them on cubism, Jeff Koons or Damien Hirst before they are ready for it? Just because their work is fashionable? I think students need some sense of security before they venture out into the wilder reaches of art.

A couple of weeks ago I was showing some students how to draw apples. They liked their results and they were starting to realise that they could draw. Confidence was building. So, after drawing apples we looked at Cezanne and went onto still-life paintings. Next year they will have a look at Picasso and see what he did with the same subject. So there is a kind of order but that does not mean that we do the whole history of art, starting at year 7. We might look at landscape, then at colour and we might then look at Monet. Chronological art history is not dead in the sense that to some extent western art history is by nature chronological. It is a constant series of movements as opposed to some kinds of art which are not chronological. Chinese art, for example, is more static by nature. It is supposed to be constant. Egyptian art was virtually static for thousands of years. A static tradition is not a better or worse state of affairs, it just is. That was the beauty of it. But western art is not, and that's the beauty of that. It moves onwards quickly. You can appreciate an elephant. You can appreciate an eagle. But you don't criticise one for not being the other. They are different things.

In considering new technological developments in art and design computers have certainly made a significant impact. Computers certainly could be regarded as ideal vehicles for postmodern art. When I wrote my thesis in 1992 I had already been working with computers for a couple of years. I came across them initially when I was teaching Foundation Studies about 1986. There we used Apple Macs with the black and white screens which we thought were great at the time, especially after using Letraset for years. I knew the potential so when I returned to working in schools I sought out the Information Technology teachers and got students onto whatever machines they had available. Initially it was BBCs (a basic standard issue educational computer sponsored by the BBC) using simple drawing packages. Cheshire LEA were quite advanced in terms of IT. The art adviser started courses at their 'Micro Centre' and arranged six month loans of computers. By 1990 my school had bought a powerful computer and set it up in the corner of my art room. It had advanced graphics programs for that time and a colour printer. The students were doing all kinds of work then including video grabs etc.

The problem at the moment is that we have the people at the top telling us to use more computers but where are the computers and the technicians? I moved schools five years ago and it was only last year I finally got a computer for my art department again. It's a nice machine but we haven't got the time to learn to use it. We have a couple of computer suites in the school but again we have problems accessing them. Four years ago we were managing to use them as part of year 7, 8, 9 and 10 courses. In fact, we used it for the cubist project with year 10. We scanned in several of their still life drawings and they broke up their images using cut and paste. So they played around with positive and negative spaces. It was a way of experimenting; of cutting up an image or putting two drawings together. We also did simple graphics in year 7. But as the pressure for all areas to use computers has increased our school facilities are totally overloaded. We find it very difficult now to get students in there as a group. We now have 50-minute lessons and that doesn't give enough time. The rhetoric from the politicians at the top is not matched by the number of computers and technicians in the schools.

Leaving aside the problems inherent in the current English education system and returning to the bigger philosophical issues, I would like to expand on the nature of postmodernism a little further. It should be noted that postmodernism is not another 'ism', along the lines of cubism, abstract expressionism and other movements in modern art. It is the end of modernism and therefore an end to the 'isms' which are a feature of the modern movement. And that's the problem I have with trying to explain what postmodern art is in a modernist context. You can't. It is a different paradigm. Postmodernism is a step sideways and you can go as wide and as far back as you want to. So there is nothing wrong with abstract painting as part of postmodernism. You can be an abstract painter in a postmodern world because postmodern theorists are not interested in whether this is the latest 'ism'. They just say 'This is OK'. I am effectively a figurative painter and there is no problem with that being labelled as postmodern either. It is not an either/or. My next painting could be an abstract. Art can be formalist within modernism. Postmodernism allows us to go for anything. If I wanted to become a neo-classical artist I could. There are a number of neo-classical artists who you could put under the postmodern banner. I don't see any problem with that, or with Joseph Beuys or Jeff Koons or anyone. There is no hierarchy in art any more; artists are all equally valued. Postmodernism does not privilege anything.

I think the features of modernism have in one sense been tied to Clement Greenberg's ideal. But if you take the abstract expressionist work of artists such as Rothko, Greenberg's suggestion that his work is purely a formalist statement about colour or the nature of paint, is absolute nonsense. Rothko's work is actually a deeply spiritual art. It is just that few critics at the time gave it that interpretation. The problem lies in what people define as modernism and the kind of rewriting of art history that has been done by someone like Greenberg. Greenberg said that you just follow the line of abstract painting right through from Monet to Jackson Pollock and that this is all a logical line of progress. For example, it is ridiculous to study Picasso's development of cubism, label him a genius, and then to ignore all of his later changes of style. Then to skip to Kandinsky etc as the successors in the development of abstraction, ignoring the fact that Picasso lived on and worked for fifty years or more but never went abstract. So if you take the Greenberg/Darwinian type of evolutionary approach it seems that Picasso gave the world cubism and then disappeared. Then cubism is said to surface again say in the work of Mondrian and then perhaps Frank Stella. But Frank Stella is not on about the same things as Mondrian. Mondrian was interested in theosophy so they are not just formalist paintings, they are deeply symbolic. Hence you have the art history of modernism as it was written, after the event, and then you have the reality which was a lot messier. The Modern notion was to find a nice, neat scientific progression through art. The theory of modernism is a logical scientific system. It goes back to the 'enlightenment' and it is kind of neat and tidy. The reality is a lot messier and so is postmodernism. It is a lot more pragmatic. Postmodernism allows for people doing all sorts of odd things, finding out what works for them, conveying meaning in their own way.

Meaning in art is something I emphasise with students, especially once they get to GCSE. There are all sorts of reasons for this including the practical one of class size. The GCSE students work on longer projects than the younger students and sometimes you can see when the penny drops with them in terms of them taking the reins themselves. That's when I say to students 'You know, you are not doing GCSE now, you are doing Art. You are really doing ART'. That is when art starts to have personal meaning and importance for them; when they start to feel that there is something important that they want to get across. It could be about all kinds of things such as semi-abstract works about the Holocaust or works dealing with gender and personal image, but when they take ownership of their work that is a turning point. At GCSE students 'get it' at their own level and in their own way. I do some teaching in a modernist/formal way, through a few exercises based on the visual vocabulary of art. I set a number of whole group briefs, introducing key themes, ideas and techniques. It is important that all the students have confidence in their basic drawing skills as well as the experience of painting on canvas and printmaking. I introduce them to a few key artists, and arrange a visit to exhibitions in London, which tie in with the work they are doing.

Eventually, one by one they start to take off in their own way. You just hope that each year they will all take off. It is a risky business. We could actually teach in a more formalised way and all do projects together and get reasonable results. But I think we have to take the risks and students have to make mistakes, because through mistakes you find out what to do. I think it is a plate spinning act where you get all the plates spinning and the idea is to get them all up there and to keep them all there by just wiggling the sticks and all the plates just keep going around. And at the end of the project you have to get all the plates down without breaking them. That is really what I am doing. I am not quite sure what is happening. There is a structure but the structure is an open structure and I allow students to go off in their own way. That is what art should do in the future.

Although some of my student's work can be fairly unconventional I ensure that all my students are well-grounded in traditional techniques. All the children at my school regularly work in sketchbooks from the age of eleven. We teach different drawing techniques, as well as encouraging the use of sketchbooks to explore ideas in a loose way, using thumbnail sketches and written notes. At GCSE the students are shown how to stretch and prime canvas for their paintings and drypoint etching is a popular medium for many of my fifteen year-olds. Life class is also key element of our sixth form work. Trips to exhibitions and galleries are an important feature of our courses, exposing the students to new ideas. This year we took the sixth form to Paris, last year we went to Amsterdam. We have seen the Sensation exhibition and will probably go to the Apocalypse exhibition. But I have also taken students to Monet and Rembrandt exhibitions. So I am not excluding anything. I am just throwing lots of different things in and hoping that they will take some of it on board and put it together in their own way.

Culture is not an issue in our school in one sense because we haven't got a significant multi-cultural group. But it another sense that makes it more of an issue because students are not in contact with other cultures in the same way as students from inner city Birmingham or Manchester would be. So it is an issue because our students do not mix with Asian students or Black students, for example. We have one or two non-western students scattered throughout the school, so their impact is fairly minimal. For that reason we almost need more of a focus on multiculturalism. It is very hard to put students in contact with the world. It would also be very easy to become very patronising about the issues.

Multicultural considerations do play an important element in the courses the students study. We produce the courses for the younger students through a kind of 'mix and match' process. The staff sit around and determine which processes and skills we should teach with each year group, which content or themes to be covered and then we have a critical studies element. Teachers pick up what they feel is appropriate from them. In year 7 the continent of Africa is a theme and at year 8 Asia (we now include Australia and Aboriginal art in that). In year 9 we look at the Americas. Obviously these are very broad headings but it means that the students don't end up doing the same thing two years running. It allows the teachers to dip into all sorts of possibilities. In one sense it doesn't matter what cultures they look at, it is the process of considering and appreciating a culture different to their own which is the key aim. They can look at Islamic tile patterns, take it into fabric pattern, tessellations, then screen prints or whatever. Or another teacher might prefer to extend the pattern idea on the computer and then it can become a cut and paste exercise. This allows the teachers to take different approaches so long as they can cover it all by the end of the year. I don't want to be dogmatic about it. I want teachers to teach from their own enthusiasm. I have just appointed a teacher this year who has worked for several years in a Kenyan village. She has a great foundation for teaching art based on African culture, and I would expect to see her expand that expertise through her own classes and the rest of the department.

I have tried to rethink that old notion that art is about self-expression and imagination. It is, to a point, but I have reinterpreted that to think about it as creative response. The students already have their own cultural background and heritage. You feed in new ideas and stimuli, and hopefully fill in lots of gaps about other cultures etc. Then somehow they will make a creative response by drawing on all these inputs. They will synthesise bits of this and that, and bring in some of themselves to it to make new art of their own.

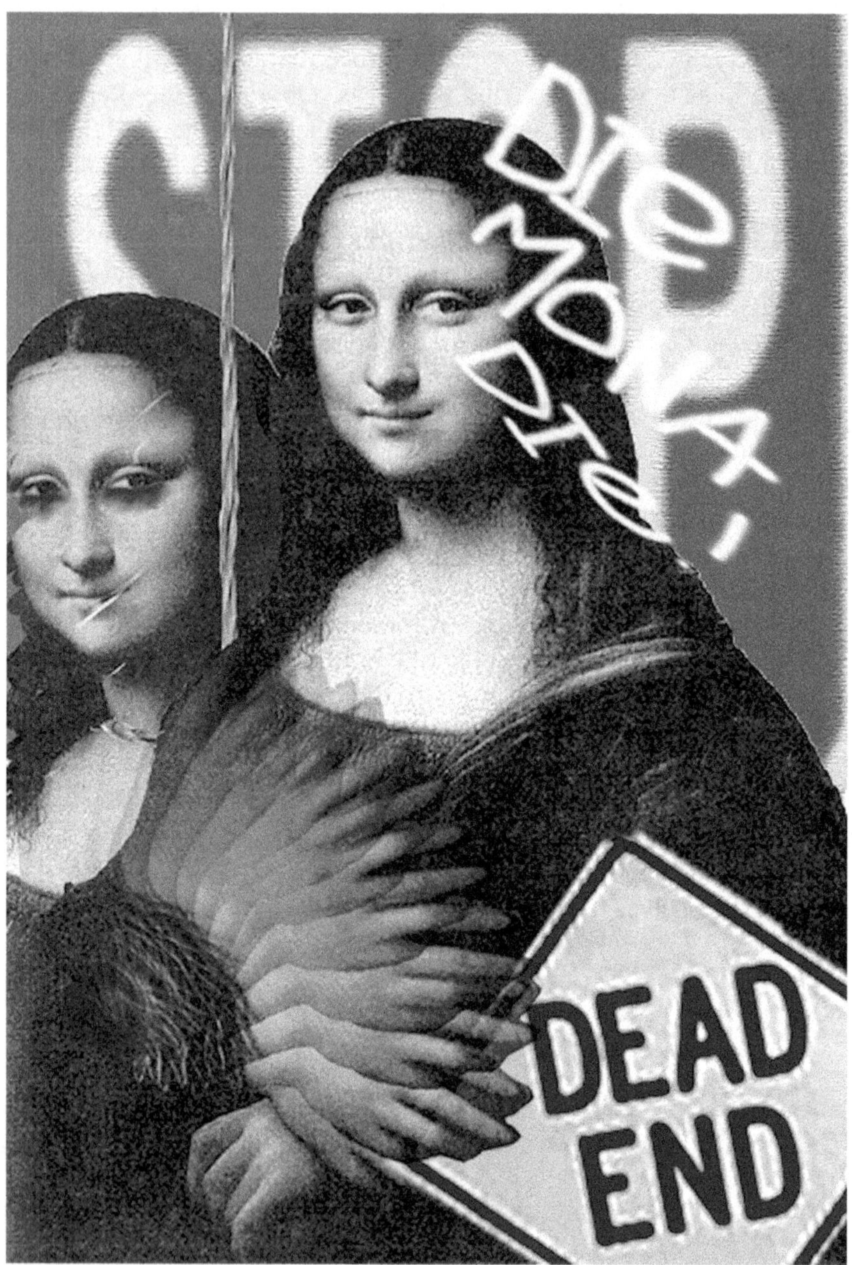

Figure 2:
Catherine Wilson, Year 10, Presbyterian Ladies College, Melbourne

Chapter 6

Malcolm Beasley

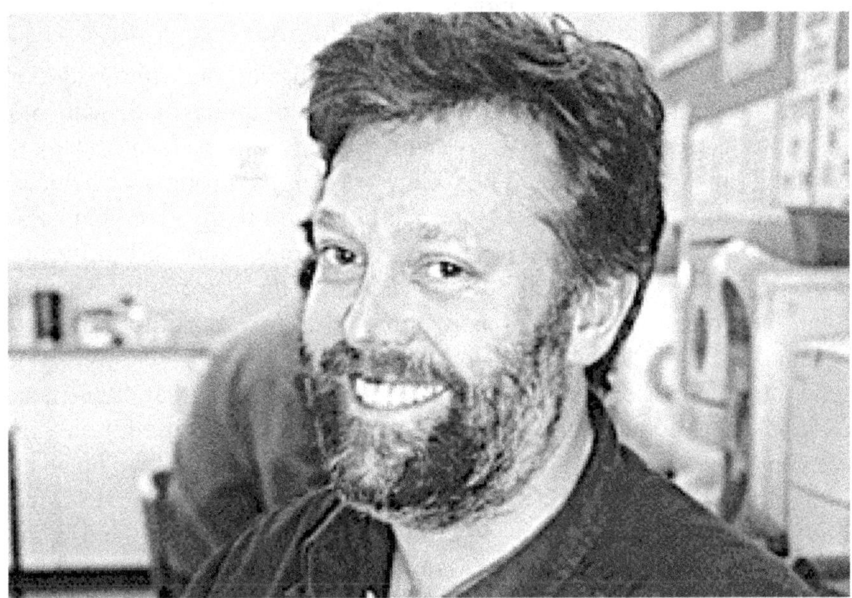

Malcom Beasley teaches multi-media in the senior school of Eumemmering Secondary College in an outer south eastern area of Melbourne. The school polulation is largely Anglo-Saxon but many students are from low socio-economic backgrounds and have tended to leave school after year 10. Malcolm has fully embraced technology and established a media company within the school. He employs an ex-student as a technical support person and attracts media development work from industry and education institutions. While I was at the school students were developing a CDROM on science education for the Curriculum Corporation. Another job underway involved the making of an engineering program for a local industry. Malcolm insists that his students use their own hand drawings as the basis of their animation and digital imagery work. The non-linear and multi-dimensional aspect of digital imagery is postmodern in process and Malcolm has noted his students' fusion of aspects of reality and fantasy as they work in multi-media. Malcolm has been instrumental in developing multi-media as an artistic medium for senior art. (ed.)

Teaching art is an honour and it is something that makes us very involved with our students. When we ask students to make art, we are actually asking them to consider themselves very closely as human beings in a perceptual universe. So we have technique on one hand

and concepts on the other. And rather than students taking concepts from a book or a menu I try to get students to understand that they have two sides to their brain; they are feeling people and thinking people. And that is very risky teaching but the risk is far outweighed by the results.

However, one of the biggest changes in education during my career has been in regard to technology. In 1995 I won a computer from Apple Australia in response to my submission outlining why our school deserved a multi-media set up. The computer came with no instructions and some software and I spent the rest of the year teaching myself how to use the software. I was strongly convinced that this multi-media was a visual medium. And really five years ago is like 30 years in technology years. My computer is still sitting at home. It is not doing much but it was a fantastic opportunity because it allowed me to see that if something is drawn skilfully and then scanned in, the scanned result is spectacular. You can then create an interactive experience with that scanned thing and that non-linear experience is actually the aesthetic experience in my opinion. When we approach a piece of art, such as a painting or sculpture, we do so as individuals. What we are trying to get students to understand is that this is an individual experience. Art doesn't have to be pretty but it has to have some sort of meaning for an individual. The fascinating thing about multi-media art to me is that you have to force the participant to become part of the art experience. There is a closeness that occurs. It is rather like sculpture because you have to walk around sculpture and invade the space; especially kinaesthetic sculpture or sinaesthetic sculpture where the sound enmeshes you. Well here we have this sort of thing.

In 1996 I offered a year 11 subject called 'Studio Arts: Multi Media' and 27 students chose the subject on the strength of a little display that I had at the School Expo. I only had one computer for 27 students but the students were very happy. They really enjoyed it. I taught them storyboarding, drawing upon my experience working in film, photography and sculpture (and I think of multi-media as sculpture). I also knew that industry required programmers with artistic skills. There are a lot of programmers out there but very few of them are artists. The growth of the web has now proved, beyond a shadow of a doubt, that I was right. So in 1997 the first group of year 12s came through. In the end we had the students achieve A's and they have each year since. Mind you I think we owe it to the public to have interactive multi-media demonstrated in the State level year 12 exhibition to show what students can do.

So I don't have any worry with change but a lot of other people do. Managing change is a very important part of the teaching profession nowadays. And being involved in information technology I have seen the sweat and fear, the real fear, on professional people's faces as they confront this technology. There is absolute fear and many schools do not manage change effectively. The only way I can see technological change being managed effectively is for it to be based on need, and this is from personal experience. For example, in response to a need I designed a report writing system using the internet, that the school has used for three years. If the need is there and that need is expressed completely, succinctly and it is demonstrated physically, then change will happen. In a lot of cases teachers don't even know that the need is there because often staff don't know what they don't know. Yet, surely we are education professionals and you would think that we could teach ourselves more effectively than any other profession, as this is what we do. However, I think we are very poor at that. And usually it is because we don't know what we don't know.

In this computer lab we have a commercial illustrator. He is in here every Thursday. He is working with two of my year 12 students at the moment showing them how to do some scanning because that is what he does for a living. I have Diploma students in here doing some work on their own. I have year 12 students working on a school-assessed task. They are scanning their drawings and they are preparing solutions. I have another Diploma student doing some coding and I have an ex-student sitting in there finding out software prices for purchasing. He was my year 12 student two years ago and now he is a full-time employee of mine. This is a company here. We are a multi-media production company and a national internet service provider. If I am to deliver real-life to post-compulsory aged students, I can't do it unless I am doing it properly. And the only way I can do it properly is to run a company. Multi-media companies within Australia are too small to be able to give students real hands-on client-based type of experience. So I have a client coming later this afternoon to review some of the things we have done and I have further clients' interviews tomorrow. So what we do basically is real work.

There are 20 computers in this lab and we have another studio arts computer room with a multi-media studio arts class running. I have employed two young graduate teachers who have both expressed a real interest to learn this 'stuff' and I really worry that they are not taught this in their undergraduate program. I think this is critical for them as practicing teachers; not just for art teachers but for all teachers. I did a seminar at Monash University two years ago to show the entire teaching and learning group what students were doing. They are so terrified that kids know so much and they know nothing about it.

One of the great changes that the technology has brought on is that my role (with which I am now so much more comfortable) is no longer that of the master. I am not the person that knows everything. I am committed to providing an environment that facilitates learning. If I don't know something, then I will find out. And in this field I don't and can't know it all. If I did, why would I be teaching it? I would be out earning a hundred million dollars somewhere. So one of the things I am getting the students to learn, is how to learn. De Bono's macro-learning notion implies learning how you learn so that you can then learn how to learn the software. Then you can apply the software directly to your needs. So you use these things as tools. They aren't the 'be all and end all'; they are just tools like pencils and paper. And the students treat them like that whereas some teachers treat them like hallowed objects. They are not. I have run Professional Development sessions and sometimes teachers are the hardest ones to teach because they sometimes don't listen to the answer as they are so busy thinking of the next question.

In terms of artistic processes we have a student here who is working on one of his assessment tasks. Stephen feels under-confident with his drawing skills but he is getting better. One of the things that I am continually trying to revise is that the screen is a picture plane. Stephen is doing an animation from his drawing involving a guy who is going to get run over by a truck (that's not unusual for my students - they tend to do that.). And with the scanned image the artistic quality of the coloured pencil on the screen comes up so well on the monitor. You cannot get that effect with software. It just doesn't work. Whilst Stephen is developing his aesthetic skills he is also working as a computer programmer; the two are not mutually exclusive, in fact, they have to be enmeshed. In terms of creativity, I want Stephen to develop confidence in his drawing. He is now managing to get perspective into his work and he has gained confidence in his ability to place things on the screen, create the illusion of depth, understand tone, texture, line, form, shape, colour and all those sorts of things. I want Stephen to follow certain design principles to get the desired outcome, just as if he were using the picture plane on a canvas or a print plate, using ink or photographic emulsion. It is exactly the same.

I would not allow students in year 11 and 12 to scan in other people's images and manipulate them. There are millions of clip art images on the web. I have to genuinely authenticate that the students' artwork is their own. Now they certainly may download images from the web and I allow this to encourage image generation. They can scan those images and then use Photoshop to manipulate and change the image but it must be distinctly different to the original. The visual form here is very important. Some students want to use clip art images because they are under-confident about their own image making ability. Stephen is one of those. But I want to see the sort of continuous improvement that I am seeing in Stephen. I can put a standard on image development but basically what I want to see is individual development. I want my students to demonstrate improvement from where they start with me to where they finish with me. The degrees of improvement is just an individual concern. So I grade students using criteria but those criteria are transferable from conventional mediums to multi-media.

Gaston, our graphic illustrator, has found that his practice as an illustrator has moved from print to delivery by disk and web. His entire career has changed. He hardly buys any art materials now. His work is all done on computer using such tools as the drawing tablet. There is still a delay using this tool; it is not the same as using paper and pencil. Students here draw their images on paper and then scan their images and then they manipulate them using the tablet. For example, the car image that one boy is currently working on has been drawn and scanned and now he is enhancing it using the tablet. So it starts by hand and it is enhanced using the computer. And with the help of Gaston the students are getting first hand experience with a professional from industry.

Schools are getting closer to industry and this unit is as close to industry as you can get because we make money from clients. We produce commercial multi-media for real clients who pay real money for the projects. My Diploma students get that money. So IMPACT Creativity Centre is a member of the Australian Interactive Multimedia Industry Association. We are a member of the Internet Industry Association and the Australian Telecommunications Ombudsmen. We get all their stuff just like a registered company. We are a registered business. We are a national internet service provider. We have national clients. We host commercial internet sites that we design. We produce commercial CD ROM-based multi-media for real clients. We have been contracted by both the Australian Broadcasting Commission and a manufacturing exporter who has used our product in an export sales push to China, Finland and Thailand to great effect. That was an engineering project and the person who was liaising from that company with us, has found that he is now the multi-media guru for his company and it has done a huge amount for his career.

One of the things that I have discovered, in terms of the commercial aspect, is that multi-media and website design involves student learning the whole business. When I have clients come to talk about their brief, which I often do in front of and with students, we take on a communication role very similar to the role of medieval artists. In other words the patron outlines what s/he wants, for whatever reason. Then the artist takes on a role of saying 'OK but I think it should have this or that'; ideas which the patron had never thought about. So this gives the patron a new idea, which s/he often goes along with. This is the future of paid art making in schools. In 1985 I went to a seminar about future work and the instructor's line was that the preps of today are going to end up working in areas we haven't even dreamed of. Well I am teaching the stuff that 'we hadn't even dreamed of'. You really are seeing a horizon industry here.

However it is not only the multi-media students who are benefiting from this venture. The art students are also getting the benefit of the production wing because they are seeing the direct application of design principles, elements and processes in a money making venture. I can't think of a more exciting time for an art teacher than the present. It offers students new opportunities. In my career I have only got two students into art school straight from here. Most of the time they have to go to a TAFE college. The two successful art school students said to me in year ten that they wanted to be artists. So we started in year 10 developing their folio of work through Art and Studio Arts. However now I have students leaving my class at year 12 and earning money by making art. It is not art in the traditional sense but it is a visual form and they are earning money doing it. They go straight into careers into multi-media and web-based production. Some work for our company. That is the really exciting part of it all. I can now say quite confidently to students that if they choose year 12 art I can get them a job. I have never been able to say that before.

When we first started teaching multi-media my colleague, Anne, was saying that my students were 'nerds' because all of a sudden I had this influx of students who had not done art since year 7 or 8. When art was offered in a non-compulsory way, they stopped doing it. And now they are coming back to do art because they love computers. And they love computer games. And what they can make for me is computer games. I have a student making a computer game with a flight simulator at the moment. He is trying something with a 3 dimensional effect. Admittedly he is using stick figures but he is wearing the 3D glasses to create the illusion of depth from the monitor. That sort of thing is exciting. Unfortunately our computer 'nerds' are male and the course is very male dominated. By comparison, senior art is usually female dominated. There are no females in this room at the moment. However in my year 12 class there are 3 girls and that is the most I have ever had. In my VET course last year I had 22 boys. By comparison Anne's year 12 classes is mainly girls with just 4 boys. The demographics are incredible. I am hoping that this is a bulge. I have spoken at staff conferences about this and I have noted that this is a bulge. Of course, computers weren't around 6 years ago and you had to be a bit of a 'boffin' to be into it. When these students were in primary school they would only have had access to very simple early Macintosh computers.

Currently the students are making a Science multi-media presentation for the Curriculum Corporation. The presentation shows the molecules of water in a glass. We want to show that water molecules are not blue. One of the things that the year 12 students are starting to understand is that we spend a lot of time talking to each other about the look of what they are doing. In fact we probably spend more time doing this than in the normal art class. In multi-media the visuals are critical because there are implied messages that are non-linear. In linear work we know where the start and finish is but we don't work this way here. Here the structure is based on a web structure. The structure looks like a family tree and we have branches although often the family tree is inverted with things referring to other things. The students have to learn how to design non-linear storyboards. I have a technique that I have developed to help students with that and this seems to be quite effective.

In this Science piece we are showing a beaker of water and we are trying to show that it zooms in and then it will go from blue to white. Then from blue to white we see these things emerge in the white and then it zooms in again to another point. The aim is to get the viewer to feel as though s/he is in a space ship zooming through atoms in space. And of course the science teacher is excited because we are in a position where we can represent water in this way. The science teachers say that there are five ways in which students represent water. I asked my children at the dinner table the other night what water was made of. They said 'What do you mean?' They said that is just is. When you pour it out it is all one thing. And this is what children think. That is called the continuous model. But through multi-media we can show them what happens when you heat the water molecules. We teach here by abstraction. We take the child's model, test it and see that it doesn't work. The child can then take that away from their understanding. They don't need that model now. This is learning by subtraction or elimination. So the medium is very powerful.

I was part of a thing a few years ago where the multi-media industry asked specialist teachers to advise the governing body how to use good learning materials. We talked about a constructive model of learning and how students learn and how they learn with their own strengths or with collaboration etc, and this medium is perfect for all styles. This is not a postmodern medium. It is not a post-postmodern medium because it doesn't deconstruct, it reconstructs. As opposed to Foucault's notion of deconstruction, here we have a non-linear universe. This allows us to go anywhere we want and when we want. What this means is that we now have a generation of students coming up who will demand to do things their own way, not the textbook way. So all the students who have difficulty reading in a linear fashion or who have difficulty with linguistic and other concepts can work with this medium. I am very fortunate to be in a position to be teaching students how to author this medium themselves. This means that they actually have to look very carefully at the way they see things but also at the way future clients can see things. It is very exciting. It drives me crazy sometimes because there are so many turns and twists. In this particular science program with the molecules, there is going to be a little animated character called young Frankenstein who will talk the viewer through the program. He will have a little sidekick called Egor. Egor is going to take on the fall-guy role and they are going to come on with Egor saying 'Hey why aren't the water molecules blue?' and Young Frankenstein will say 'You idiot, you idiot. Don't you realise that the colour is not made by the atoms.' So you pre-empt the dumb questions, and that is a really powerful learning tool. So the client is very happy with this so far. So we will see how it progresses.

In order to look at artworks in multi-media by other artists I have had students look at Alfred Styglis and the Photo Successionists. Now why I have done that is because 100 years ago we had a group of artists use photography for the first time and everybody canned them and said you can't make art with a camera. But of course you can. It is a visual form. In photography, as in multi-media students use design principles and elements, tension, tone, lighting and any effect they want. So in looking at photographers doing that students feel quite privileged that they are on the cusp of a thing like that 100 years later. There is also a mystery thing that multi-media is high tech. But it is really only like a medieval craft like carving.

The exam questions include one appreciation question and another always involves a discussion of the impact of change on practicing artists. So with an exam question like 'There is nothing new in art. Discuss this', the same issues apply to multi-media as to all other mediums. Design principles remain design principles whether you do it on a 640 x 480 pixel screen or whether you do it on a 200 x 300 cm canvas. We use the same compositional devices. The arrangement on the screen, even on the news, is now carefully organised. Filmmaking is the same.

In looking at other multi-media artists we do find that these artworks are so often collaborative. One exercise I get the students to do is do screen shots of browser windows. They surf the web. They do screen shots. They print them off and then they get a piece of tracing paper for each design element and one for each design principle and they overlay them and try to see whether someone has thought about it or not. We do that with screen dumps of multi-media productions as well to try and get students to think about whether people have consciously thought about design. And it is usually obvious and students can ask why something is not so attractive.

Another exercise that I use is to show students products by others. I have had to become an IT person here and I have set the network up. This piece of multi-media is one which I have downloaded from a CD on to our server. It is by an Italian, Luigi de la Loisia and it is called Strand Cose and I wish I knew what it meant. But on the screen he has this beautiful metaphor where you move the cursor over the screen and it activates these amoebic shapes and lovely colours which jump and flow around. So we do screen shots of this and ask ourselves what the rules are which underpin this work. How would he do this? And the images change all the time and sometimes rules can be broken. You can use that notion to great effect. I love the Tango screen where the images follow the mouse. These images bounce and move about in very clever ways. I don't know how he does this but I would love to find out. We have been pulling things apart trying to do this sort of stuff. We can use this work because it really is like a succession of paintings. There are hundreds of paintings in this work. Just look at the metaphor for the menu. The more I pull the cursor across the more it moves or then you go into the middle and it slows down.

In multi-media the viewer has to be active and involved. We are at the start of a new aesthete but it is an aesthetic which is easily assimilated. It is unlike the conceptual period of the seventies where the aesthetic was so 'highbrow' and intellectual. This is also intellectual but there is a serious aesthetic and each frame is a picture and I am trying to encourage the students to see that. But of course game-playing comes into it and that is interesting because you are actually enmeshing people in the environment.

I am convinced that students transfer into virtual environments. I know that for a fact because when I go to turn off the Nintendo at home my 12 year old says. 'Don't do that Dad. I am nearly finished. Look where I am'. He is not there. It is a character. But he is there, right in it. They transfer. I am doing something for the Department of Education at the moment, testing whether students transfer into environments. Students can change their avatars (virtual simulations of themselves). So these are Gaston's images which allow me to enter a space and I am that person. When I talk my avatar talks. I can move around, for example, from room to room. Other people can log in and they can appear on the screen too. What I discovered when we first started trialing this, was that students learn to work collaboratively. I also developed a control system. Once I started doing this the students entered a dream world. I made myself into an avatar and when I wanted their attention I appeared in the top right hand corner of their screens as a jester. I then started to say something and THEY DID IT. Now to me, that it is transference. They are IN that environment and when I say something they respond. Whereas they wouldn't respond to me as the real person, physically standing in the same environment. It is actually MORE REAL.

Now I had students in both rooms and I could say on screen 'Right now you can go for lunch' and they would go'. Now I said it on screen. We had a brainstorming session between four students and one student said something really interesting and I said 'Hey that's really interesting' and the other student said 'Yes that is really interesting'; just like a teacher does. I was being a teacher in a virtual environment. And of course, we now have our BOTS (Bionic Organic Talking Servants). So these students will be able to go into a room where they will meet a producer, which Gaston has drawn. The producer will talk to them about being a multi-media producer, but it is pre-programmed with AI. So if a student says a word in a sentence like 'repeat' he will repeat what he said before. Or if a student says a word like 'How' it will go to a question that I have pre-programmed. And so we have designed this system to be autonomous and the students won't know because I can jump in any time and take on that personality. So they will not know whether it is me talking, or a real producer or it is pre-programmed. So this is a system that I have devised and patented. Can you imagine students studying Hamlet in English and being able to interview the characters? Why did you do this or that? And the characters talk to them about their role etc. They can have the play but the characters can be interactive. The teacher can be anywhere. Of course, I could teach from home—only joking.

As an artist in the digital age, you are facing bandwidth levels that will allow for full interactive art in your bedroom, or wherever you have a television screen. As teachers we have the opportunity to engage students in artwork more than ever before by transference. You will be able to imagine being in Picasso's 'Guernica', with all the noise and sound that is implied. Students can be there. The ideas are completely transferable. A Studio Arts multi-media student is doing the same art process as students using other mediums. It is the same artistic design process using the same conceptual analysis and development. The physical mechanics of making something look good are exactly the same. It is just the medium that is different. But the only difference between multi-media and traditional flat uni-dimensional art is the non-linear ability to enable participants (not simply viewers) to be involved. The participant is in control and that control makes this an awesomely powerful medium. As long as we keep focussed on making good-looking things then we are making art.

Chapter 7

Anne Carins

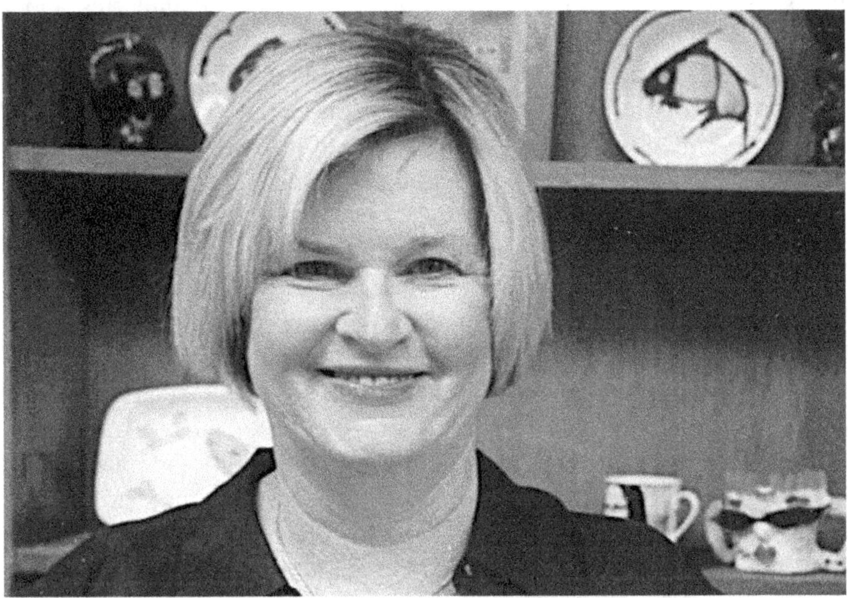

Anne Carins teaches at Eumemmering Secondary College in Melbourne and is Head of the Art Department. Anne teaches art while Malcolm Beasley teaches multi-media. Anne has overseen the development of a large new senior art wing in the senior school and instigated some key projects in the department. The new senior art wing at Eumemmering is a lively place with resident artists, a courtyard sculpture garden and a central large gallery space. At the time of writing this account Anne was working with the resident artist to plan and mount a sculpture installation on the front outside wall of the art wing. Anne is keen for her students to learn basic modernist and formalist values yet acknowledges the importance of introducing students to contemporary artists and art practice. (ed.)

During my 27 years of teaching art in secondary schools there have been many changes in education, some political, some educational. One of the major changes has been the 'Schools of the Future'. This scheme involves schools being accountable for their own educational philosophy and financial management. Also introduced was the 'Professional Recognition Program'. This was an attempt by the previous government to 'corporatise' schools by making teachers accountable for their own performance at the end of each school year.

A problem with the change of government is that schools with specialised subject offerings may find their program in jeopardy if they are required to conduct a general curriculum.

In order to keep up to date with modern trends I attend professional development programs in art education, I read articles on art issues and artists, I attend exhibitions and I visit galleries and I subscribe to various art institutions and outside agencies. One of the major initiatives that I introduced within our art curriculum was the introduction of the 'artists in residence program'. This program has been time-tabled within the VCE (Victorian Certificate of Education) art curriculum for the past two years. The concept for the artist in residence program came about when I was seeking information about employing a professional artist and one of our local art suppliers mentioned that an artist was using his attic area as a workshop. So I approached the administration and we organised a fee based on the Casual Relief Teacher budget. This year I have managed to obtain $15,000, which pays for 80 days at $172.65 per day. The artist assists, rather than teaches, the students, as in this case, the artist is not a qualified teacher. The concept of this program is not to adopt a formal teaching structure but to allow students to experience an artist's approach to art methodology and to create a studio/workshop atmosphere within the VCE art curriculum. The program is to accommodate the 'gifted' students but it is also 'open' to all art students who wish to experience particular knowledge of different studio forms.

At present the artist is involved in organising a design for the facade of the arts building. This will incorporate sculptural wall panels made from an assemblage of copper pieces. The artist was also instrumental in the planning and construction of the art courtyard situated at the back of the arts block. The artist's first commission of work was the construction of the assemblage, which confronts the viewer as he/she enters the arts building. This spectacular piece was constructed from a variety of different materials and was linked with the Unit 1 VCE art program 2 years ago. The artist worked with a team of 11 students and assisted the group through the planning/design brief processes and was also instrumental in the final decision-making tasks. One of the main roles that the artist undertakes is to oversee the technical assistance that the art students may require on an individual basis. Students also have the opportunity to question, challenge, and inquire about their own potential by working with professional artists. Students witness the planning, the methodology of working practices and the constraints that artists at times have to address.

I believe art teachers have to adapt and exhibit the ability to cater for all individual learning differences within the art room. They need to understand and cope with change within the art curriculum. They need to link the role of technology and art as not necessarily two separate entities but complementing one another for eg. 'multi-media' processes; the use of photography and material technology metal constructions. Teachers need to encourage the visual art student and the technology student to see combinations and or extensions within the VCE curriculum. Art teachers need to possess a firm understanding of art history. One of the major concerns regarding the new VCE structure is that students will be expected to write art essays articulately. Therefore the art literacy skills must be addressed within the 7–10 levels. Students must be able to write both formal essays and short reports. Art teachers therefore need to be able to teach the process of 'visual analysis' and to be able to teach the students the formal qualities of artworks. For example, I might present a Breughal painting for discussion. I talk and discuss the background to the artwork, the actual diversity related to the work and the historical context. I also talk about the 'structure' of the work. I use particular art jargon and introduce the use of art terminology to the students. These procedures are very important within the new VCE course and students need to address these major components.

Schools like ours are in geographical areas away from the inner city galleries and exhibitions. It is important that art teachers be able to access resources from a wide variety of agencies, as excursions may be limited to once a term or dependent on socio-economic standing of students' families; students may only avail themselves of first hand experiences once a year.

I also hope art teachers will encourage students to be creative and not inhibit the students' natural ability. Teachers need to be able to 'pitch-in' to assist students to achieve, and to help them extend and refine the idea. To familiarise myself with a group of students I initiate brainstorming exercises. I ask the students their likes and dislikes, personal interests, where they are obtaining their ideas, who inspires them, their favourite colour and their hobbies. This exercise frames a pastoral care situation. From a list of twenty ideas the student focuses on three. From this structure, the development of the folio is created and this year the VCE students must produce a broad, innovative and experimental folio.

A sense of humour is also important in teaching art. The art teacher must consider the delivery of the curriculum as a performance and you have to sell the product. The art teacher allows or entices student into the teacher's world and relates to the students an awareness of the teacher's interests and passions regarding the art scene. I recently brought into class some articles on David Callum, winner of the Archibald Prize. And whether I like his work based on 'David Wenham, an Australian actor', or not, this award is a current event within the art calendar. Students respond more effectively to current issues, controversy, and on-going feedback regarding art exhibitions and awards and art issues.

The art budget here is $4,000 per half year. At this campus a school contribution fund has been structured. Art students pay $45 per year, but the anomaly regarding budgeting in school programs is that this process is not always a pleasant experience for the school Principal. The school cannot force parents or guardians to pay the specified amount. The Principal works out the percentage that the art faculty is allocated. The program budget has to include accountability for materials, repairs and the payment of guest speakers for specified art classes. Students are provided with all materials apart from the sketchbook and folio. In the art curriculum we have to be aware of our clientele. Our school is based in an outer-suburban area comprising a medium to low socio-economic population. We have to be quite pragmatic about what and how we are delivering the curriculum and the availability of materials that are affordable for the benefit of our students. The library is very supportive of our needs regarding the art curriculum resources. Some of the books are ordered through the library and the art department provides some assistance with the accounts. Art books, as is widely known, can be very costly items.

I am very passionate about art teaching. I want students to be able to enjoy their art, to be creative and individualistic. I believe students enjoy their art at the point when all the processes are completed and the student actually visualises the refinement of the artwork. Michael, one of my students for example, has worked constantly through all the stated criteria and has finally reached the selected outcome;

throughout these tasks he had his initial goal/s. I believe once you start reinforcing the goal to them and say, 'Where are you going with this task? What is this idea all about? What do you want to achieve from this experience?' One of the major roles of the art teacher is to reinforce the importance of witnessing the design process from point A to point E. Some students are satisfied with this outcome, while other students desire an instantaneous image. In the VCE Art course and in the years 7–10 art curriculum the student must demonstrate itemised results from the designated criteria and reach a final outcome. Art students gain enormous satisfaction from these experiences especially in their final year 12 course work. Again this process comes back to experience. The student's confidence develops after they have had constant exposure to the design, trialing and refining processes.

Art is an academic subject as well as an aesthetic experience. The art program is not a soft option for students to view as a 'fill in' area. It has become commonplace, almost mandatory, to begin a discussion of the definitional separation of 'art' and 'culture' with reference to the work of Raymond Williams, the British cultural theorist whose understanding of culture underpin the interdisciplinary academic field of Cultural Studies. Williams (1981: 10) identifies three categories of usage of the word culture:

- A general process of intellectual, spiritual and aesthetic development
- A particular way of life
- The works and practices of intellectual and especially artistic activity

Students should also be given every opportunity to fulfil their personal potential. I believe that some students 'sell themselves very short' and that as art educators we have a personal responsibility to praise students at every opportunity; even if it is about the 'smallest image' in the sketchbook, this process is important. Quite a number of students do not possess confidence; many are going through periods of uncertainty. Problems outside the classroom may be affecting their work and art may be the vehicle to allow them to explore and escape from problems emanating outside the sanctuary of an art room. Art is one subject within the school curriculum, where the student can 'explore from the soul'. The art teacher has the opportunity to communicate and listen to the student; then explore the options of what each student is capable of achieving for a potential outcome.

I also prefer students to experience the professional artist's viewpoint within the art curriculum. There is an on-going connection and continuity with the students when this approach is applied with each student's coursework.

We use CD ROMs, web sites, the internet and other independent resources. Sometimes students bring in books from their own personal library and I use my personal art collection for the gifted students. I encourage students to use external agencies. I also network with the art teachers from the different campuses and the other schools in the area. It is beneficial to see what other teachers are working on regarding individual projects. We do not have the regional network of teachers that existed several years ago. Now art teachers rely on the individual contacts. The cutbacks in school funding have affected these programs. The VCE symposium, conducted by the National Gallery last year, was a wonderful opportunity for me to meet the state assessors in the Art and Studio Arts areas. One of the major losses within the assessment area in art has been the abolition of the art moderation program.

I use the art texts by Gombrich and Hopwood because a certain percentage of art history students arrive at the VCE campus with no prior knowledge or understanding of timelines regarding art sequences. These two resources explain in chronological order the art terms and art periods in a succinct language. These texts are good starting points for the art students. I still believe these texts are relevant within the art curriculum. There seems to be an 'air of paranoia' that these two texts are out of date. Well, the art teacher would never use these books as one set reference. The art teacher explains the relevance of the period, the main influences, characteristics and qualities that frame the period. By using these texts as introductory formats, the art 'jargon' and terminology are able to be understood by the student. There are other references that are useful. Betty Churcher (an art critic and author) addresses the visual analysis strategy successfully, but unfortunately the text that she wrote is out of print. There is a great series on television called 'Take Five' in which Churcher discusses Australian art.

I like her approach and the way she addresses the artwork. The explanation and her style of delivery are appropriate for the VCE art history area. Eventually I will show my students these videos. At the end of each week, I conduct a session on practical work and then the class views a selected video. I also want to show the year 11 art students 'Lust for Life'. This video is based on Van Gogh's life. I introduce the art periods in an informal way. If I use the internet material or the website, the Board of Studies has indicated that these resources are only to be considered as options. They are not set texts. The art student must present a range of resources regarding specific artists studied; these include journals, periodicals and selected art books and articles from newspapers.

In contemporary art, I believe it is important to appreciate the artist's intention and method, to see how he or she has communicated an emotion or an idea of that moment. To me this strategy is important, I like to know what underpins the artist's philosophy. I understand that an integral feeling or involvement can be an instantaneous message. Unfortunately a percentage of the community does not appreciate the artist's output or production. This view is probably applicable to all studio art forms. I have recently acquired a contemporary painting for my own personal collection. The work was produced by our artist in residence; a Mark Rothko inspiration. I do not know how you can successfully educate the public about contemporary art. I suppose the most effective approach is through the art teaching methods we use with the students under our care. The art teacher needs to broaden the student's awareness to art criticism. For example, students can interview 'the art critic' regarding a recent art exhibition or gallery visit or they can interview the professional artist in their own environment. I believe that training students to read as many articles on art issues or regarding specific artists is the most effective form of learning.

My view of postmodernism is that the term reflects the society that the individual inhabits; the events that happen, maybe at a particular time, for example, a revolution, flood, the Vietnam and Timor war, a strike or an abstract moment. The artist attempts to reproduce the moment without any inhibitions about art or art cultures. For example, 'John Perceval' creates a moment. His work is wild and full of energy. He captures a particular feeling or imagery that he wants to convey irrespective of other people's viewpoints. There is a source of vibrancy that occurs within his work. There are complex issues contained within his art apart from his love of colour. You have to brush over all his personal breakdowns and acknowledge the artist's skills, values and beliefs regarding the art process.

I do address gender and cultural issues within my teaching program. If students have for example, a 'Koori' heritage I encourage them to pursue their derivation within their art making and cultural research. I also include gender issues in the art curriculum. This is particularly relevant where the students examine art commentaries in the Unit 4 VCE Art course.

Artists of the calibre of Elizabeth Gower, Jenny Watson or Howard Arkley are interesting artists to study. Several students have been interested in Arkley's work since his death and the recent retrospective exhibition held in Melbourne. The concept of the artists' work determines the outcome or focal point unless gender issues are the prime reason for the construction of the particular artwork.

In respect of popular culture and art in the media I like to notify students about current events such as the 'Archibald Prize' for example the recent issue about Henry Bolte and Jeff Kennett are relevant to art issues; Andres Serrano's 'Piss Christ' controversy and the art pieces pertaining to Alan Bond are issues that have also been featured in the newspapers. I introduce these issues within the VCE art curriculum.

Technology is an important area for generating art images, however the basic knowledge and skills need to be 'hands on' and understood before they are applied in the multi-media area. For example, knowledge of the design process, the elements of line, shape, colour and texture need to be studied. Awareness of the formal qualities in art such as balance, proportion, perspective and composition needs to be included in the teaching program. The use of imaginative imagery generated by hand skills must be implemented before the usage of a machine dominates the process. I have concerns about honesty within the art production experience. How much is the student's input and how much is the machine's final result? So issues of plagiarism are important to consider. Also, the notion of students who use the computer as a 'crutch', for example students can lose that ability to have original images and concepts that enable them to be individualistic within their art making experiences.

Creativity is still relevant in art because without it you may just as well have a computer and press the buttons all day. Art is about creation, thinking and personal inquiry. Students need to know how to use tools, processes and specific techniques within the art experience. I want students to enjoy their art experiences. I want them to challenge concepts and not to be complacent. I do not want them to simply accept that one way is the only way. Students have to use exploratory devices and to produce broad, innovative folios. I want students to be assertive and confident. I would also like them to be continually exposed to contemporary artworks by artists so that they could discuss the content and the intentions of these artists' works. If possible, I would like the students to view artists' workshops, studios and working places outside the classroom. I would invite artists into the classroom on a regular basis to give students personal insight into the origins of their artwork and their personal world.

The art teacher training system is questionable. At times some of the graduates are not realistic about the classroom situation. They live in a Utopian world regarding art programs and art budgets. Schools do not have a 'bottomless pit' of money. Students are individuals and teachers must accommodate all of the needs and expectations of students' abilities. Art teachers must note the clientele and the delivery of the curriculum that they are addressing and overall be realistic.

In conclusion 'art', however one defines it, must still mirror (favourably or with hostility), the development of the society to which it belongs. Inevitably, contemporary art too reflects the complex and diverse social, political and ethical state of our civilisation.

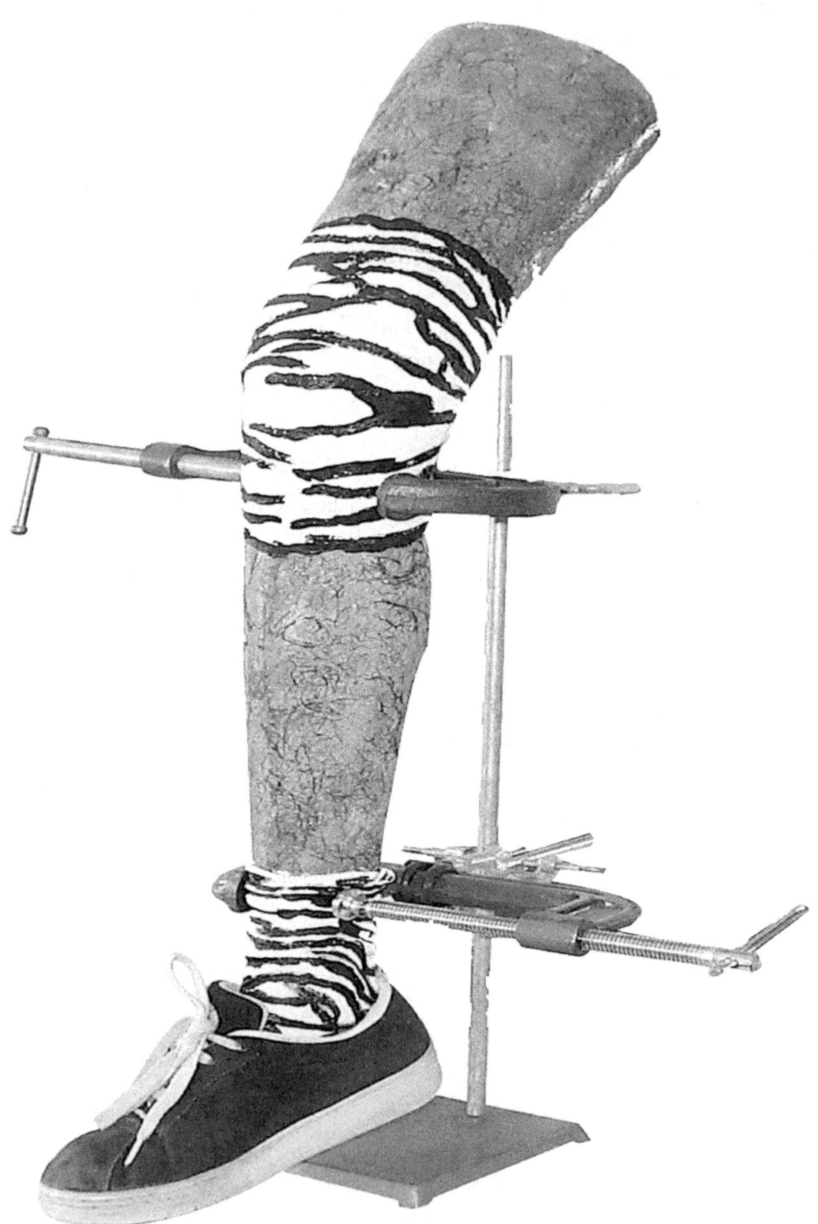

Figure 3:
David Halliday, Year 12, Camberwell Grammar School, Melbourne

Chapter 8

Mark Fenech

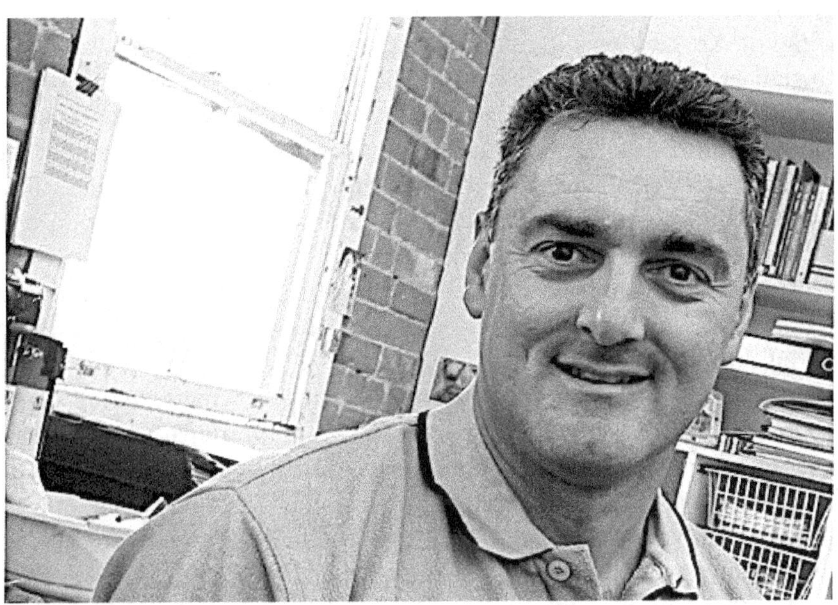

Mark Fenech is the year 12 Coordinator of Studies at St Joseph's College in Hunters Hill, Sydney. Opened by the Marist Brothers in 1880, St Joseph's College is a large Catholic boarding school for boys. Michelle Tinta also teaches at this school. The school population is predominantly Anglo-Saxon with a large percentage of the boys coming from country NSW areas and thus boarding at the school. Mark has a mostly administrative role in the school but still teaches the senior art history program. Mark is also nearing completion of his Ph.D. studies at the University of New South Wales. His studies have involved him in reading contemporary Marxist social theory which he is keen to discuss in relation to the use of interpretive 'frames' in the NSW art syllabus. (ed.)

I didn't do a lot of art when I was at school. But like many other art teachers I had one teacher in my schooling who really inspired me. I was very fortunate to have a brilliant art teacher by the name of Mary Brown, in years 11 and 12. She taught me about art history, which was a totally new world to me. I had never read about art history as a youngster. I had always liked to draw and paint and thought that was fun but the world of art history, theory and philosophy was to me, at that young age, quite inspirational at that time. Surprisingly from that group of students who did HSC art in 1980, we had 4 art teachers come out of a very small class. The four of us went off to the Alexander Mackie art school, now called the College of Fine Arts. So I finished my undergraduate degree in 1984 and just did what a lot of new teachers do. I wrote to lots of schools and Joey's was looking for an art teacher at the time. The numbers were growing here and the Head of Art here was looking to take maternity leave. So I was lucky to start at St Josephs in 1985 and I have been here ever since. I have enjoyed various roles, first as a classroom teacher and then Head of Department. I was Head of Department for about five years and at the end of 1986 I accepted a position in charge of year 12 studies. This took me out of the art department to do more administrative work. It is a challenging and highly regarded position within the school. If I had to be honest I would have to say that, at times, I regret the decision. I felt so much more challenged as a head of the art department than I do in this administrative position.

My area of focus within the art department is the teaching of art history or theory. We tend to specialise within our department, at least amongst our senior classes. I concentrate heavily on the art history and criticism aspects of our course. In year 12, I solely teach the art history and theory. Michelle Tinta and Michelle Marcuse, for a want of a better way of putting it, are studio art teachers.

In 1993 I was a very late applicant to the Master of Art Education course at the College of Fine Arts (COFA). I spent 1993 and 1994 enrolled as a part-time student in the Masters program by course work. I thoroughly enjoyed that and found it very stimulating from the point of view that I had previously spent eight years reading only the work of my own students, so just the level of reading and the diversity of the program were very stimulating. I enjoyed the writing and assignments and all that was involved in the content of the course work. From that I intended to commence the Masters at an honours level. After almost a year pursuing that, an application was made for a Postgraduate award and that was granted on condition that I upgrade to PH.D. level. So I commenced doctoral studies at the beginning of 1996 in the area of art education, with a focus on art museums.

Essentially my doctoral work revolves around the disclosure and interrogation of opaque forms of communication within art museums. I am using the theorists Habermas and Adorno to help me to disclose forms of communication which occur in art museums that may not easily present themselves to individuals, whether they are museum professionals, visitors or tax payers, however I want to define the various groups that use art museums. It is an educational investigation into art museums and it focuses on museum practices at the Art Gallery of New South Wales and The Art Institute of Chicago. Both sites are places where there is quite a bit of educational practice. Certainly The Art Institute of Chicago is an extensive department which is a very well-funded and staffed department. In 1998, when I was there, they had about 48 staff in museum education. It was very inspirational being with a staff of such high calibre in terms of their knowledge in both art and education. I am looking at those two sites in a very broad sense. I have looked at museums as cultural sites. The Chicago Institute is very much a city museum. It is in the middle of a very big metropolis. The trains in Chicago run underneath the building. Sydney on the other hand is more a park museum that lends itself more to contemplation. Chicago Institute as its name suggests is more of a place of learning and teaching which has more of a tradition of art education practice than the Art Gallery of NSW. So I have been looking at instances of communication that occur through things like exhibition display and catalogue notations, also trustees' documents and annual reports. I am interested in the way that those messages may mask certain meanings. It is political and I really enjoyed that dimension of the work. I maintain that the art museum in contemporary society really has the potential to be a place where individuals, especially art educators, can enhance the dimensions of learning about art. It should be a place for argument; it should be a place for discussion and disagreement and activity; a site of struggle. And so I find art museums to be exciting places. At times they can be frustrating places. They are institutions; they are guided by a system much larger than themselves and certainly they rely on taxpayer money.

I don't think the director of the National Gallery of Australia in Canberra made the right decision when he refused to show the controversial 'Sensation' exhibition in Australia. I think places like museums need to be arenas of debate for better or for worse. It is interesting though that Kennedy didn't allow 'Sensation' to come to Australia. It is interesting in relation to the wider ties that he has in the broader bureaucratic political system in which he operates and the different agendas that run through that. I think his refusal to go with

'Sensation' is interesting but it does deny the public the opportunity to be confronted and challenged. I don't advocate that the museum should be a 'free for all' place where anything goes but certainly in a democratic society and in an arena that is typically a place of political activity, I think it is disappointing that 'Sensation' didn't come to Australia.

In relation to censorship of artworks in art education I think the context is important. Certainly within the domain of art history and theory we have discussed works such as 'Piss Christ' by Andres Serrano and we have looked at it very intelligently I think. I have also recently spent a fair bit of time in class discussion of Gilbert and George. A lot of their recent work is very confronting, concerning bodily fluids and homosexuality and other such issues. I haven't censored that dimension. I do however create a certain type of buffer zone when discussing work with students. This puts us at a distance so that we can look at such works in a critical way without being offended or personally challenged in a negative way. That distance just helps us be a little bit more rational about how we deal with those confronting works. I have from time to time, in the area of art making, advised boys, although certainly not censored them, about some of the imagery that they have been using. This has not actually involved prohibiting them from using certain images but I have advised students that this is a religious school. It is the home of a religious order of brothers; that being a boarding school the students and the brothers live here 24 hours a day and that some groups do take offence at certain uses of imagery. I have made them aware of those type of things. Very often religion and the crucifixion finds their way into senior artworks. Even this year we have senior works that involve the crucifix. I think it is such a potent symbol in itself but the narrative that surrounds the crucifixion then touches upon different areas of this school context of which the boys are a part. I think it has been my role to highlight those connections and make students aware of them. However I have never actually been in a situation where I have said 'no you can't do that'. In fact, perhaps the area that I have advised students against is the area of graffiti rather than the use of religious imagery. I have discussed the artistic value and context of their HSC study and asked whether graffiti is an appropriate avenue of artistic exploration for a HSC student to pursue. What does it say about their conceptual ability, their technical ability and so on? I have been more restrictive about graffiti than other issues.

This school is very Anglo-Saxon in its traditions. Our population is not culturally diverse at all. We do have a growing contingent of students from Asia but their numbers are really few. The tradition that we work within is predominantly white Anglo-Saxon. However in the art department here we do go out of our way to present issues that the students may not confront in other domains of their education here or even in their home life. We present issues of a feminist nature and we do a lot of study of women artists. Racism and dominance are two other issues that we explore. Because it is my belief that art comes from social action I tend to teach from a Marxist point of view and I am quite open in the way that I present that to the boys. And they are very responsive to that. I present it to them that we look at our art and our world from a critical point of view as a way of gaining understanding. Certainly the areas of gender and indigenous issues are areas that students in this school find hard to grapple with. We have a high proportion of students here from country backgrounds and they bring a lot of baggage with them in terms of race relations and so on. We deal with issues such as reconciliation and the importance of land rights when we study Aboriginal artists. We don't study traditional Aboriginal rock or bark paintings in an anthropological sense, however we look at a lot of urban Aboriginal artists. This term for example Trevor Nickolls will be one artist that we look at when we look at 'leisure and lifestyle' with year 12. In this study we look at the urban environment as a place for, not only white Anglo-Saxon Australians, but also for multi-cultural groups and indigenous peoples.

The model that this school presents to its students on the role of women is also problematic because I think it does seem to present the notion of a woman in service to the students; in the classroom as a teacher, in the dining room as a helper etc. We do go out of our way in our art programs to discuss issues of gender and the construction of values in our society that are based on gender and race. I think we also introduce those concepts quite early in the art program. We deal with certain issues in year 7 but not at an elevated conceptual level.

Just for convenience I have tended to use the seminar room and theatre to do a lot of my art theory lessons. I have moved away from using slides to use of colour photocopies and colour scans. I have been making art 'recipe cards' which the students carry around. They can be seen carrying bundles of cards that deal with artworks. These have notes on the back and summarise aspects that help them with written expression. For example I include paragraphs on certain frames. We might write a paragraph on a cultural aspect on the back of a card and on the front there is always a topic sentence. Literacy is a hot potato in NSW schools and I try to do everything I can in order to strengthen my students' written skills. In particular I try to help them prepare for an exam. That is why I have started working with the cards. Coupled with that, is the notion that I strongly believe that students need to be out there in the art world, ie galleries and museums. We do take students on gallery tours, not just to the Art Gallery of NSW, but also to the Brett Whitely studio etc. We have also had visiting artists talk to the boys. As recently as 2 weeks ago we had Anne Zahalka come in and talk to the boys. We have also done a tour of the commercial galleries. I think it is important for our students to see art in its art world environment and to see the authentic art object and not just the reproduction. My presentation of art theory and history to students is a discussion about art and art issues. It is not a picture study. The reproduction facilitates the discussion of the issues but certainly it is no substitute for that one to one confrontation with an artwork.

I am a great fan of our NSW year 7 to 10 syllabus. I think it is a great syllabus for the student and the teacher. It allows great scope for the teacher to approach the making of art and the study of art images. I think the four frames, structural, subjective, postmodern and cultural are terrific tools to work with when students make and explore artworks and when they study art issues and art history. I have found that students are much more confident in dealing with art within those frameworks. I have found as a teacher that using those frameworks gives me the scope to investigate art from the perspective of a product that emerges from society rather than something that is separated from the normal activities of life. The syllabus has allowed me to do that. I think the 7-10 syllabus has also allowed me to work with students in the museum setting in the same way. I can take the concepts that I present in the art room and talk to students about those same concepts when we are at an art museum or when we are reading an art review in a newspaper. I think the conceptual elements of the years 7 to 10 syllabus are transportable.

The new syllabus that we are starting in years 11 and 12 is essentially an outcomes-based syllabus. It is a measurable outcomes-based curriculum. I think there are great strengths with it but I think there are also some great drawbacks for art teachers. The great strengths are the conceptual frameworks that support the syllabus. The notions of art world and artist, artwork and audience is a real holistic way of looking at art as part of our culture and not just a separate phenomenon which is devoid of social contact. The syllabus helps to de-objectify art teaching. I must say though that the red tape that is caught up with the measuring of outcomes is quite stifling because I need to cut back on content to be able to satisfy other curriculum imperatives to do with the measurement of outcomes. I need to make students aware of certain assessment criteria and levels. Michelle spends a lot of time on paperwork to help students become aware of outcome issues. I am realistic enough to realise that accountability is a cultural condition that sweeps throughout society and we are caught up with that. I find this challenging because I like to work at disclosing some of those hidden meanings within our study of art that aren't always obvious.

We have had some passionate discussions in our department about the new year 11 and 12 syllabus and the whole idea of outcomes-based curricula. I am coming a little more relaxed about it because I am living it now. But I often think about that element of wonder that is meant to be part of learning and whether there is a place for that in outcomes-based learning. The other thing is gut reaction. I really believe in teachers, and especially art teachers having a gut reaction to a student's work or something that we are reading. Is there a place for that type of learning? For example, there is a boy in year 12 that does great charcoal drawings that are very powerful. I sometimes think about how we measure that power and vitality. We can measure conceptual strength; we can measure use of materials and a whole range of other components but those very subtle elements of what we teach that make us different from other subjects are difficult to grasp. How do we reach into those areas? I am just starting to come to terms with this. Ultimately learning about art and teaching art involves people and not papers and paper work. The minute it does just become a checklist we have lost the whole thing. We have lost that holy grail aspect of art. As long as it involves people we are going to have those subtleties and we are going to be able to recognise those subtleties.

I remember just last term we were looking at traditional art with year 11. We had studied some classical Greek art and we were looking at the Parthenon at the time. I wanted to take them into the controversy of the Elgin marbles; to look at the art world issues that surround these objects. Part of that comes from my first experience of going to the MET (Metropolitan Museum of Art) in New York. I think this experience must hit everybody. It is such an incredible experience to see an Egyptian temple inside a museum and to wonder how it got there and who put it there. This really stopped me in my tracks and to me that was a significant art experience. Seeing great artworks like a Botticelli at The Art Institute in Chicago or a Picasso at the MET, these are numbing experiences. But to also contemplate the power structures at work that enable a temple in an art gallery in New York that should be in Egypt is equally numbing yet stimulating. The frameworks within the syllabus provide us with the scope to tackle issues like that. It also gives us scope to talk about art from a philosophical and sociological position. I often talk to parents at parent/teacher days about how difficult it is to study art as a student at school because students have a grounding in numbers when they study maths but they don't have a grounding in philosophy when they study art. Students are dealing with a lot of the conceptual elements of our subject for the very first time and it is hard for them to get their heads around them. But I think the frameworks of the year 11 and 12 syllabus allow us to manage those. They allow students to put those elements in context so that they can understand why we talk about Marxism when we deal with the ownership of art or the place of Aristotle or Plato when we look at more traditional aspects of art. It helps them to put the pieces together.

More than anything in art I want students to ask the right questions. What they learn I don't know. I can tell them about some of the historical aspects of art and artists and about my experience of learning about these things, but ultimately my job is to get them to ask the right questions so that they can do it without me. I want them to be able to go to these places and question and not be passive viewers. Idealistically I want them to be involved, active viewers. That is an idealistic hope but I think that's what drives me to teach art. I often jokingly say to my students 'Art's up here with the Gods and everything else is a very dull second'. I say to the staff I work with, that we are so lucky to deal with a subject that can touch areas of learning and human experience that nothing else can do in the same way. Music can kind of do certain things as well but other subjects are just pretending.

I think I am teaching very differently to Mary Brown. She gave me such passion for art history. She was very much a Gombrich and Gardiner person and she was a product of that time. Mary was a teacher of ancient history too and so there was always a very social connection to our study of art. I think what Mary did, in her own way, was not only to present the material to me, she also encouraged me to ask the right questions. However it was in a different way. It was through some other means of debate and discussion. I must say the classroom that I was in with Mary Brown was a much more active classroom as far as discussion goes, than my own. My own classroom can be a place of debate from time to time but I think that has a lot to do with the mentality of students here anyhow. Students here like to be fed. They like handouts. They expect the notes on the board. That's not something unique to my classroom. It is an overall mentality and I think it is a great challenge to this school to manage that. It is slowly changing but it's inch by inch. I think part of that is that it is a private school. The fees are high and when it comes down to it, people are talking and thinking about value for money and it is a bit of a vicious circle really.

I think the various art forms are very separate in NSW schools. I feel that more since returning from 7 months in Chicago two years ago. At the Art Institute I was very close to a person who ran the Elder Hostel program which was a seniors program. It involved people coming in for a week, being accommodated at a hotel in Chicago and it was just a cultural experience. People went to the Art Institute for lectures and tours and various practical activities. They also went to the symphony across the road or architecture walks. It seemed so integrated. It struck me that people in NSW don't readily connect the Art Gallery of NSW with the Opera House. It seems so perfect an opportunity to make that connection yet I just find, in Sydney, (and it may be my ignorance of theatre and opera etc,) that there just isn't a strong connection. If there is it certainly is not obvious to me as a player in the field of art education. I wonder whether it is obvious to the layperson not involved in art. I really doubt that it is.

I think that any graduate coming into teaching today needs to understand that they are entering a difficult work environment; a work environment from which they will not become wealthy. There needs to be something else that motivates them to want to come into schools. I think they do have to be passionate about the content that they teach. They do have to, in themselves, have a wonder for that content. I teach because it really excites me to teach art. I know that sounds easy to say and I do find it difficult at times. I find it difficult now to teach practical art classes. I find, even after 16 years there is a bit of lack of confidence in the way I teach in the studio. I am absorbed by art theory and criticism and I want my students to be absorbed by it too. That is what is exciting about teaching. It is something that I can put myself into. My administrative position which occupies 70% of my time basically involves making lists. It is a very mechanical separate experience. It is not something I pour myself into. It is something I do and I do efficiently and well but it is a different experience.

Technology has been useful for me in the teaching of art history. Occasionally I have had the internet hooked up and we have gone looking into various home pages. I remember we looked at the home page of the Chicago Architecture Foundation and we went on a virtual tour of some of the architectural sites that I was lucky enough to visit. That was fun and the students liked that, and they were good at it. The art staff and I have had discussions about this over the last 12 months. I feel that this technological advancement is just passing me by. I recognise that young art teachers are familiar with computer-generated art and multi-media. I don't have those skills and that worries me. I feel very confident in my place as an art teacher but I recognise that is an area that I am not keeping up with. I do blame myself for that but I also blame the school for that because this is an insular school. It is a bit of a comfort zone. I have been here 16 years because it is a good place to teach. The facilities are good. However, more than anything the students are good to teach and that's what keeps me here. I do recognise that I have sacrificed a lot by being here and that is the diversity of being at other schools. In terms of my marketablity as a teacher I have made certain sacrifices by staying here I think, that may make me possibly less attractive to other employers. This was one reason why I began postgraduate work. I have also done some consultancy with the Board of Studies in connection with the preparation of support documents for the years 7 to 10 syllabus. I entered those activities to extend my involvement beyond this school.

Chapter 9

Michelle Tinta

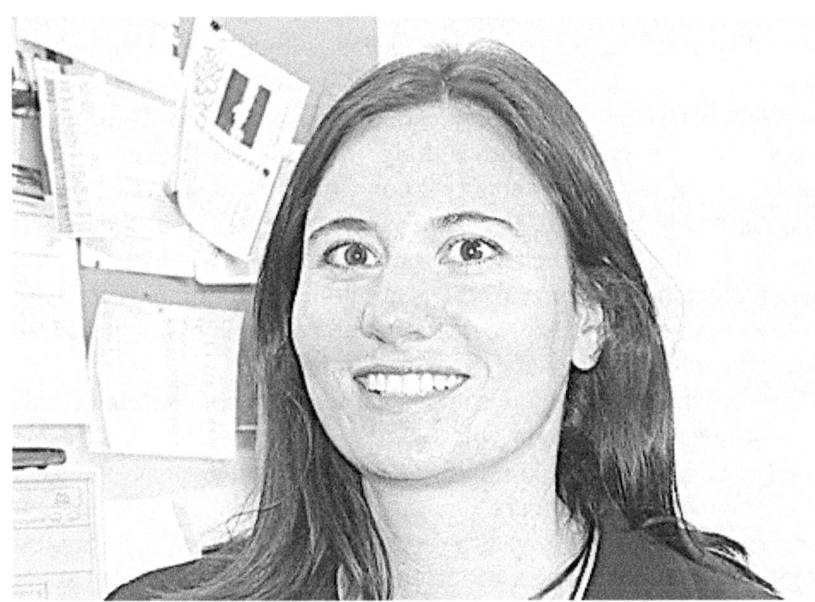

Michelle Tinta teaches Visual Art at St Joseph's College in Hunters Hill, Sydney on the same staff as Mark Fenech. Michelle teaches studio art practice in a refurbished converted dairy in the large school grounds. The art studios allow boys to work on large-scale paintings and senior boys are given access to good quality materials and equipment. Michelle also teaches photography and this involves use of digital imagery. As the New South Wales (NSW) curriculum specifies that students explore artworks through one or a combination of four given frames I was particularly interested to find out how the 'postmodern' frame was used in both art theory and art practice. I was also interested in the ways in which difficult aspects of postmodern practice were handled in a conservative 'modernist' school climate. (ed.)

I have had just ten years of teaching experience. I studied at the College of Fine Arts (COFA) which was the City Art Institute at that stage. That is the basic visual arts grounding for a lot of Sydney art teachers and I think it is a good one. After the normal casual teaching stint while looking for a job I got a phone call from a friend who asked me to come into Miller Technology High School. So that was my first school and I stayed there for three years. It was a very different school to my second school, the one I am in now. The three years in a new technology high school was interesting but a very different experience to St Joseph's College. The place that visual art takes within the school is very different.

I think that this is a traditional school and in that sense there are subjects like English and Maths that are pursued more vigorously. However visual art does have a strong role. A lot of boys take visual art and they enjoy it. It is quite a respected subject within the school so that is very good. The numbers tend to reflect how the boys view the subject. They know that they can achieve academically in visual art and that is a really positive thing in this school. We focus in specialty areas so the students know that if they want to do photography for example, they can pursue that for one and a half years. So I think art is well respected and parents do understand the value of visual art. Whether the boys are going to continue with art as a profession or not they still get to understand that looking at culture provides an important balance in their learning.

The department was quite established when I came here and staff were working quite strongly with the new junior syllabus. So I came into some very strong programming within that junior area. Numbers tend to fluctuate and numbers choosing to do visual art do change. It depends what is on offer in the rest of the curriculum. The biggest change would be in the area of technology. That has redirected some of our programs particularly in photography, the area I was employed here to teach. So technology and use of the computer has been an area that we have had to develop since I have been here. We need to keep up to speed with the students here. We tend to think of computers as tools for digital imaging when it is the art area. If we are using technology for research then we go outside the art rooms to the resource centre. So the use of computers is differentiated between the areas of digital imaging and research. I think that is a distinction that we make. If students want to use the internet, and we encourage them to do so, they use computers in the resource centre.

I think the NSW syllabus is good because it does allow flexibility for content. So we structure our content around teacher resources and specialities. And that is how we work within our department. I think one of the strongest things about our junior syllabus is its focus on literacy. It encourages strong use of literacy and uses the frames as being the most recent change within the junior syllabus. The senior syllabus has allowed incredible freedom. We have tended to customise it within the school so that it suits our programming. Even though the syllabus suggests an integrated approach to criticism, history and art making we tend to separate these areas. We focus a lot of effort on history and criticism and this is taught separately from studio time. We divide the visual arts into theory and studio time. And we do specialise within the practical area. So students tend to follow a teacher. For example, I teach photography, so students who want to do that come with me. That specialisation within the senior area has been quite good. We also offer painting, drawing, sculpture and computer generated images.

Visual art is offered from years 7 to 12. It is mandatory in years 7 and 8. Our year 7s do two fifty-minute periods a week. Our year 8s do three periods a fortnight and year 9 art is an elective and students choose that for two years. So the additional studies course is a two year course. From there students can select to do that again in year 11 and 12. It is not essential for students to have done visual art in years 7 to 10 in order to continue in years 11 and 12. In year 9 and 10 they do 3 periods of art a week, the focus being on art making. The balance is 60% art making and 40% art criticism and history. In year 11 and 12, that changes to 50% each and students have four periods a week. Basically students do one compulsory subject, which is English, and the rest are chosen by the students.

I want students to appreciate the cultural value of the visual arts and the place of the visual arts within the context of community living. I also want them to understand that it is quite a noble pursuit to be able to continue with visual art as a profession. I want them to understand that there are many professions that they can continue with and that art is not limited to art making. At school here I like students to understand that writing about the arts is a profession that they could continue with. That interest need not only be temporary but is something that they can pursue for a lifetime. I think that is important. The awareness of culture and the development of a sensitivity to objects and images is important. I want them to know that visual language is important and I want them to have a respect for visual art and art making.

We study a lot of western art here. From time to time we do look at other cultures but a large part of our program deals with western traditions. This is something we may need to address. We do have students from overseas but many are Anglo-Saxon. We have about

50% from the country and 50% from the cities. It is quite different to previous schools I have been to where there has been a larger cultural mix. I do believe that it is important for the students to have a sensitivity towards and a respect for art from other cultures. They need to experience them and be aware of them.

There are some fundamental areas that I consider important to study in visual art. I think that it is significant for students to understand classicism as a basis for looking at historical objects. For example, from Greek and Roman traditions students can study the revival of classicism throughout various periods of time and then see how these revivals lead into postmodern art. When students are reflecting on images they can then see that art can be eclectic. Some would say that students do not need this grounding in classical art. I also think that modern art is pivotal as an area of change. The three areas of classicism, modernism and postmodernism are three key areas which we focus on from years 7 to 12. I also think students should be looking at contemporary art from early years.

In classicism we look at Greek and Roman art and we look at the ideology behind works and a little bit of philosophy. Students look at the world in general and they understand that what we are looking at are cultural objects which are not isolated. I want them to get an understanding of broad aspects of the world. We then look at Renaissance works such as Raphael's The School of Athens which features Aristotle and Plato. So students play off these different ideas and see that we can look at artworks from many different viewpoints. Romanticism is also a period of change we deal with, looking at the subjective and the emotional aspects of art making. We study Gericault, Delacroix and Goya. Goya is a personal favourite of mine because of the narratives involved. I think students love stories and these are brutal and ghastly stories and of course, boys love them. We work thematically in the junior years. We do select contemporary and historical examples side by side. For example, in year 7 we look at interiors. We might look at an Australian example and a Renaissance example. As an example, we might choose Tom Roberts' 'Shearing the Rams' because it contains stories and images which appeal to a lot of the country boys here.

Modernism is the most interesting period in respect of change. The notion of artists having freedom to do what they want is something that appeals to students. But I think it also confuses as well. It is working through that confusion that is interesting. Students like the notion of artists doing such radical and revolutionary things to objects. Picasso and Pollock are the two Big P's of modernism; Pollock being the full stop of modernism with his destruction of the image is seen by students as fascinating. They also find the lives of the artists intriguing.

Postmodernism can appear threatening and I always look at it as an age of cynicism and questioning. The positive part of postmodernism is the questioning of moral attitudes and the examination of the way things are done. I think that questioning is quite a healthy thing. Modernism was a period when artists were breaking boundaries. Postmodernism is more of a blurring of those boundaries and that whole eclectic notion is a perfect reflection of our society. So there are many positive aspects of postmodernism. We use the term postmodernism with the boys and they have a sense of what it is. I think they have an opinion about it. I tend to look at the attitudes within postmodernism and then I look at the strategies used by postmodern artists. So students get to understand that postmodern artists do work with strategies and probably the basic concepts that we introduce at year 7 would include appropriation. They understand the idea of borrowing images. This is a very basic concept which can be expanded on later when they deal with eclecticism and pluralism. It relates to broader notions about globalisation; the idea that we live in this globalised world in which everything is blurred; cultures are blurred, images are blurred and they no longer come from just one source. So we do introduce postmodernism very early and it is compulsory because it is one of the frames within the syllabus. And it is fascinating and interesting even though it is sometimes confusing for students. I do find that it is an area which the boys find difficult to grasp.

When we teach postmodernism in year 11 students have already looked at modernism however I don't know whether students need a grasp of modernism before they can understand postmodernism. I think it does help to have a big picture when looking at postmodernism. We do study feminism. A few years ago we looked at some of the recommended areas of study and looked specifically at women artists. One group were doing technology and women artists. We immediately began with 'How many women artists do you know? Write a list of them'. Then we asked them to write a list of the male artists they knew and list them. It was quite apparent that that they needed to look at women artists and we needed to address this in the program. I actually found that they were really fascinated and interested in the artists that we looked at. We looked a Gentileschi but we also looked at very contemporary artists like Barbara Kruger and Vicky Varvaressos. I think they got a lot of understanding about minority groups at a particular period of time. There certainly wasn't a resistance to looking at feminist art at all. We make a point of trying to have gender equality when we are programming.

I see postmodernism as an opportunity to create awareness of key issues. I see feminism as a really gutsy topic to tackle and one that shouldn't be shied away from just because of the gender of the group you are teaching. Sometimes it might be just more interesting to one class than another. We look at Tracey Moffatt's work a lot; we look at Julie Rapp and we have guest speakers. Ann Zahalka came in recently and so did Julie Rapp and Robin Stacey. And we have had them here not simply because they are women artists but because they are contemporary artists who have very interesting art practices. They also have enormous bodies of work for students to look at. I think that access to an artist is important for students to experience.

I think since the new syllabus teachers have taken the postmodern frame on board. The junior syllabus has been in place for five years. I would like to think that it has been embraced and used constantly and that it is a general part of the program. The in-servicing of art teachers is very strong in NSW. It has a lot to do with galleries or the Art Education Society. I think the people at the Board of Studies seem to be in touch with teachers' needs. There has always been an attitude that visual art is a very academic subject and I think the new junior syllabus has done a lot for the status of visual art in NSW.

I think postmodernism is fascinating. The issues-based nature of it is interesting. I think the brighter students will relate the key issues to their own lives. They work and operate on an issues-based level. I do find that there is a lot of modernist art practice. For example, our painters are often just dealing with painting. We have students who may be working in a very subjective way. I sometimes think that students are sometimes doing these practices but may not realise what they are doing. They may be operating in that way but may not be able to articulate that their technique is postmodern. This may also be the same with many artists. It is the writers who are theorising this. In my ten years experience I have always treated art writing at the same level. I would never shy away from writing no matter how much the students enjoyed the practical side of art. The theoretical side is of equal value and is interesting for the students. The teacher has to tap into what makes it interesting whether it is the stories, the artist's world etc.

We introduced students in year 11 to notions of classicism and romanticism. We looked at David's 'Death of Marat' and we selected specific romantic works such as Bill Henson's photographs and compared them to the work of Turner. So we presented students with a series of writings on these artists. We discussed the narrative of 'The Death of Marat'. We examined the horror of the skin disease that possessed him and we explored his political beliefs. The boys found these stories about the things that led to Marat's assassination very intriguing. Bill Henson's photographs also have very controversial leanings. They are very subjective but they are controversial because of the way that he employs his models. His images are dark and mysterious and they revive traditional romantic notions. It is that brooding aspect of his work which is useful. It is also the large scale of the work and the mystery of them that captivates. It is the notion of looking for something that we don't know is there. They are very challenging works to look at as they don't give away too many clues. They challenge the viewer to engage in finding the meaning of the work. They are also confusing and difficult works and the boys recognise that. However, it is up to them to put their own interpretation to them.

When we asked students to choose the artists they wished to write about Turner was not a popular choice. David however, seemed to be a concrete image with literal connotations. It allowed them to bring quite a lot of information they knew about classicism to that work, so they had a lot of material to use. The Henson image was also popular because students could write about photographic processes related to their own photography work. The Turner painting however was more difficult to unravel for them.

We deal with contemporary Aboriginal art rather than traditional. We look at the work of Lin Onus and Gordon Bennett. In the postmodern world these artists are operating very politically. In particular the boys find Gordon Bennett's work fascinating. They are very gutsy paintings but they are also very issues-based and the students recognise that these issues are happening around them. Some students don't recognise them and it is very interesting to present these ideas to them. Some boys have a lot of questions and their naiveté to some of these issues shows through. When we look at Aboriginal art we are able to tackle these issues without having any other art background. We are focussing on the issues and we are focussing on the appropriation of styles.

In selecting art for students we don't step away from controversy. When the Andres Serrano issue arose concerning the controversy over 'Piss Christ' we looked at it with both juniors and seniors. Students asked us about it and we didn't steer away from it at all. We spoke to them about an artist who was being censored and we looked at the issues of censorship with them. We talked about the images and what their personal opinions of them were. We discussed how their opinions might differ from that of the artist. We asked why the artist would present works like this. We certainly didn't steer away from the issue although being a Catholic school the broader issues of the real world and the specific social issues of censorship are there. I think you can deal with those issues in a sensitive way so that students can come to understand them.

We haven't had problems with discussing controversial works such as the recent work by Damien Hirst involving the dissected cows presented in formaldehyde. Last year we looked at dissent and disorder as a theme. Obviously they not only looked at dissent in modern artists but also in postmodernism. This was a recommended area of study and there is a place in art history for dissent and there are always going to be artists who are pushing the boundaries of accessibility and creating art 'on the edge'. I think it is particularly important for senior students to be aware of the larger picture and if there are artworks that question those boundaries then we would look at them. But we would be sensitive and we need to respect the institution we are working in. But I think that the institution would also respect the needs of art.

The students are starting to use digital imaging in my area of photography. They all use cameras and they all use the darkroom technology. Digital imaging is an extension of the foundations of photography. Digital imaging is a process I use and I think that combining of images is important and the computer software does that well. Students can combine images manually and digitally and it is just a question of what works best for the individual. I think cameras are here to stay and I don't think the digital camera will replace the conventional camera.

In the studio area students are constantly moving from one medium to another. That is how artists work. They don't necessarily have to be purists. You do have some students who will just work in print making for example. But for others their artwork develops through broadening the use of media or they might need to use digital imaging for part of the process to get to their subject.

I am still teaching because I actually enjoy being in the classroom. I love art and I think the students here like learning about art. That is what keeps me here.

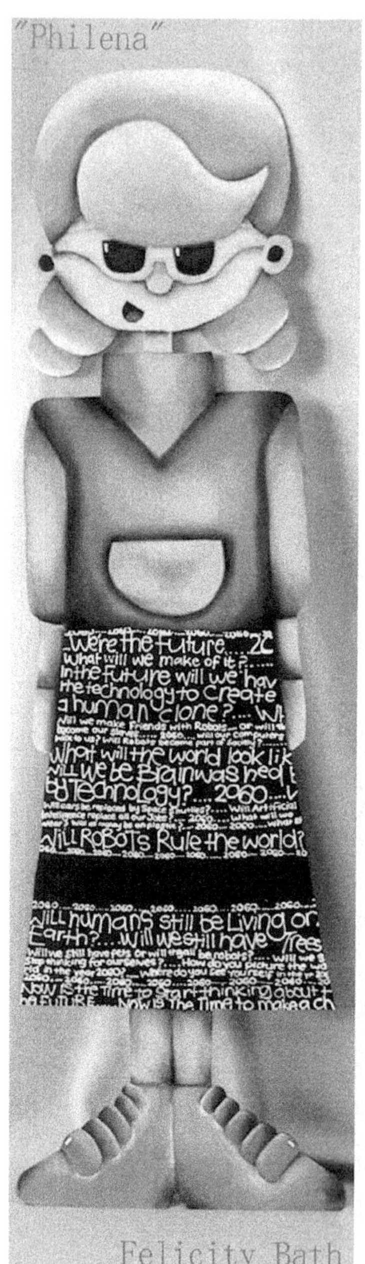

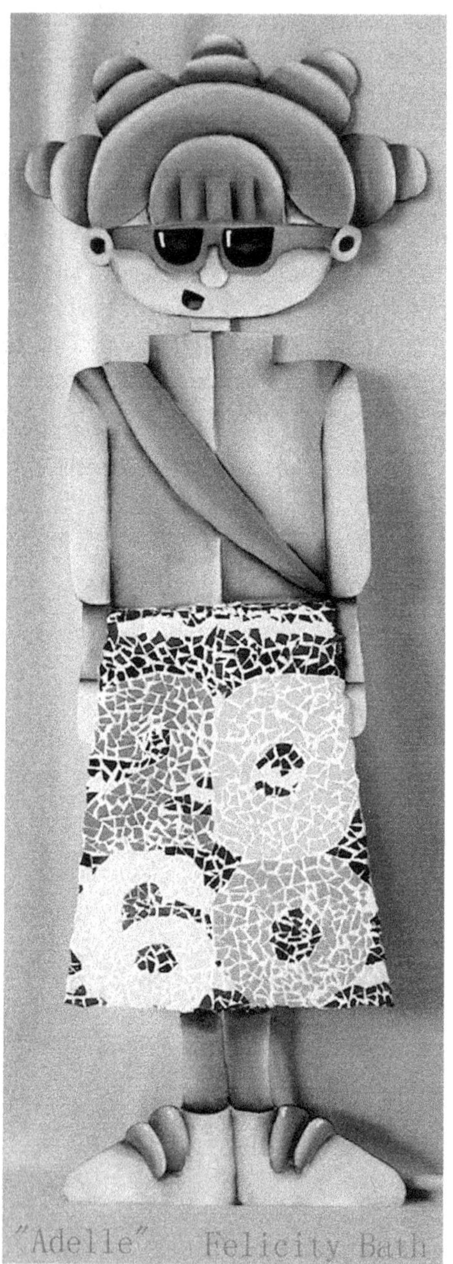

Figure 4:
'Philena' and 'Adelle', Felicity Bath, Year 12, Colac College, Victoria, Australia

Chapter 10

Nick Wright

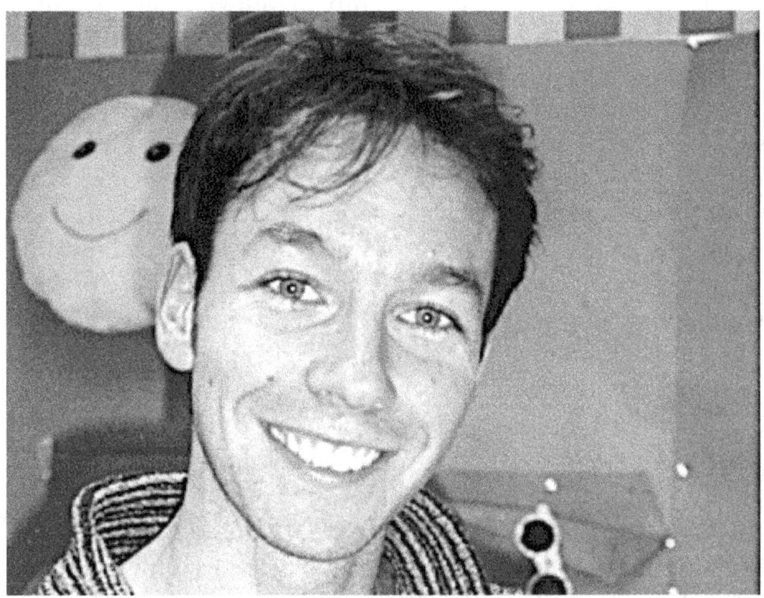

Nick Wright has been a teacher of art at Ellen Wilkinson School for Girls in North West London for 5 years. This is his first teaching appointment and he teaches art to all levels in the secondary school. The art department is housed in a new building comprising three art teaching spaces and a separate space for computers. The school has a population of 1063 students and students come from a diverse range of cultural backgrounds. The religious education program of the school embraces the religions of Christianity, Hinduism, Islam, Judaism, Sikhism and Buddhism. (ed.)

I think art is one of the key subjects in the curriculum because it is really literacy and I think that more and more we are surrounded by a visual world in terms of communication. So for pupils to be actually able to interpret that visual information in the wider world and to read those conventions through the media and advertising is obviously very important. And then on another level you have basic coordination skills such as hand-eye coordination, problem solving skills and the skills of craft involving the use of materials and drawing etc. It is complex and we should be able to define what we do but it is difficult to pin down what it is that pupils are going to go out there with.

There have definitely been changes in art teaching in recent years. When I was at school in sixth form we had a very successful art department but it was very much based on the formal elements of still life and the figure. It was a more traditional approach to art and design. It was much more limited in terms of visual literacy. But one reached a high level in terms of the craft of drawing and painting. That, on a personal note, as an artist, has always held me back because I didn't necessarily have the art and design skills of investigation, research and development. And I didn't have the critical and historical aspect because I didn't study art history. So I found it very difficult to access art and to be tolerant of art in the wider picture. One of the great things for me as an art teacher is to gain a greater understanding of those aspects I missed in my own education while enlightening pupils. It works both ways. Teaching has to be fulfilling for both teachers and students and that's where it gets exciting. So the most interesting and vital projects tend to be those where I am tackling new ground myself and therefore there is greater response.

I think what has brought in changes in schools is not so much art in the wider world but the changes from the examining boards and the understanding of the role of art education. If you get the criteria for the exams the purposes of art are set out clearly through the separate elements there. So I think that has been what has brought about change in the classroom. I think artists and teachers have always been influenced by what has been going on around them because we are interested. We go off to galleries and we know what's going on. That might not have a direct influence but it certainly has an influence in the classroom. I think what is needed is a greater understanding from the examining boards and those who are setting out the criteria. The influence very much stems from the Institute of Education. You could almost say that they are bulldozing an art environment in schools which is art, craft and design-based; that deals with a range of artists throughout time; that looks at art in terms of context, place etc. They are the real force behind it. They have a lot to take credit for but they also need to be realistic about the resources that schools have.

However I do have my own way of teaching despite the attainment targets etc. The beauty of this subject is that you design and create student projects. They are not prescriptive and therefore as long as you are meeting the criteria it doesn't matter what you do. And this is quite an interesting point because I think it is about learning to learn. We have been doing a project on Turner and while doing this I go through this conflict thinking why would the pupils at this school be interested in studying this particular man? And then I say to myself 'Well no it doesn't matter who they are studying, it is how they go about the study'. So we are teaching students to understand various things; the historical aspects and context, the use of techniques etc. So one part of me says it doesn't matter which artist they look at, as it is more about learning. So sometimes I get a little disgruntled with the Institute for advocating that students study particular artists (contemporary or whatever), suggesting that for some reason we ought to be studying these people. But as long as students are gaining the fundamental skills I believe it doesn't matter which artists are used. What does matter is that the classroom becomes a relevant environment for pupils. For me the Turner project has cross-curricular links with history. So I talk about the slave trade and things like that. The context is what makes it relevant to other subjects. But I also take students through the very formalist elements of watercolour techniques so they get fulfilment out of learning some traditional craft and design skills. Pupils here are very open, they accept art in the curriculum and I don't feel the need to find things that specifically motivate them.

In terms of issues-based projects students would work in some sort of medium, say a poster, but they would choose some sort of issue that they are passionate about; an issue which comes from them. Issues-based teaching is one of the key ways to get students involved. Some of the issues they might come up with include protection of animals, prevention of cruelty to children and other key social concerns. In relation to gender issues I try to just use relevant artists. I won't just use a woman artist because this is a girls' school. But if a particular artist happens to be a woman who is going to be able to create exemplars for a particular way of working, then I would use her work. But obviously one is limited by the resources that we have in the department, so we are always conscious that we get multicultural resources in and we make sure the gender balance is there.

In order to get resources I, or another teacher, might come up with a project that might well have come out of a personal visit to an exhibition. That might be followed by a school visit to the exhibition. And then a project will be generated out of that, so the catalogue of the exhibition is purchased and books by related artists are sought. For example with the Cindy Sherman work, we have books by other artists whose work has a similar feel or ilk to that of Sherman's. So this gives a more diverse set of examples. The Cindy Sherman project that I run in sixth form was initiated by the Cindy Sherman exhibition in the Saatchi Gallery. The students also went to the Sensation exhibition and they responded to that in a very positive way. This influenced undercurrents in much of their work. So I used that energy, at the time, to explore self-identity and make connections with media studies. The project basically uses the work of Cindy Sherman but is not as explicit in its content as some of hers. I used her black and white photographs which she calls 'film stills'. Students look at these and go away and invent themselves in a scenario involving drawings and studies of the time-based scenario. One of these is then selected and developed in different ways. They also take the design into IT as well and so they add text to the image. They scan their image and then develop it using Adobe Photoshop and they import them into publisher or Adobe PageMaker.

They also do larger scale work where they take an individual image, rework it on a larger scale and exploit it through materials. So they create something with a finish or realisation that is important for the examinations. I say realisation because it is one of the things that is always an issue. The big people up there in education circles are advocating process and realisation and I feel that it is given a disproportionate amount of marks. This is substantiated by the art moderators. For example, if we think of Claus Oldenburg and a GCSE year 12 project which looks at soft sculpture or cast objects, the process may involve looking at balance, building armatures and looking at the underneath structure, but often as not the realisation is not as good as the two dimensional work, and it takes a lot longer. So it is very difficult to keep up this sort of work when you don't feel it is being appreciated by the examining board. And that is something that keeps on coming up again and again. Some contemporary artists such as Oldenburg might take a shirt and dip it in plaster and it would dry and he might paint it with enamel paint. But he may not be dealing with any of the formal elements at all. So you need to balance the use of an artist like that, who has a contemporary idea that pupils will respond to, while at the same time building into that some of the other more formal aspects of art and design. Often an artist's response shows the realisation on the outside but not all the work that has gone into it. It is very difficult for young students to do both.

There are some works not suitable for use in school art programs. At the Apocalypse exhibition (Royal Academy of Art) there is work that is Certificated for over 18 year olds and that was so in the Sensation exhibition as well. Mike Kelley's work in the Apocalypse exhibition shows violence between a man and a woman and some explicit images. Even with Cindy Sherman's work I have to be careful about which images I show. I mark the pages to be looked at and I keep that book locked up. I think in the school context it would be wrong to show students some works. What I do depends on the pupil and her interests. I can tell them that there is an exhibition on and they can take themselves there. This was the case with a very mature group of year 13's I had a few years back. They responded to the 'fuller' aspects of the Cindy Sherman shall we say. That was fantastic and one of these girls got into Foundation College from that work, but it was not something that the whole class responded to.

I never introduce the term postmodernism to students. I always just use the name of the artist. I never talk about postmodernism. I only describe my own schooling as being modernist because without artists at the turn of the nineteenth century I wouldn't be responding to art in this way. I cannot help being influenced by art around me. But I don't know if you could describe a school as modernist; I don't think it ever really works like that. My teacher in sixth form was a wonderful painter and actually would sit there and paint on your work, and you would see the technique that he used. And he would also take on board your natural technique and develop that. I learned a huge amount from him as well as learning a huge amount about energy from my life-drawing teacher in the classes I went to on a Wednesday evening. They were totally different responses but I couldn't narrow them down into a particular 'modernist' classification.

If I think about how this particular art department might be in 20 years time I can imagine much closer ties between media and art and design. I could imagine a lot more time-based media as technical hurdles are overcome. So the use of digital video cameras, down loaded images and editing will change things. You are always restricted by time. The technology involving still images using Photoshop is very plausible but for pupils to learn the software and be able to handle that involves a great input of time and energy. And it is a virtual time that often cannot be seen and recognised. For example, the moderator said he was a bit worried about the amount of work evidenced, But you have to realise that there are weeks of work learning how to use the software before you can apply that. You can say we could use IT in more simple ways and we do that at the lower age groups, knowing that their skill-base will be higher by the time they come through the school. But I think there has to be a more realistic understanding of how long it takes for someone to learn to use something in order to achieve an expressive outcome. I get very excited by computer art and the computer used as a tool. It breaks my heart to feel that I am almost doing students an injustice because the time spent doesn't necessarily correspond with the grade. Yet I feel that in relation to the wider world of vocation in industry and the work place students with computer skills are getting a massive service and a great head start.

Computers will change the notion of originality, although I don't really think anybody is original. Maybe artists such as Cezanne can shut themselves up for years and come up with something different, and make massive leaps forward. Maybe people can work without influences, just look and then come up with new ideas. But the majority of art is montage. It combines influences and if you look at the work of any artist you can generally reel off about three names with which the work might be associated. And although artists would probably deny it, they really have been influenced at some point. I think if computers are used in the right way, they are very useful. If used as a tool, for example to look at composition to see what works, or maybe to try different colour separations for a fabric print, or to realise a design for a package then it has a real place. I just think computers are incredibly difficult to use well. I think it would be too extreme if computers were the only tool used in art. The tactile aspect of art and design and the affiliation with materials are important. You can't let go of that and let art be taken over by something that is completely virtual. You will produce some interesting work but it won't be giving the pupils a broad art and design education.

At the moment I think I do like artists with fashion overtones because the students love fashion. So there is a very strong emphasis on adornment. This means fashion in the widest context and from different cultures. Associated with this are studies of identity and we do a lot of work with that. We construct hats, wearable items and non-wearable items and discuss the boundaries between fashion and art and where they meet. We look at artists that influence designers and designers that influence art. We try to understand that these things are overlapping and interchangeable and that they work together; you can't really see one without the other. Actually an interesting exhibition was the 'Hundred Years of Art and Fashion' exhibition at the Haywood Gallery. This introduced the idea of the non-wearable garment and the students really enjoyed it.

As far as originality goes I use copying a lot. I certainly don't think it is the place of schools to be producing something that is original. So there is no issue about schools imagining that they are at the forefront of contemporary art and setting the way, breaking new boundaries. That is just not what it is about and never will be. Copying as a way to understand something and as a way to look hard, is imply that, a way of looking. Drawing from observation is copying. It involves analysing what is in front of you, working it out and improving your skills as a result of that. So much contemporary art is about ideas. It is ideas-based and I think ideas-based work is out of the boundaries of school art classes. At the end of the day it must be about tangible work that is realised in some form. I am thinking about Winnie's A level exam in which she has manipulated text. And in looking at Winnie's work you can think of the dada movement but I don't think Winnie was ever introduced to the dada movement. It is just been her response to the exam question. She has manipulated the text to create an image which is quite innovative in one way, especially for a school environment. But she has used the word 'deforestation' in the shape of a tree and she has shown parts depleted etc. to convey the idea. But I think she has picked up these ideas from outside influences rather than anything I have talked about. But maybe students apply general educational ideas to their work. Even though we haven't studied dada she has still come up with dada-type images.

There are cultural restraints that apply to certain cultural groups in the art class. There are certain things that are quite taboo for some cultures and we have to be sensitive to that. For example, when dealing with personal identity we are aware that some of the students can't be photographed for religious reasons. So we have to be aware of that. We talk about these issues on the staff and it is the sort of thing that was discussed in lectures We have had some parents very concerned about certain things. We don't really therefore deal with the nude figure at all. I think the ethos of the school is that everybody learns about everyone else and there has to be an understanding that people do things different ways. So part of schooling is about learning different views and opinions. But we do check about photography and ensure that no cameras are taken out if the student is not allowed to be photographed.

For me a lot of exciting contemporary work involves artists looking at archaeology or science etc. One of my favourite artists is Naum Gabo where he starts off as an engineer from a very different background and somehow it tends to make more exciting work than 'art for art's sake' or art about art. I really like the constructivists. Probably the way forward is to make sure that we are developing cross-curricular links. The Force Fields exhibition at the Haywood Gallery was a great example of this because it showed art using magnetic fields and all sort of scientific things being used in a creative way. Unfortunately we didn't take the students to it but it would have been interesting for them and they would also have thought about the physics behind the works. I think cross-curricular work is something that needs to be really explored. It tends to depend on enthusiastic individuals. I think that is where the exciting artwork will develop in the future. There is no style in contemporary art. If I talk to people and they are upset about art today I say, 'Just relax, don't worry so much about it. Stop asking yourself whether this is art.' When galleries buy works using government money there is a question about whether the art is good or bad, but on a wider level all the boundaries have gone, so we cannot make a decision about good or bad. It depends on just responding and respecting the fact that the artist has followed an idea and found the time to do it and take us forward. I think there has always been a lot of pessimism around. If you look at Goya, Breughal and Bosch you can see horrific, apocalyptic images. I think art has always been shocking and it is just a question of how shocking. I think the Chapman brothers hit on the question of whether we become numb to shock and I think we do and have.

I think art education is such a huge thing to understand and it is sometimes very difficult to motivate yourself in the classroom and think that you are actually doing the right thing and that this has a purpose. I do feel that art in the classroom is sometimes very unrelated to everything that is going on outside.

Chapter 11

Graham Nash

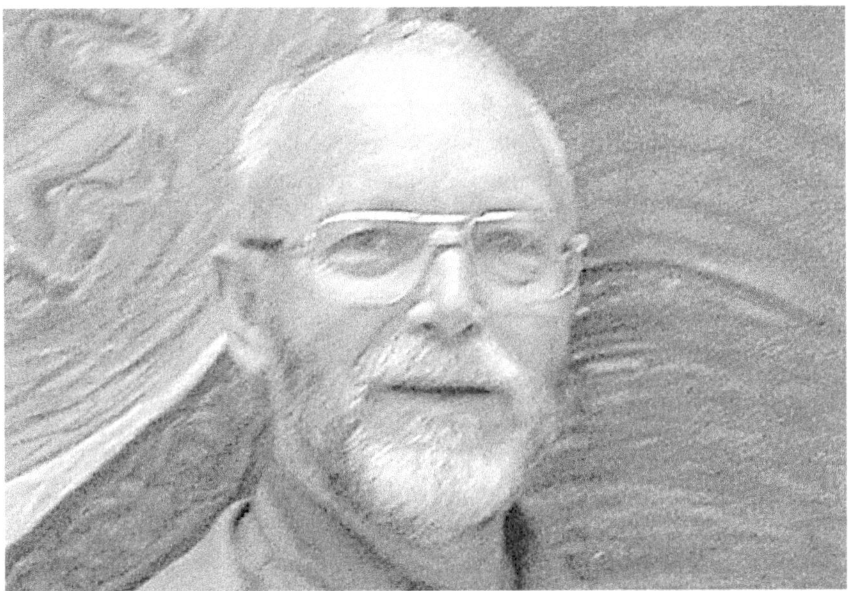

Graham Nash has been Head of Art at the Anglican Church Grammar School in Brisbane, Queensland for six years. Prior to this appointment he was head of Art at a large co-education independent school in Melbourne. He has established a large art gallery at his present school and the school has a fine collection of artworks displayed around the school. Graham is interested in gender aspects of boys' education in art and takes a keen interest in contemporary art practices related to cultural issues. In the belief that 'boys love toys' he is currently working to establish a computer lab in the art wing for digital imagery work. (ed.)

What I want my students to achieve is comfort in being able to express themselves. I teach boys from 13 to 17 years. Adolescent boys are subject to a phenomenal amount of pressure through that period. It seems to me that they have a lot to express, but often have very few vehicles to do so. I hardly ever set topics for major tasks but I set lots of topics for drawing, composition and structures that they do at home. All of the students draw. They all have visual diaries and no matter what studio they are in they always have to be drawing. It is the homework activity twice a week. When a student approaches the painting studio and I think it is time for him to undertake some type of resolved form, we go and have a look at his drawing. We go into the visual diary and start to talk about what he thinks he would like to represent, what he is interested in expressing. It can be the shed on Uncle Tom's farm. It can be that wave that he caught on the weekend. It can be the girlfriend with the big breasts. It can be a whole range of things.

The idea of students being comfortable to express themselves is important. There has been a lot written about boys at this particular time in their education. I am loathe to say that feminism has achieved its task but I think in a lot of ways girls, are finding it easier in schooling than boys, particularly in the sort of schools I am in. Private girls' schools can accelerate learning but boys are still under the misapprehension that just because they're boys and they are going to a good school, they are going to become brain surgeons. They are just so far off the mark. I think somewhere in these years they start to see the problem. They are under a lot of pressures. Adolescent maturity is an interesting thing. A lot of parents say to me: 'But the subject matter of their painting is so adolescent'. We have Dungeons and Dragons and violence, but the student is an adolescent. If he is still doing this at age 25 seek help, unless you have a very large bank balance that he has made from the work. But I don't see a problem with a 15 year-old doing that. I invariably say to all the students as they are seeking ideas, that essentially, I think they are intelligent. They feel deeply about things and there must be things that concern them that they are interested in. We do not necessarily have to problem solve here. We are not trying to solve their emotional problems but there are things that they feel deeply about. Making images and talking about them can be one way of externalising that. Boys don't do this. Men don't do this. We know that this is a major problem in men's relationships and maybe, by drawing, painting and expressing it; by putting it out into a public domain, is a way that males can be more communicative of their emotions. I think that this is essential for my students, and its one of the things that makes me hostile with curriculum planners who would like to make the arts an optional frill.

I am pushing the eight key learning areas in our new middle school structure with the Arts being an essential part. It is that notion which is important. I think there is great room for improvement in the ways boys are able to express themselves. My generation never did. My father loved me greatly but found it difficult to express it; couldn't express it. I never felt unloved but the communication of that was restricted. Now I have an advantage that I can see that and I consciously am all over my son and daughter—to the extent where it is almost forced. Maybe my son's generation will be able to do it a lot more easily, more naturally. I think that is a legitimate ambition.

There are two dimensions to the comfort notion. One is that they are able to express themselves and then that they don't feel constrained and embarrassed by displaying that. Essentially what I ask the students to do is work publicly. I encourage them not to hide in the corner and do it. I am aware that if there is a particular case where this might be difficult, then I make an exception. But essentially I ask them to perform in public and we constantly display their work. We will mount it, frame it and hang it on the wall in the gallery next to professional artists' work. It is not 'Blu-tacked' to the wall. My essential argument is that the act of creation is not entirely complete until you have exposed yourself. Once it is up on the wall however, it has to be a valued item. It can't be the B grade item. I would challenge people to walk through our gallery and pick the students' work. Sometimes the level of skill and adolescent subject matter gives it away, but it is not often.

I just see our gallery as being the centre of what we do. It grew out of an experience I had on the Gold Coast when I taught there. I started the school art collection and the only place I had to display it was in the office foyer. The headmaster thought it was wonderful and he gave me a few hundred dollars a year and we framed a few bits of work. Then I started an artists in residence program without money. I would release one of my staff from one of his or her classes, bus duties, playground duties and I would cover that for them, so they became our resident artist for a period of a month. They in turn donated a piece of work to the school collection. So that became a very interesting exercise and everyone thought it was wonderful except me, because the students never really saw it. They saw a bit of the artists in residence but we weren't able to extend it completely to make it accessible. The gallery was in the office foyer but the only students who went to the office foyer were those that were going to be 'whipped'. It is a nice idea. It sounds great but the students don't benefit from it. The artwork not the whipping! It was window dressing for the school's administration. Now there is value in pushing it in the public domain and getting the headmaster across the line but it wasn't a teaching aide.

Essentially, what I have been able to do both at Wesley in Melbourne, and at Churchie in Brisbane is create gallery spaces. At Melbourne we had a small space outside the art office and we constantly maintained that as a gallery and I thought that was brilliant because students walked through it all the time. When I came to Churchie, I just had a big space. I don't know what the dimensions are. It is probably 2 cricket pitches long. That's about 40 metres. It has plenty of wall space. I have currently got 40 professional works from recently emerged and emerging young Brisbane and South East Queensland artists curated by Doug Hall, the director of the Queensland Art Gallery. They come from a private collector. Now to get that many works up I have taken most of the student works down. However within that collection there are a number of 3 dimensional pieces but I had space for more. So the students' ceramic works and about 15 other student works, sit side-by-side with those professional works. Essentially you can't tell the difference.

I take the attitude that the students see a changing variety of works. They see their work valued. Of course, we display 'Curated by Doug Hall, director of the Queensland Art Gallery' in bold type and announce that it is a private collection etc. This is good PR. but it is done for several reasons. It says to the students, 'This is not Mickey Mouse stuff' and 'We're there too'. It has an effect on the school's teaching community. They want to come and have a look. We have two or three parents a day who come in and wander through, just to check out that 'thing' that I have written about in the school paper. They drop their children off and have a look. I see teaching the broader school community as being an essential part of teaching their sons.

This is South East Queensland. This is the white shoe country; the white shoe brigade live here—a conservative community. This is a stereotype that isn't always the case. When I taught on the Gold Coast, right in the middle of the white shoe brigade country, we had a phenomenal amount of support from parents who lived in that area. They didn't understand art but they knew it was something that they hadn't had exposure to and could now afford to expose their children to. That in essence, was what they were saying. Now I don't see quite that support here but there is some very deep support. It shows in the way parents come along to exhibitions. We also have a couple of benefactions from parents who say 'These works have been in the office and we have remodelled and they no longer fit'. I got a Charles Conder out of that. They are prepared to give it to us because we value it and because we will look after it physically, and we will use it. It is not going to be locked in a vault.

I see the gallery as being the centre of what we do, as the centre of looking. I see the building as being our art room, rather than the classroom. The students are moving between spaces all the time. We timetable all of a year level at the same time. The dark room, the painting studio, the printing studio and the ceramic studio are all functioning at the same time. The students don't have free movement but if I find that Johnny wants to do something or he needs to do something he can be shot off to another studio. I don't have a problem with him wandering through the building if he can get that contact to make that particular work. We would generally have a couple of staff on each floor of the building and I would consider that to be professionally under control and it doesn't confine the students by a timetabling grid. And the students take advantage of the freedom and don't abuse it.

I would consider that my staff is old [sorry guys.]. There are three full time staff and a couple of part timers. I would describe us as 'boring old farts'. I am the oldest but the others are set in the same sort of ways as I am. We teach a term unit in postmodernism to all of our year 10s. In the year 11 component we deal extensively with some of the Robert Hughes 'Shock of the New' topics at the end of that series. We stretch that into contemporary practice. Our students have just done a joint production with a couple of other schools and the Institute of Modern Art here with our year 11s. They did an installation called 'ReDo It'. It was an instructional piece that came out of Paris. A curator in Paris has set 14 different proformas that you can give to artists. Fourteen different artists will make their artworks from these proformas and you will exhibit them in a group show. The organisers gave these to seven schools and we did one. Now because we were aware that we had more staid practice than that, we went looking for this collaborative process. The students loved it. It was an outstanding success. We had the Minister for the Arts open the show. The parents didn't understand any of it but thought that it was absolutely amazing that their children were doing this.

They had a brief that said they had to make a piece of work from a photographic source. That photograph had to be a portrait of some sort. In front of whatever was made, it had to have a vase of flowers that was left there during the course of the exhibition. They ended up making a face based on some contemporary supermodel's face. Each of the fourteen students in this group made a 60cm x 80cm panel. They constructed a face out of that and it included a whole range of things. One student had a lick of hair that was a wave cast in plaster and painted. The other side of the hair was done in spaghetti. To continue the supermodel theme they had in their year group two ceramic legs which they placed as the vase and they placed paper flowers in the vase. In the course of preparing for the exhibition they needed to dry the spaghetti. So the night before it was due to be hung they decided with their teacher that they would dry it over a low fired kiln. She forgot about it and when they came back at 3 o'clock in the morning they had ashes. In one hour they constructed 'Spaghetti Head' again and they took the ashes and put them in a wonderful black ceramic bowl and they presented the ashes in between the two legs. It was vaguely erotic. It was a beautiful piece. A number of schools had formerly written pieces about their works. We didn't feel that it was appropriate that the staff write about this. So when we installed it we took all the boys to the gallery and they negotiated the writing. Now because the incineration was the latest thing that had taken place it was high in their minds. But they wrote about the whole thing in terms of the journey of its production and I was amazed at their level of understanding. That is what we had been hoping they would come to, but they came to it at a very, very high level. They were very articulate about the process of their making, although they didn't attach any value to the end product at all. They weren't upset by the incineration. In fact they saw that as a chance to go further. They liked the fact that they had gone somewhere that they hadn't expected to go.

We saw that idea as an opportunity of extending contemporary practice. We teach theoretical units and we teach an art history course embedded in the art course. All of our students are taught an art history/art appreciation course of some form or other. In the next term we will do a unit on the Asia and Pacific Triennial exhibition currently on show in Brisbane. I will be preparing this next week. The APT will form fourth term's teaching unit for all of our year 9, 10 and 11 students. I have booked a computer lab for the term which I think will give each of our students 5 or 6 periods in which to work on the APT collection. They will do a slide show Powerpoint presentation on the structure of it. They will then have access to a computer and the APT website. They will work on the website probably for 4 or 5 periods. They will then go back into the lecture theatre and I will lecture again on what they have found from the website. That will be a matter of me negotiating with them on a regular basis about how they have discovered things and what they have done. We will then run through the website again in the computer lab and then we will do an extensive tour of the gallery. Every year we teach that fourth term around that exhibition of Asian and Pacific arts. I think that is crucial. It has to be. It is the future of our students.

We teach European art history and North American art history because we are familiar with it. We are derelict if that is all we teach but these art forms are an essential part of our culture. But the future is going to require some understanding of the cultures of Asia. It is not enough to simply learn the language. I think you have to understand the cultural ethos and we are talking to the language departments about some cross-cultural studies. We are going to do a French immersion program next year. A French-speaking artist will teach our French art students their art course. She can also teach their Phys. ed. course because she is a marathon runner. Once we have that in place we are going to have a look at a couple of other language studies and it may be that we can do a term of Indonesian art with an Indonesian speaking art teacher, if I can find the right sort of people. We are going to trial the French program for a month at the end of November.

I don't think our students really understand what modernism is about, and yet that is what we are trying to do. In a potted history we take year 9 students through some of the formal elements of composition. We do some work on appreciation and a lot of looking and talking and writing. We do the fastest history of western art you have ever known; essentially so that the students gain some understanding of chronology. This tends to be teaching chronology rather than major movements. I get these students for three periods per week. So if I start taking too long it becomes a history course rather than an art course. So we would probably in a course of 10 weeks get five out of 30 periods in the theory class and they will do a research project as a result of those five periods. They will do some essay writing; we do some research essays; we do gallery critiques; we ask them to research a topic and present it visually. One of the postmodern assignments involved giving students a photocopy of David's 'Oath of the Horati'. They were asked to construct a work from that and write what they thought they were trying to do and how this fitted with what they understood to be postmodernism. We got some high levels of understanding and some poor work that displayed no understanding. We are looking for notions of appropriation, understanding of issues, aspects of media reference.

In year 10 we do a potted four-lesson version of Australian art; wonderful but brief. We deal across some of the early 20th century movements of modernism. I talk about modernism as being a search for the new, a constant quest for the new. My briefest explanation for postmodernism immediately after that is a reference from an architect I met from London in the sixties, who said that history is no longer a dirty word. You can go back and look and reference. I try to make that as the separation between the two. Modernism is constantly seeking something new. Postmodernism, amongst all its other components, is prepared to say 'Let's go back and dip and take something from behind and drag it forward'. Then we would look at some issues such as feminism, racism, war. Boys often want to deal with issues of war and I am surprised how many pacifists there are among 15 year-old males (who will immediately leave the room after having handed their Pacifism assignment in and kick the shit out of the kid next to them). But there are tensions and they write about pacifism and the destructive qualities of war quite intensely and then not model it in their physical behaviour. That is an interesting one.

I am not asking them to be aware of social justice issues because I don't really see myself as a social engineer in this context. But what we do teach when we teach about postmodernism is that social issues are just one of the parameters of it. Now they may pick up on that and 'The Oath of Horati' task was excellent for that. There was a whole range of opportunities to take that image of war and loss. We had the grieving girls over on the one side and they picked up on the female side of war. They took mateship. They took one of the sub plots and extended that. One student presented his deconstruction of that on the top of a shoebox. I can't even remember the punch line but they were basically doing battle over the Nike that were in the box.

In the middle of next year we are bringing year sevens into the school and we are establishing a middle school structure. It will include some integrated curriculum units. Specialist subject areas will probably sit outside those integrated areas. I have a few problems with that because I reckon I can teach English better through my art course than they can teach art through their English course. But I can also see an advantage in it and I am saying to the school community that I think I can provide an art course for my year 7 students that is unique, invigorating and exciting. What I want is a lab of 20 'iMacs' and I think I can teach them all this boring stuff about line, shape and colour so quickly. I think I can teach all that through the machine. Essentially my thesis is 'boys love toys'. They love technology. They will come to me in year 7 and I hope to be able to say to them 'Here is your art course' and have them explode. If I give them a piece of lino and say to them 'Now we are going to cut a dog and print it", they are going to say to me, as we have all heard before, 'Oh we did this last year'. I am looking for the step that can break that cycle. When they move from the prep school to the middle school, we need to give them an exciting introduction to the arts. I can teach them all this stuff that I think they need to have as language, both visual and verbal, without them realising they have been taught it. And then I can introduce them to the other studio spaces where I can deliver their theory, history/appreciation units through their machines as well. That is where I would like to do that history of art. That is where I would like to take my postmodernism. That's where we want to use technology. I have got a submission for that in the pipeline at the moment. I do battle with the technologists soon.

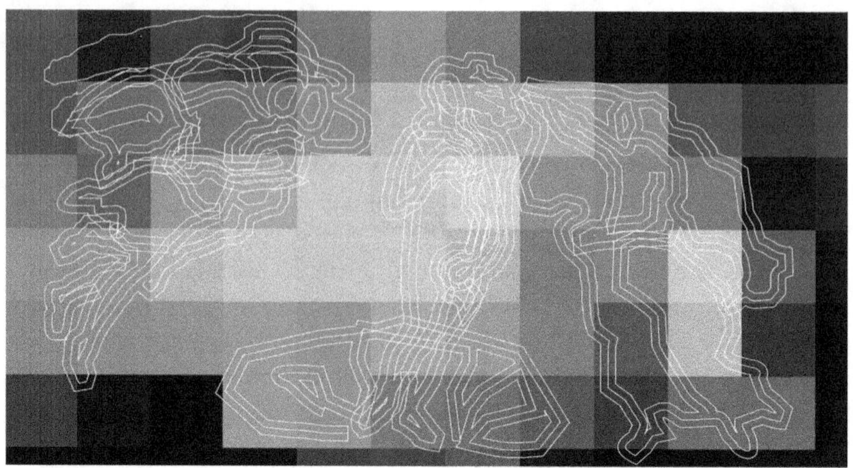

Figure 5:
Simon Manley, Year 11, Camberwell Grammar School, Melbourne

Chapter 12

Colin Simpson

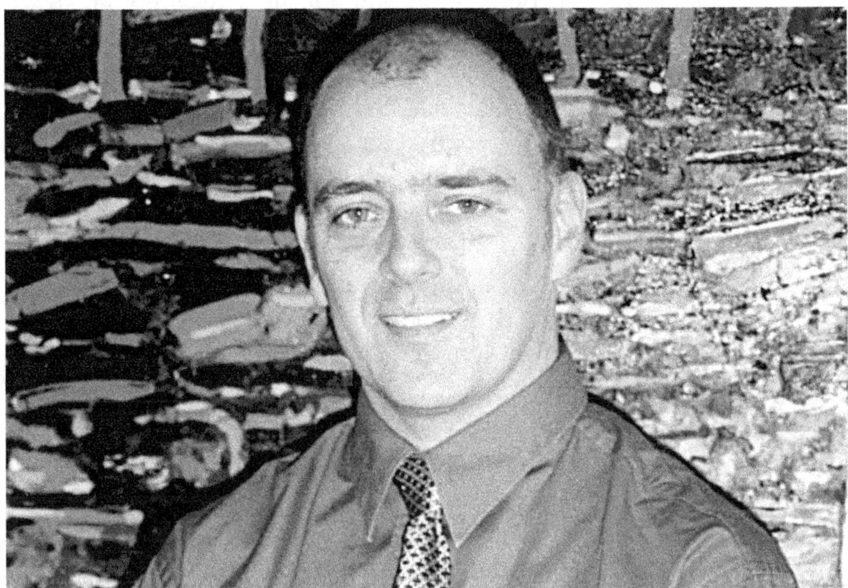

Colin Simpson, at the time of this interview, was teaching at Heatherhill Secondary College, a State co-educational school in an outer southern suburb of Melbourne. The school has a multi-cultural population with most students being born in South East Asian countries. The school buildings are nearly 40 years old and in some need of upgrade. Colin had, at this time, taken on an administrative position in the school and was only teaching a few art classes each week. His own textbook for secondary students is called 'Art Now' and this was used as the basis for his art classes. 'Art Now' focuses on Australian artworks and deals with contemporary issues that relate to postmodern thought. He is now teaching art full time in another school. (ed.)

My school is in the Southern metropolitan region of Melbourne. This school has been here since the mid-sixties and it was one of the experimental courtyard schools. The Department of Education built about six of these designs. There are two left. It was a design that didn't work; the open courtyards are a bit too open and cold for Melbourne's winter. So the school started with a working class Anglo Saxon population. Most of those people would have moved out here from the inner suburbs when the area opened up as a housing estate. There was a middle European wave of the seventies and early eighties.

That settled in for a while followed by more eastern European and after 1975 there have been increasing numbers of Asian students from different countries in the region. So we have students born in Vietnam, Thailand, Cambodia or Hong Kong. They will have an ethnicity that is as confusing as is South East Asian politics. The school is in a low socioeconomic bracket. Our indexes are high so we get grants based on being a disadvantaged school. The students are from less well-educated families—poor English speaking.

I transferred here knowing that this was a multi-cultural school. That was the clear decision. I applied for two schools and this was my first choice and I imagine I was the only applicant. They were really pleased to get me. I think they thought it was Christmas because I had so much experience by that time. The quality of teaching staff at this school has been down for about twenty years. It has been a school that has had a lot of excess staff. It has been a school that has not been in a desirable location. We advertise senior positions and no one applies. Whereas some schools could advertise for an assistant principal and get two hundred applicants, we could advertise and get a handful of applicants at the best. We could advertise a leading teacher position and possibly no one would apply.

I think one of the key changes in my life as an art teacher has been the introduction of learning outcomes and having to define indicators of these. I don't think my actual classroom practice has changed greatly over the years but the curriculum has changed and it is much better. The type of physical activities I do with students and the way I approach these has not changed too much. I think I was lucky to do the B.Ed. (Art and Craft) course. There was a strong curriculum component to that course, which I think, set up my strong interest in the curriculum. We now have a highly designed curriculum and we have quite strict ideas about what we want to get from that. When I first started teaching art teachers would often make up the topic as they walked towards the class without anything written down. The first time I ever saw a written curriculum was not until 1987, so I had been in schools for 6 years before there was a written art course. I still have a copy of that first course and when I look at it now it seems so basic even though I, along with the other art staff at the school, wrote it. However, at the time, it felt very revolutionary and I remember at the time being very excited that we had this guideline of what we were going to teach in classes.

A concern that I do have about our current art programs relates to sequential learning. In art we still get large numbers at year 12 even though the Asian background students tend not to select art because of their vocational needs and pressures. We have however been quite successful because we have developed a sequential but flexible curriculum that can be adjusted to meet the needs of individual students. At this college the arts teachers have always been responsive to change and are flexible and creative enough to put these into place. We spend a lot of time looking at our curriculum and are always looking for ways to improve it, even if it means that some of our individual views and the rigour found in some schools, is not present. We balance this by making sure that the VCE course is very demanding and we raise the bar of expectation dramatically. Our students handle this because they seem to say, 'Yep now its time to get down to business!' As I have said, sequential learning is not possible and we cannot presume prior learning in art appreciation. Rotation of art at junior levels gives good basic skills, but nothing revolutionary that is not part of any normal adolescent skill. We have developed a program that most students seem to like and we are very careful not to frighten them off in year 9 by making too many demands on them; we let them enjoy art. They then come back in at year 10 and that gives us some basis for our healthy VCE classes. Year 11 numbers have increased and it is clear that even though curriculum agendas have changed art still fulfils a vital part of the experience teenagers want.

The role of computers is one of the biggest changes in the last ten years, if not the biggest. They are a useful tool and provide great opportunities for art teachers and students to develop practical work, write and connect with other technologies. Certainly being technologically advanced never hurts an art teacher, and because we are visual thinkers the skills often come quickly to us. This has been my experience, all the art teachers at this school are high level computer users. We have an art computer and scanner with a colour printer attached. Our year 12 students do computer-generated artwork and they hand it in on CD or email it to us. We encourage this sort of approach. In terms of hard to find resources, I scan in contemporary art images and pass them on to students on disk or e-mail them to them. This means they have ready access to images. The Internet is most useful here too. When I wrote 'Art Now' there was little information around on the Internet about artists like Bill Henson or Jenny Watson. The other day a student and I were researching together and we found a huge amount of material, including fantastic images she can use in writing and practical work development.

As I have said, there is great comfort here with technology and we encourage students to use it. Our art teachers are retraining all the time to build up their skills. I myself have been a learning technology leader and that has increased resources for us. We are setting up a CAD computer lab now which is attached to the old craft, now technology, rooms. This will be available to all arts classes. There will be computers in the art room itself within two years. My students have been making computer-generated work for a number of years, and have created beautiful works. I feel comfortable assessing this work and in my experience, art teachers are very good at getting the right balance in assessment between system and student needs.

I treat students as individuals in my art classes. I speak to them rarely as a group. I generally start by giving them a quick overview of the topic and what I want them to achieve. Sometimes I don't even give them the whole picture. I might say 'For the next half hour I want you to do this' and I show them very quickly. I get them all around me and make sure they are really close to me. Then they work at large tables in groups which they choose, and I leave them alone to make key decisions. They can then ask for help as they need it. We give them a lot of one-to-one teaching. I also take a real hands-off approach, which some students can find frustrating, but I then watch them grow as they make decisions. I rarely if ever touch their work and expect that the artistic struggle needs to be theirs. In my role as a Board of Studies examiner I have been in schools where every students' work is the same, however I would feel a failure if I saw that in my class. The work must be as different as the kids themselves. Anyone who knows anything about art and artists must know this.

I do not believe that a chronological approach, as set out in Gombrich's 'The Story of Art', is useful today in art classes. This approach cannot work any more. Teachers need to be able to quickly slot students into concepts and data along the broad timeline with little former knowledge. One of the biggest challenges to art teachers now is how to achieve high-level outcomes in this structure. When I am teaching art appreciation I give a lecture to the students and discuss relevant issues and background. I use slides, notes, other books and my own, and use language to lay the conceptual framework. This might involve some broadening of general knowledge or cultural information, which is necessary because of the sequencing problem. I engage them in discussion and do a lot of visual analysis. If drawing is the basis of practical art, then visual analysis is the basis of art appreciation. The style I use is similar to the one I learnt and used at the National Gallery of Victoria (NGV). It involves questioning, pointing out, discussion, offering opinions, story telling and cultural and historical positioning. I think this works well and it is a shame all art teachers do not feel comfortable with it. I use the collection of resources we have in terms of books, slides, the internet and posters. We have an excellent poster collection and it is highly flexible and effective. Visits to the NGV are difficult because of our position in Melbourne and finances, and like many schools we cannot use them as a regular resource.

We have a very diverse and largely Asian population in the school so we must consider their needs. We are encouraging our diverse population to take art as a subject and in art we need to have multiple expectations and goals in each classroom if we are going to meet the needs of all the students. The immigrant students often have special and complex needs and these are dealt with as a matter of College policy and as a mixed ability grouping issue. We are part of the Asia Education Foundation Asia Network of schools, which means we have Asian studies within each learning area and have it as a focus. It is not a major priority any more as we have gone to a school focus which promotes literacy and health. We encourage the Asian students to use their own heritage in their artworks and we certainly talk about culture broadly and as a western and eastern thing. That is we don't just talk about western culture.

We also still teach craft at this school and I do believe that craft courses are still legitimate though we lost so much to technology in the early 1990s. We still teach a craft elective at year nine. It is quite a traditional course that is very well selected. We can sometimes have three classes over the year. It is well cemented in our school program and students do textile, leather, basketwork and sewing, all with a strong culturally diverse focus. It is a real success and I feel that in the next ten years we may feel, from a visual arts point of view, that we let craft go too easily. I also use my own textbooks in VCE teaching and I would be one of the few authors of such texts who are teaching in schools. I enjoy that and the kids are very pleased that I am the author, even if sometimes they don't believe it's me. I read my writing to my own students, which is so exciting and they see me as a writer and an artist. Unfortunately few teachers write or make art after they leave university. I certainly don't do nearly enough of my own artwork, and it is ten years since my last exhibition

In my view postmodernism has greatly affected art and education and it has particularly impacted on year 12 practice. It is vital that teachers deal with and understanding recent contemporary art. Art teachers seem poorly equipped to handle these issues because they mostly draw on their last experience at art school, university or teachers college; this experience remaining their last in depth contact with art. The workload in schools, busy lives and proximity to artistic centres are all hurdles in them remaining connected. Recent arts writing as well can be quite alienating and this is why I have felt it important to interpret contemporary art for teachers.

Contemporary art is not covered in the junior years and we talk about little contemporary art at year 9, but at year 12 it is our main focus. This is because of my special interest. Other art staff are getting better at handling it, though they would not be completely on top of it. We talk about modern and postmodern art in terms of the history of art and explain the fundamentals behind art movements and cultural trends, We talk also of the Avant garde and issues of the human condition and 'Why do individuals feel the desire to create?—that type of thing. We talk about a variety of topics, themes and issues and complete a range of drawing, painting, ceramic and print making topics. We are also re-introducing photography this year.

I do have particular artists that I find useful in teaching about contemporary art and the artists I selected for use in my book are representative of the artists I think are good and accessible to use with a variety of students. I use Jenny Watson, Roslyn Piggott, Jon Campbell, Gordon Bennett and Howard Arkley as starting points, although links are made to other artists. I use a strong personal narrative approach and am not too directive in terms of category or framework. Gordon Bennet provides a wealth of material for students: issues, culture, gender, etc. I ask the question 'why?' a lot, and this enables students' personal views to form and is most challenging. I find the concept of interpretive frameworks in the VCE too narrow. It forces teachers to over-define because they are so scared of doing the wrong thing. I myself don't tie it down too much and encourage teachers to be broad. For example why talk about restrictive frameworks when 'self' works as well. This concept is much closer to the experience of children. Teachers can still talk about politics, feminism or the landscape but they can tailor their discussion to meet the needs of the class. I don't take the soft approach with the VCE students. I don't care if they live in Springvale, South Yarra or Prague; there are human concepts that educators should and can discuss with them.

I realise that I may need to carefully consider some contemporary art which may offend some students but I do not avoid controversy in the art room. I would certainly discuss the British 'Sensation' exhibition, although I am always clear on what I want to achieve from the discussion and I need to be sure the artists are serious about what they are doing. The 'Piss Christ' controversy in Melbourne, for example, raised interesting questions but the selection of that name was done to create effect. I am always clear about this with students and the nature of controversy is worth talking about as well as artistic merits. This school is a conservative school so I use some self-censorship in terms of content when I am talking to a class. In terms of directing students to artists, I have few restrictions, just my personal judgment that they would benefit from it and can handle it. I use Bill Henson and his works have some soft-porn elements. I find kids more shocked by technique than images usually.

I will finish my account with a more formal definition of postmodernism as I have discussed it in my book and as I discuss it with my senior students. In my view any discussion of art produced over the last twenty years needs to be held with an understanding of the relationship between modernism and postmodernism. This must involve discussion of the decline of the idea of an Avant garde and the way the debate between modernism and postmodernism has left its mark on works of art and artists. I think it is very hard for students to read and understand contemporary arts criticism. It simply does not operate on enough levels. There is the 'hard edge intellectual' stuff that involves its nuances and exists for itself and this alienates teachers and students. Then there is the school-based material such as I have developed. However, there is a need for art writing that sits between these two levels. Teachers and students need clear writing that they can tap into. Much of the sophisticated writing is too esoteric and teachers just find it all instantly hard, incomprehensible or lacking in detail.

I explain modernism in this way. Modernism in art history terms, refers to the period dating from the 1860s to the 1970s. It has been the dominant cultural form over this century, shaping works of art, ideas, taste and education. It was a period in which each 'new' generation rejected the past, creating the notion of the 'avant-gardé', or advanced guard, meaning those who were ahead of their time. They were independent thinkers who challenged middle–class ideas and values. The content in works of art was often a celebration of technology, spirituality or a reaction to materialism or politics. Artists were also interested in the exploration of the art medium itself and how a range of aesthetic effects could be created. The key feature however was that each idea built upon, or reacted to, the previous generation's innovations.

I see postmodernism however as rising after modernism. postmodern thinking is based on a loss of faith in this continued technological and artistic progression. Modernism's optimism had given way to a broader, darker, emotional range and something more cynical, with an interest in recycling and revisiting of forms and ideas from the past. The term postmodern first developed in relation to architecture, and described the large number of contemporary buildings developed over the 1980s that no longer adhered to the ideas begun with the international style (1920–1976) earlier this century. Postmodern architects were more interested in forms both historical or technical, than a primary interest in space and mass. Their designs tended to be imaginative and symbolic, relying on historical details and over emphasised structural elements. The distinctive style of structures such as 'Lloyd's Building' in London reflects postmodern ideas.

So in conclusion, I will close by suggesting that postmodern issues of gender, race, culture and popular culture are very much a part of our art program here. However, we have not thrown out 'creativity' and it is still very much the centre of our art program; so we cling to elements of modernism while we deal with issues of postmodernism. They exist side-by-side here.

Chapter 13

Catherine Middleton

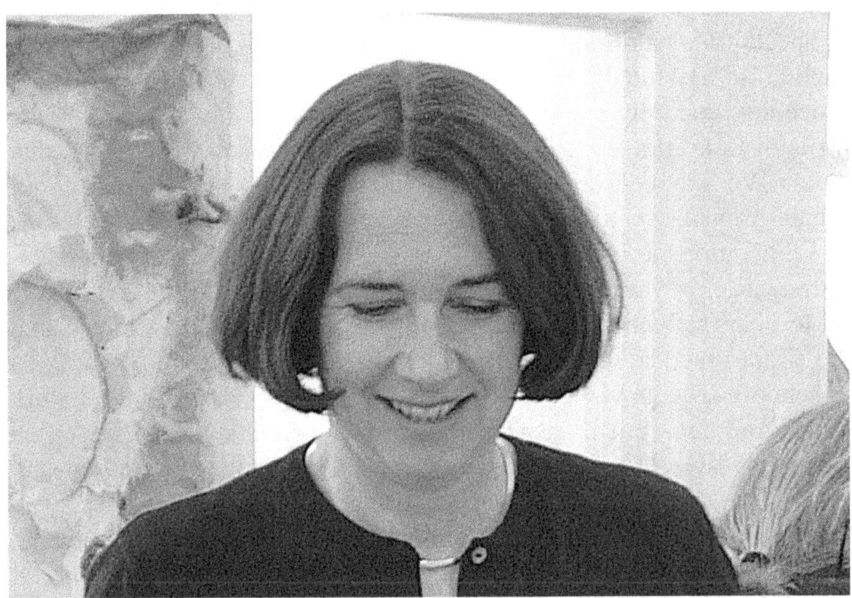

Catherine Middleton teaches art at Maiden Erlegh School near Reading, England. The school has 1530 students from years 7 to 13. The school is obliged to follow the National Curriculum in England and thus 'art and design' is offered as a compulsory foundation at years 7 to 9 then as elective in GCSE, years 10 and 11. In the sixth form (years 12 and 13) students can elect to do art and design at A/S and A' level. There are four full-time and one part- time art staff members at the school and a wide range of 2 and 3 dimensional studies is taught in well equipped studios. (ed.)

I have been teaching since 1976. I did a B.Ed. course at Reading and taught for eight years in a comprehensive school before having children. I then completed a three year M.A. at Reading University. Following that I taught in adult education and then began a job-share with Sue Hall. We worked in several schools and started here part-time in 1988. We have both been here on a full-time basis since 1990 and enjoy the stimulation of working within a large, lively department and a good team of staff.

Within the department I have responsibility for mentoring four Postgraduate Certificate of Education (PGCE) art and design students each year. I also worked as an external examiner for the University of

Brighton PGCE course for a period of four years which expanded my personal professional development. I have pastoral responsibility for a sixth form tutor group. My teaching involves me with all age ranges which can be demanding in the amount of planning and assessing for every year group. All the art staff teach all aspects of the subject from painting and printmaking to textiles and 3D work. Although my area of specialty is painting I try to attempt all areas as it is important that each child has the opportunity to experience a wide range of media, processes and techniques. This can be exhausting and it can be difficult to keep a track of stock and resources when we are all using them. We are constantly striving to find ways of improving our organisational structure to make our teaching even more effective.

Education has changed rapidly in the last ten years. The introduction of the GCSE examination has broadened the outlook of art teachers reflecting the greater diversity of our cultural interests and the wider practical experiences which are now on offer to most pupils in schools. The new A level syllabus has really been exciting to work on and our department has achieved fantastic results with this over the last ten years. The personal study invites students to research and investigate an area of their own choosing which really helps them to mature in their thinking and engages them in reflective personal analysis of an artist's work which they have seen at first hand. It seems to prepare them well for study in higher education. The structure of the new A level syllabus which was introduced in 1991 did give our teaching a fresh impetus just as the new GSCE course did. It lead us to work in a tutorial way with the sixth form treating their learning as something for which they should take more responsibility as individuals. I think that has had a knock-on effect right the way down the school. Critical and contextual studies are introduced with every practical project and aligned with the pupils' own work. We also try to let individuals develop at their own rate and to set them personal targets and goals. The new programmes of study, which have just been introduced as part of the National Curriculum, allow this process to take place. Although there have been many changes introduced within the curriculum and external examinations these have not been viewed in a negative way by our department but more as a challenge which has enabled us to stimulate our pupils as broadly as we can. I think the increased role of critical and contextual studies linked with practical work has been really beneficial. In the past teaching Art History was often taught as a completely separate subject which had little relevance to the pupils' own artwork. The emphasis has changed and criteria for assessment have changed. We do also work in a much more intense and pressurised climate than we used to.

We are now much more careful to record, document and structure schemes of work, although we find that we update and change these from year to year as we don't like to be bored in our own teaching. We also keep very detailed records of pupil performance and have to target individuals to improve their performance. We have had two OFSTED inspections which certainly keep you on your toes. There is more administration and form filling. We also have different means of assessment which are more time consuming and slightly more rigorous, particularly for GCSE. Marking our own examination work at A level and GCSE is also demanding, when we are not given a lot of time to do it. We don't record our results on computer as we only have one in the department. The use of ICT within our art department needs to expand and we are awaiting funding for more computer technology. We need a computer suite that we can use with whole classes of pupils. We are all quite computer literate but we need better facilities.

I think issues-based art comes in throughout the curriculum. In year 7 we work on a project on identity or self-image as they call it in the KS3 programme of study. We look at the different ways in which people have recorded their identity and image and how this reflects their personality and their physical make-up. Looking at contemporary art on this issue can be quite challenging. The pupils are encouraged to make self representations through drawing self portraits and through discovering expressive use of paint and colour. They may also have the opportunity to work three dimensionally on an identity box or on a ceramic portrait. This project can also be taught to older pupils in year 11 or in the sixth form and can lead them to think about other ways of using the body to show identity. Pupils are shown work by such contemporary artists as Marc Quinn and Jenny Saville and are encouraged to develop personal responses which might include body casting or photography.

Within years 12 and 13 we address a wide range of issues stemming from contemporary art. These can be challenging and will provoke class discussions. At other times issues arise with individual students where and when appropriate. We have many books in the art room which students can access freely. We are careful with the younger ones using the book collection because work can be misunderstood and misinterpreted. For example if they came across work by Jake and Dinos Chapman in the Sensation book then they might find this disturbing. I think if students are looking at images without some sort of explanation then their response will be different from the one from which one might hope to elicit with careful explanation about the intentions of the artist. We don't actually provide any formal sort of safety net for students. The books are all here and generally the students have open access. We are slightly selective in what we choose to show the younger students within the classroom but we are not afraid to shock them into a response. I haven't deliberately shown any of the students the work of the Chapman brothers. Personally I found their work the most shocking and distasteful in the Sensation exhibition and found it hard to come to terms with. Some other controversial works, such as the Myra Hindley work, were damaged in the Sensation exhibition. Students have some quite strong reactions to works at times especially if they have read things in the tabloid press or their parents have said that the works are shocking and shouldn't be allowed etc. So then you do try to have some kind of discussion and open it up for debate.

I have one female student in year 11 who is researching some very disturbing work on body mutilation and artists who suffer pain from hanging themselves from their skin. She has been getting information from the Internet and is fascinated yet shocked by it. It is quite horrific to look at her research studies but she is very thoughtful about it and it stemmed from her investigations into Salvador Dali's work. She has made interesting and intelligent connections between the two. She is now making her own body cast out of latex and stitching it together. It is her intention to suspend it from the ceiling with fish-hooks. We talk about the fact that sometimes art is there to shock. Maybe that is part of its duty to shock. We discuss the need to have some people pushing boundaries. Much of our work beyond year 10 is through individual tutorials and issues arise from the pupils' own interests. We are able to judge the pupils' levels of maturity and their ability to understand controversial and challenging contemporary works of art.

I don't introduce the term postmodernism to students generally within a class situation although again it might be referred to with an individual student for whom it might have some significance. Unless they are able to put it into a context of what came before and how it fits in then I don't think it would be useful, especially at the younger levels. With the older pupils they may have heard it but generally they would not use the term. I don't think they would understand the term modernism either. Because we are not teaching art in a chronological way they don't always have an understanding of timelines. Sometimes we have put up a timeline to show where things fit in and we do introduce a specialist vocabulary from year 7. However, we don't consciously introduce the term.

We do introduce students to art from a range of cultures. In year 7 we introduce students to world art and we encourage them to draw from artefacts. We have links with the local Reading museum service and we borrow artefacts. They have a fabulous collection which is available to schools on loan. They have such things as papooses from North America, coats from the Sioux tribes, puppets from Java, fabrics from West Africa, carvings from the Inuit tribes of Alaska, African musical instruments and just about everything you can think of. We recently went to look at the new housing of this collection and to identify more objects which might be useful within school. We start the pupils with observation drawings of the artefacts and then bring in some of the cultural aspects. Each case we borrow is accompanied by a specific description of the origins of each piece. This idea is particularly helpful with KS3 classes as it is difficult to arrange to take them all on a visit to a museum as we are such a big school and have such large numbers. However when we want to introduce a cultural topic to year 10 we take them to the British Museum where they can work in a wide variety of different rooms each representing objects and artefacts from different cultures and from different periods of time within those cultures. We have quite a number of Muslim students in our school and I have enjoyed looking at the art of Islam with year 8 pupils particularly. It is interesting for western students to look at the design representations and the lack of human form. The focus is away from the individual artist and rests on the religious and cultural significance of the work. Muslim students have brought images from home that might be fantastically ornate mosques, or designs of rugs used in the mosques. If you look back in Islamic art there is story telling and narrative and it is only recently that the human form is not to be represented. I found all of the students have been very responsive and interested in such differences between eastern and western art forms. Muslim students would be restricted to certain forms of imagery if they were studying art within religious teaching but in school we have never had any parents who have said their children may not draw from the figure. I don't want to be guilty of stereotyping but many of our Muslim girls do have a fantastic facility with pattern work. They have a natural intuitive sense of colour and pattern. We also have Afro-Caribbean, African, Chinese and other European countries represented amongst our pupils.

Issues of gender would surface on an individual basis or might be challenged with whole classes. We use women artists here as a matter of course. We look for example at; Georgia O'Keeffe, Frida Kahlo, Paula Rego, Barbara Hepworth, Susan Hiller, and Cindy Sherman to name just a few. We find that many of our female sixth form students will choose a woman artist to work with for their personal study. One of our students in the upper sixth is currently doing a study of Cindy Sherman. We also suggest that they read feminist viewpoints and feminist critique. We also talk about women's issues and women's work. We do bring that in lower down in the school too, in terms of asking why there aren't any women Renaissance painters represented in books. We ask them why we don't know about them and why weren't they recorded. I would say that much of our work on critical and contextual studies starts at the turn of the last century. As women have been strongly represented since that time then they occur as part of our teaching as frequently as men.

We are eclectic in our choice of artists and will show contemporary work alongside more traditional work from previous centuries. With year 7 I am working on an identity project so I have used a range of self portraits from Renaissance to contemporary. Cubism was just a feature of the still life project which I have just completed with year 8. With year 9 I have been looking at artists who use sculpture in specific locations. We have been looking at our local town and at making art for public spaces. Year 10 at the moment are looking at natural forms and have been investigating the work of Barbara Hepworth, Georgia O'Keeffe and the English sculptor Peter Randall-Page. He sites his work in such places as the Dorset coastal path. Year 11 are using a whole host of different artists in response to the questions they have been given as part of their GCSE mock examination. Year 12 are looking at 'A sense of place' and they have a list of artists to view including Hodgkin, Hockney, Turner etc. but they are able to expand upon this list and find their own sources of inspiration. Year 13 are really directing their own study and from time to time we suggest artists that may be appropriate. I think we are quite eclectic in our approach. I tend to use whatever I have recently seen myself. If I have been to America for the summer then I come back with a whole lot of Navajo stuff and use that. Or if I have seen a fantastic exhibition somewhere then I will turn to developing work from that. I think it is important that you recharge your batteries and work from what is fresh, lively and challenging. So it is whatever I see as interesting. I tend to get bored if I use the same ideas over and over again.

I think art education is changing so much. But if I was to advise young graduates I think that having really sound subject knowledge and being confident with practical skills is very important. I also think keeping abreast of what is going on and seeing as much art as possible is also crucial. You need to be inspired and excited by what you see. It is difficult to know where things will be ten years down the line. Things change so quickly that we don't know where we are heading. I think more computers would help us in this department and would introduce another dimension to our teaching. It would be a useful resource and a tool for developing art. I think that is the next step for us. I think digital imagery is something that we haven't got into yet. I think that this would enable us to prepare pupils for using art packages which they could then develop within the world of work.

I hope students will go away from art education here with a deeper understanding of themselves as individuals. I think what we try to do is to help each individual to grow and develop artistically and personally. I hope that students acquire a broad range of skills and that they feel a sense of excitement at the experience of working with materials. I hope that they gain a love of the visual elements and that they can put them together to gain a sense of satisfaction from working with materials and ideas. I also hope that they acquire a love of looking at art and that they make the effort to visit galleries and museums when they can. It is amazing how successful the Tate Modern has been compared with the Millennium Dome in London. It is interesting to note that many students have chosen to visit the Tate rather than the Dome. It seems that people are still excited by art so we begin to think that maybe we have been motivating students. I hope that our students will gain all of these things. Many of our students choose to pursue courses in Art in Higher Education, initially taking a Foundation year and subsequently a degree. Many of our ex pupils are successfully employed within the art world, some as teachers, some as practising artists, some in film and others in graphic design. We love hearing from them and delight in their visits when they return to share their successes with us.

I think teachers don't deal with the word postmodernism because we don't really understand what is meant by it. I have never had it very clearly defined and I have never really known where the line was drawn between modernism and postmodernism. I think it is clearer in literature but not so much in art. I think we are very liberal in our approach in that we try and get students to switch on to whatever it is that motivates them. So we are very wide-ranging in our practice and this in itself may be postmodern.

Chapter 14

Sue Hall

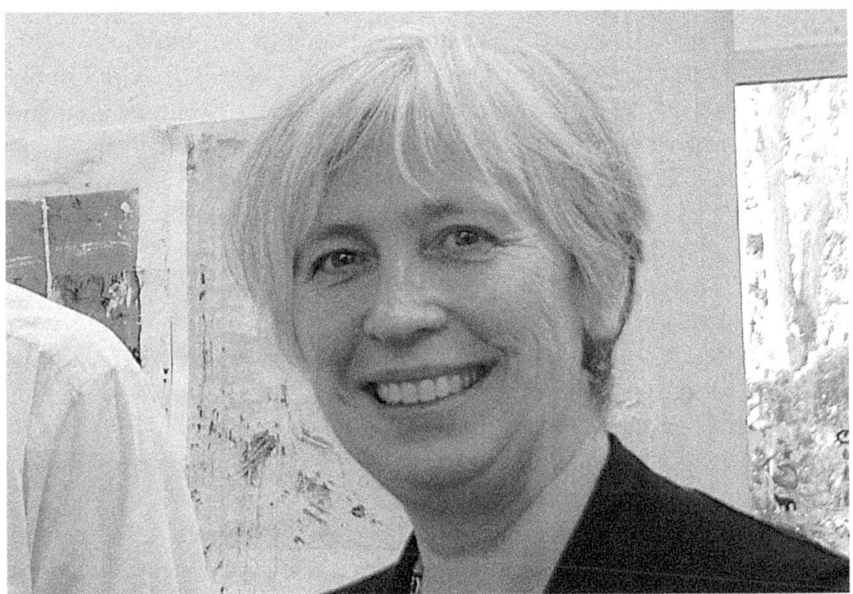

Sue Hall is deputy Head of Art at Maiden Erlegh School near Reading in England. She and Catherine Middleton have taught together for 12 years at the same school after job-sharing for several years. The art rooms are large and quite well equipped and a large collection of books and catalogues is held in the staff room for senior student access. (ed.)

I am an art teacher at Maiden Erlegh School. I am second in the department of four teachers. I moved to Reading about 15 years ago and for 3 years Catherine Middleton and I worked as a job-share. We worked in 3 or 4 schools and we went as a package. We enjoyed that, it was very positive experience and it suited us both as we had young children. We were both appointed here and became very involved with the whole school. We have seen the work at AS/A (years 12 and 13) level develop and the numbers of students opting to take a General Certificate of Secondary Education (GCSE) in Art and Design. We have introduced new and different methods of working partly in response to the National Curriculum and also because of new developments at AS/A level. We have also brought in our interests and enthusiasms into the department and developed our own skills in theory and practice.

There have been a number of key changes in our art programs. A lot of my time is spent with AS/A level students so I will just start with them first. In the AS/A level group (ages 16 to 18) the introduction of the Cambridge University A level Examination Syllabus about 10 years ago allowed students to build on skills acquired during the two-year GSCE Syllabus. There is freedom in the interpretation of the syllabus so the students are really empowered and given a lot of responsibility for the development of their ideas. They are allowed to develop their own strengths through their own interests. The role of the teacher has changed in that after the key foundation course in the first term we have developed a more tutorial-based approach. The teacher is more the facilitator, or the tutor who listens to the student and then introduces methods of working in line with student needs. I think the course gives students more responsibility and allows them to get more involved with their work in greater depth. The ownership of the work is paramount.

Critical studies are an important component of the present A Level and the new AS course introduced this year. There are many changes at AS/A Level and we are currently introducing the new course with our present cohort of year 12 students. Both courses involve a personal study, coursework units and examinations. Over the years students have produced very exciting personal studies. One student interviewed Tom Phillips, another Norman Ackroyd. The A/S, A level builds on everything we do in the school. We are trying to build confidence and a personal voice; an increasingly personal voice as the students get older and more involved in their own ideas. In A level the group size has gone up. There were about 12 students doing A level when we arrived in the two years, and now we have about 60 in the sixth form (i.e. in years 12 and 13.). We love it. It is very exciting and the work that's being done now culminates in a major exhibition in the summer. This highlights our calendar.

From year 7 we aim to build students' confidence, through experimenting and trying new methods of working. We also use the sketchbook, which is at the core of everything we do. This involves students recording, analysing and keeping a record of their own progress so that they can look back at what they have done, how far they have got and whether their work has improved. We also hope they gain confidence in talking about art and developing opinions. We want to expose them to varied ideas and techniques in 2 and 3D. We use the National Curriculum as the backbone of what we do but we are not prescriptive, the actual projects change according to what's on in London or what's around at the time. It is not static. We tap into whatever is happening. So taking students to galleries is important. We often take year 7 to the National Gallery and have workshops. We take year 10 to the British Museum, the V & A (Victoria and Albert Museum) or the Tate Modern and we try to expose them to the notion of working in the gallery space. We also use the A level and the GSCE exhibitions as teaching opportunities for students lower down in the school so that they work in those exhibitions. The younger children use them as opportunity to work in a gallery and talk to the artists and to look at the work. We also invite in year 6 pupils from Primary school. It is exposure to art and ideas; including drawing, sculpture, painting etc. We use critical studies in all of our projects and ensure that by the end of year 9 they will have had opportunities to work in 2 and 3D.

A project might start with the work of an artist. For example one of my year 8 groups at the moment is working with Matisse and we are doing some investigative work looking at who he was and how he worked, then when we look at still life we will look at his style and approach. The next project may start with observation drawing, for example, natural forms. We aim to give students a rich and varied diet working with imagination and memory and through drawing, recording, analysing and composing; all the basic ingredients for art making. In years 7, 8 and 9 students have exposure to ideas and methods of working, recording and assessing. We assess their work as a group. They write about their work, we give written and spoken feedback. We don't grade work lower down in the school. We start grading work in year 10 and then throughout year 11. Before that we only write positive comments and teaching points in sketchbooks. Monitoring is through the sketchbook and report writing plus parent meetings. We also use sanctions if the students do not make the progress they should. We use work or discipline detentions or we refer the student to the head of department if there is a problem.

We would use computers more if we had access to them. This school has had two OFSTED inspections and each time our department has been identified as being 'outstanding' which is very rewarding for us. However, one of the criticisms has been that we don't have enough access to computers at the moment. We have one in the department and this can be frustrating. Now that the curriculum demands it we will I am sure change the current situation. I am very keen to develop the use of the digital camera. I have just asked to borrow one of the two digital cameras in school but I need one here permanently. My own personal target for this year is to start using the camera to document my teaching for recording and assessment. We also need more training in the use of new technology.

We don't have any policy on which art we would or would not show children but we are sensitive to pupils' age but we do consider the content of the work we expose children too. With the A level students I can't think of a piece of work I would not be prepared to discuss. I feel that from 16 on, if they are doing art as one of three or four subjects at A level they have to be prepared to take on board the issues. And you can't study art without that. So we try not to censor in that way. Some A level students went to the recent Sensation exhibition and some of them were shocked. Clearly there are many issues in art at the moment. It is a challenging subject and it can be hard for students to make sense of the things they see. If you offer them this work and start talking about it they may want to use it in their own work, and that can raise difficulties occasionally, from that point of view it can be difficult. We have discussions about the nature of art and what it is about. We discuss contemporary art and artists frequently. What is the work of for example, Tracey Emin trying to say? Is she making fools of the audience or what is the message that is being communicated? We do talk about these things and students will argue. Some of them really respond positively but they do all have something to say. Some say things like 'Art is going nowhere' or 'It's the skill rather than the idea that matters'. Maybe we would only talk about things that we feel comfortable with ourselves.

We have freedom as a staff and department to structure the curriculum in a way that does suit us. We offer the students a range of working methods and subject matter. We visit other schools and see their work when we can but we work in a way that suits us. Sometimes you do get a glimpse of work in other schools that is exhilarating but other times it is disappointing. I have been to an Independent School recently, which I though was brilliant. The students were working in a very focussed way and they had lots of space and access to abundant materials. So we decide what to introduce or the students might come in with some ideas. We use a variety of approaches in our teaching. But I suppose we wouldn't choose to look at artists that we would cringe from. I don't know. For instance I haven't talked about the recent work of Gilbert and George. But then we have talked about Mark Quinn's 'Blood Head' and we have looked at lots of other issues. So it is sometimes just what comes up. I feel very open minded and I think I would be willing to talk with the students about anything that comes up. I hope I would.

All students have access to all our library books and we don't say 'You can look at this and you can't look at that'. Although mainly in the early years students see the things that we show them. We don't censor the images that we are talking about but we may not necessarily introduce very heavily political or difficult images at that age. We introduce projects that are appropriate but I don't often think 'Should they see them?' Issues-based art can come in all stages. At the moment my year 7s are looking at 'Identity' and we are making boxes about themselves. They are rather like shrines to themselves. It has to give hints and clues to their personality and some aspects could become challenging if they deal with relationships etc. So that could raise some issues about how students relate to the world etc. But I can't see that there would be anything there that I would not tackle. With issues-based themes some of the AS/A level students work with issues like conflict. At GCSE an issue may be a question on an examination paper and would be elective. I don't think we would do a whole project with a whole group but they would have opportunities to work with issues-based work if they wanted to from year 10 onwards. We have certainly looked at themes and issues.

The school is a mixed cultural population and we do a lot of work with art from around the world. It is such a fantastic rich resource. Sometimes we get artefacts from the museum. We have had North American Indian and African objects and we also bring in artefacts of our own. I went to the Aboriginal art exhibition a few years ago in London and I thought it was so inspiring that since then I have done work with children based on Aboriginal art. Last year a student brought in actual paintings brought from Australia so we have used those. We encourage students to talk about their own cultures. We have a lot of Pakistani and West Indian students here so we would encourage them to share their cultural identity. Sometimes it might be a general theme like art from around the world with year 7 and we might ask them to bring things in from home if they have prayer mats or objects which they have collected. The last time I dealt with Aboriginal art with year 8 we talked a lot about land rights and freedom and we talked a lot about the spiritual aspects of the paintings and the legacy of the culture being carried on. We talked about freedom being taken away and how we would respond, what we would feel like etc. We did this through discussion and by writing about why the paintings exist and their significance. We looked at symbols in our culture that would have meaning for us if we tried to express ideas about our history and our past. They discuss ideas and then look at parallels in our own life. We imagine how we would feel if things were different.

An A level student based a project on her Afghanistan background. Her mother is from Afghanistan. The piece was based on a traditional Afghan dress. It looked from the front like an Afghan dress but reflected the two faces of Afghanistan. The back decorated with images from refugee camps and making political statements. The whole piece was about her identity, her link with her mother but it also reflected what was happening in Afghanistan. Those issues were all documented in her sketchbook, which accompanied the final piece. So we would hope that students would feel comfortable in using their own cultural identity in their work. Some will and some will be hesitant. Others are not interested. It is not something that they all have to do.

We use a variety of approaches to gender issues. Sometimes it would come from the work when the work throws up issues that they would talk about and explore, particularly at A level. But then from year 10 onwards they might be working from a series of questions that they have been set and they can select which one they wanted. So if they selected to explore a gender issue they would develop their project around this theme. We don't have any restriction on the projects that we might use. Recently I have used portraiture and figures in environments. We have had students who have done a lot of work with their own sexual identity and their relationships with other people such as their family and friends. We would encourage them to do that if they wanted to do it. We would deconstruct art from the past in terms of male artists and female artists. We look at the rise of female artists and the fact that a lot of successful artists at the moment are women. So we do discuss these issues at A level and quite a few students work on that. One girl is doing her personal study on Louise Bourgeois and this is encouraging. We also look at the world of art being male dominated or at craft being female dominated etc.

I love the work of Matisse. I love his use of colour. I find that most students respond very positively to his work. They love it. I also have particular enthusiasm for Rauschenberg, Jasper Johns and Joseph Cornell. They for me, are major influential artists. The transfer techniques that Rauschenberg uses I use quite a lot. Students respond positively to his work. I also love the work of Andy Goldsworthy and Richard Long. I am very excited about artists who use the environment to work in and draw inspiration from. Just looking at the books we have available, there are so many artists that excite me personally and that I would use very readily with students. Tom Phillips is a superb painter, musician, photographer etc. I do have favourite artists but I would tap into any of them to introduce a project. I don't think we do any projects in which we don't introduce artists. Or if it's not in the first lesson it will be in the second or third. So if I started with landscape I might then introduce Len Tabner or Turner etc. I also love Picasso. At the moment I am doing sculpture from found materials with year 9. So we are looking at Picasso. One of the things we want is for students to have an understanding of the richness and complexity of art and artists. It really is a matter of exposure to all sorts of ideas and trying to find artists that will help students find confidence in their own ideas and abilities.

We are a Postmodern department although we do not really use the term as such. We don't discount any artists work and we get recent publication such as 'Modern Painters', 'Craft Magazine'. We also go to the Tate Modern and take students to see the work of contemporary artists. Recently we have looked at the work of Damien Hirst, the Chapman brothers, Tracey Emin, Chris Ofili etc. One student did a study of Chris Ofili last year and another a study of Damien Hirst. This is on a website designed by the student. If the students respond to the Quinn brothers we would use that. We don't consciously use the word 'postmodern'. I am not sure that they would differentiate between modernism and postmodernism. If we looked at the theme of portraiture we might look at Rembrandt, Cindy Sherman and Tom Phillips and we would select artists who dealt with that theme. We might say for example that a particular piece of work is contemporary but we might not use the word 'postmodernism'.

This year the students have had a visit to New York and we are planning a trip to Paris in the spring and a lot of them have been to the Tate Modern. Some of them have been to lectures at the Tate. One student might do William Blake while another might research Rebecca Horn. Cindy Sherman is very popular and a lot of girls, in particular, seem to respond to her work. So the students present their personal study to the group and everyone in the group will read it. I think they choose quite difficult artists and it is a free choice but to help them in their choice they discuss ideas with the personal tutor assigned to them in the department. So I have 12 students in particular to monitor through their personal study.

In the future I hope art will become more and more popular and more and more students will want to do it. If you look at the curriculum generally in some areas the arts are getting squeezed out but in some schools like ours, more students are electing to do it post key stage 3. There has never been a better time for the arts. You have students who are wanting to learn and needing to be creative and that is encouraging. The art schools are very good and buoyant. So there is a good progression for art and design education in this country. I have no idea how art teaching will change in ten years' time. I think students need to know how to use computers but I don't think it is essential. Personal expression through using materials gives students enormous pleasure and using computers as another tool is fine as part of that. Maybe our art rooms will change and there probably will be more IT. I think every art classroom should have 2 or 3 computers, a camera and a video camera. But at the end of the day you still need the skills of the teacher and the love of the subject. Students will respond to the enthusiasm of the teacher.

There are certainly things that would make a more ideal art teaching environment. I think we need smaller teaching groups. In some subjects such as IT and CDT (Craft Design Technology) they have 15–20 students whereas we have up to 27 in the lower school groups. So in terms of numbers we are being stretched. We do get a fair chunk of time in the curriculum though and that is not a problem. Financially we are quite generously funded at this school compared to others, but it is never enough. We need books and storage and I think our department needs to be totally refurbished. We have a great technician but we need more time as we are always preparing materials for lessons. I think we need smaller teaching groups and better facilities generally. We need a greater investment of money. We encourage visitors like artists coming into the school and we have had artists come in and work for an extended period of time, like a term. We feel that because we are involved with the world of art and the training of teachers it is never dull. However there are things that we would like to do and hopefully we will get around to it. These issues are common to most art teachers and one way forward for us would be to apply for special Art College status. If we put together a successful bid and raise £50,000 towards the bid we could be awarded special status and be awarded more money to promote the Arts both in school and the local community. Our curriculum is fine. It doesn't inhibit us in any way. It just helps to give us a foundation and we don't feel restricted by it. I think you can interpret it with confidence. We would like more space and I would like to build out from the staff room. We have visions for the department and so that is why Catherine and I have stayed here for 12 years. We have never been bored.

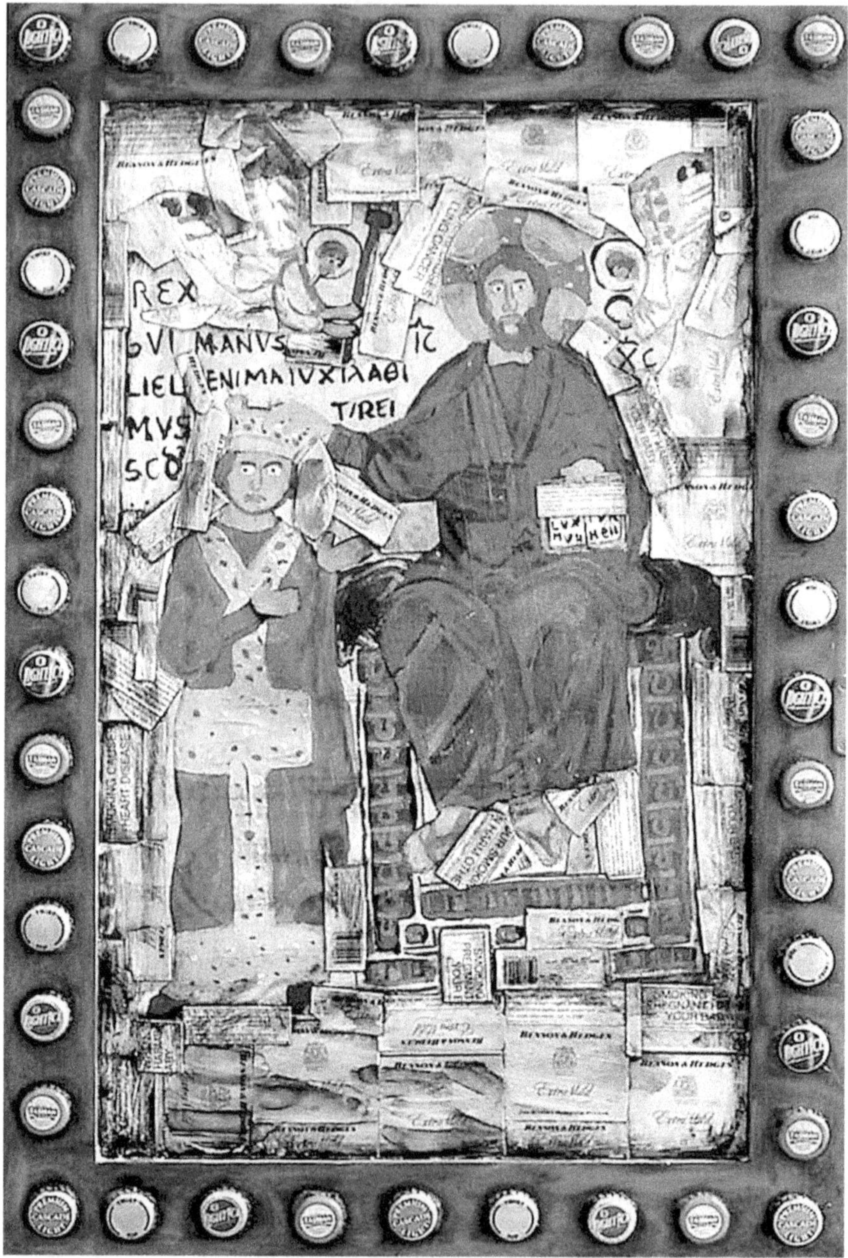

Figure 6:
Michael Salipas, Year 12, Camberwell Grammar School, Melbourne

Chapter 15

Ross Waterman

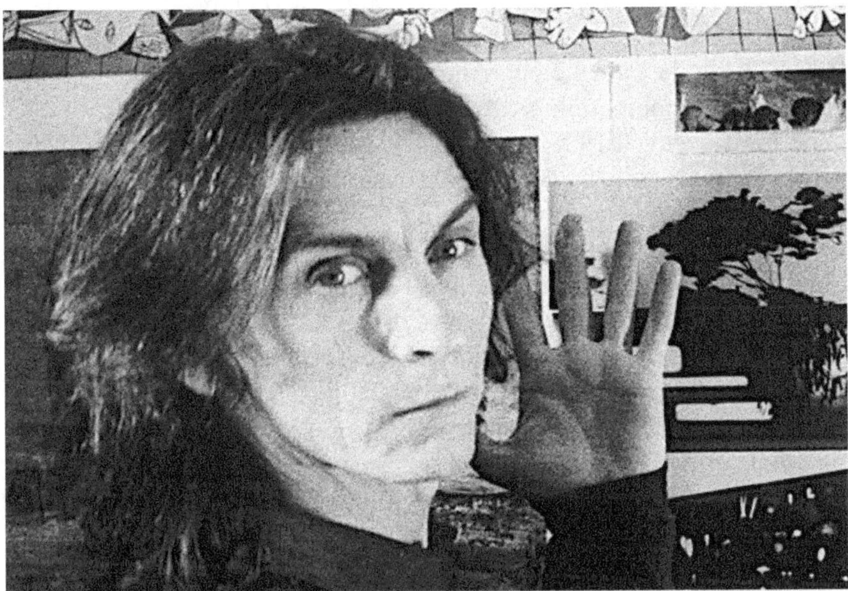

Ross Waterman teaches in the western suburbs of Melbourne. Copperfield College is a new name for an amalgamation of three schools set on different campuses. Although the school is located in a low socio-economic area, the art department is quite well equipped with facilities for art, ceramics, photography and graphics. Ross is Head of Art and maintains displays of student work in the corridors and has a budget for the purchase of artworks for the school collection. Ross has been an invited speaker at several art teacher conferences in recent years and it was at one of these that I heard him speak about his art program. I saw a long-haired 'arty-looking' person before me and wondered what he would have to say. He filled in his hour with endless strategies for having students look at and respond to artworks. He personally knew many artists and he recalled endless discussions with them. He drew on contemporary postmodern theory, but wove it into the discussions he had with his students. He described his gallery visits with students and recalled their responses and how he stimulated them to react. Although he claims that he doesn't write very much, he speaks faster than anyone I know. (ed.)

The school is located over two sites. When I began here in 1983 the school was just the administration block. When I first arrived here you could see to the horizon line but now all you can see are houses. These are brand new suburbs so our clientele comprises people who want to live in nice new suburban houses. Quite a lot of them have moved from inner Melbourne suburban areas in which there was a street life culture and inner suburban experience. The school has a large percentage of disadvantaged students in comparison to other schools. This is judged by the fact that many students are on government Education Maintenance Allowances. Many also come from language centres and are ESL (English as a Second Language) students. These factors combine to make our school a 'disadvantaged' school in terms of the student population.

I don't necessarily think about what underlies my teaching. I just get in there and do it. But when I was thinking about the aesthetic principles that underlie my teaching I happened to be listening to a gospel tape in my car and at that moment the song 'Everything is beautiful' came on, and it was like Kismet. Because to some degree, that is my aesthetic principle; the notion that everything is beautiful. And the next line of the song goes 'Like a starry summer's night' and a number of my favourite painters paint 'a starry summer's night' or 'a snow covered winter's day'. Peter Booth who is my favourite Australian artist has been doing these magnificent 'snow covered winter's days' for some time now and on the other hand, in the early eighties was doing apocalyptic, cannibalistic scenes. Both of those things have an immense beauty in them to me. And the next line of that song was 'There is none so blind as he who cannot see. We must not close our minds. We must let our thoughts run free'. There is beauty in everything, no matter how gross; no matter whether it is a Goya execution or a Bosch depiction of hell or a Rothko black or red painting. To some degree it is our job as art teachers to make people realise that if they open their minds up they can actually see a form of beauty in something like shearing a ram or someone picking up seeds out of a field. There is a beauty in nearly all things and whether it is a George Gittoes' depiction of some atrocity in Asia or whatever, it is that desire to make people want to see and to question the values that they have already gathered along the way. That is what underpins my teaching; these are my aesthetic principles.

If we get down to how you do that, I would suggest that going and seeing artworks is one of the most important ways you can do that. Going to the National Gallery of Victoria and sharing your experiences of the artworks with students is the best way. And if you can do this in a way that captures their imagination then this is great. I think a good example of this is the Peter Booth doorway paintings. For 15 years whenever I went to the NGV that was the painting that caused students greatest problem. They would see this black rectangular shape and feel threatened by it, and on a number of occasions it would take no more than about 3 or 4 sentences to engage them. I might start with:

> Have you noticed that it is hung just 6 inches off the ground? That is an instruction by the artist. Did you realise that it is a doorway shape? Have you ever considered that entering a dark space, a dark period in your life or a dark lane, could be represented in this way? And just for a moment think about this as a painting, rather than as an obscure black shape; as a shape that represents a space that we sometimes all slip into.

And when I have done this I have found that, not only my students, but people in the gallery would come up to me and say, 'I understand it now' and they wouldn't feel scared about the painting any more. So the way to get students, and adults who haven't had the opportunity to actually appreciate an artwork, is to give them something to hold on to; to give them something that they can find meaning in, that is part of their experience.

I think you have to talk with students. You have to utilise *their* language and *their* experience. In trying to explain to students why 'Shearing the Rams' by Tom Roberts was so outrageous in its own time, I ask them how they would react if they won Tattslotto on a Saturday night and they commissioned Peter Churcher or Tom Alberts or some other really good figurative painter to do a painting for their new huge area over their mantelpiece in their new huge mansion in Templestowe and three months later when the artist unveils the work he reveal that he has done a huge portrait of his mother cleaning the toilet. The artist might then explain that his mother actually assisted him through art school and she had sacrificed such a lot for him, so to him she is the most important woman in the world and she was a woman of great dignity. In that story the students begin to understand how outraged people were at the depiction of people shearing the rams. But unless you can contextualise art in a way that students can understand you are *only* speaking about your learnt experience rather than their known experiences. I ask them who learns a musical instrument and there might be one or two. I get them to explain that music involves regular study over many, many years and after 7 or 10 years they might expect to be reasonably good. So I explain that that is the same with drawing. Once students begin to understand that they shouldn't naturally be able to draw, they then might begin to look at drawing in a new way and understand where it comes from and how they might express themselves either through drawing or through other mediums.

I like to set up displays in the art room that actually take on board the issues that we are working through. In front of me at the moment I have displays that are about different approaches to portraiture and we work through portraiture as subject matter both in terms of the theory and practical content of the class. I have devised strategies and methods of working which help students produce quite realistic portraits of themselves which bring them great joy. It is something that comes from being able to point out images on the board. I can point out a Frida Kahlo or a Rembrandt or a photograph that I might have taken of an artist doing a drawing of me. They use photography. Basically what I want to do with portraiture is make them realise that there is a way that they can produce a realistic portrait of themselves. So I have devised a project where the students or I, depending on time, take a small close-up photograph of their faces.

We do this using studio lights and a camera on a tripod and I take 2 angles of each student, straight on and a three quarter view. I then get those photographs commercially processed and I then go down to the photocopy room and enlarge them up to A3 on the photocopier. So I then elongate the profile photograph by using the XY facility on the photocopier which allows you to stretch things like magic mirrors at Luna Park. You can get an image of a student's face and make it look like a Modigliani. So I present them with 6 or 7 photocopies and then we learn how to contour all the various shapes on the face. So for the first time ever they realise that the shape of an eye is not determined purely by the shape of the eye but by the shadow that falls underneath it. And originally with the previous CSF (Curriculum and Standards Framework) and with VCE (Victorian Certificate of Education) as well, I would get the students to go through a process in which they lay down their tones onto the photocopy. Later they would attach the photocopy to the back of a stretched canvas and with back-lighting from a strong light they would trace the image onto the canvas. And they would trace it emphasising all the contours of lights and darks and then they would simply fill in all the lights and darks. Simply by filling in the lights and the darks they would end up with this quite realistic portrait of themselves. And what they have learned is that you don't paint colour but you paint the way light falls on to a face. And this was a very successful project because they all wanted to take their work home. And then they all wanted to do art because they all wanted to take their work home and hang it up. Then they all paid their art levy. So this was the ultimate success story.

Katy is a year 10 student and she has been working on portraiture. We began by taking a photograph of Katy. We then enlarged it up to an A3 size and elongated some of the copies. The student then looked at about ten different portrait artists' techniques and styles. Katie chose to work with Modigliani. She started by doing a quickly copied portrait drawing of a Modigliani. She then spent a period just emulating Modigliani's technique and discovered that it is basically a pushing quality that achieved the brushy effect. At that point also, she had to go away and learn some of the words and descriptors that she would use to describe Modigliani's work. Following this she came in and on one of her photocopies she attempted then to emulate the technique of Modigliani. She used a range of orange tones and in the dark areas she used a darker tone of orange and in the lighter areas she used a lighter tone. So she has begun to understand the notion of actually describing the face through tone. And then she did a reasonably good job of putting a thin black line around the work which looks quite graphic. She then went away and had a look at some expressionists and examined their use of colour. Finally she got around to producing, on an elongated copy of her face, a work that was a combination of Modigliani's technique and expressionist colour. Katy has really appreciated this whole experience and has actually realised that if you work in a particular way with certain information, you can produce work that satisfies personal aesthetic demands.

One of the display boards in the art room has a display of portraiture and I concentrate on some key artists and styles such as pop art, Frida Kahlo, cubism, Modigliani etc. I usually put out some student works also. I won't put out exactly what I want the students to be working through at that moment because they might all end up fixating on that one very successful work. Then I also have a collection of original artworks in the art room. The school has an art collection and I get $2000 a year to purchase original artworks which are used as examples in the classroom. We just bought a range of ceramics for the Studio Arts class. We bought a Merric Boyd jug, a

Martin Boyd pottery plate and a John Perceval plate. So we do buy ceramics, textiles, photography and most mediums. A couple of years ago we concentrated on buying small expressive paintings and they just serve as a reference point in the art room. Students can actually look up close and see the surfaces and textures and it is just a good experience to have original works of art. In the art room we have three oil paintings, one collage work and a photographic poster by Bill Henson.

And on another display board I have pictures of landscape. And the idea of this is to make links between different forms of landscape and artists we are studying. We look at concepts like 'idealised landscape' and whenever I am teaching I always try to get back to a point where the students can enter and understand the difference between a landscape and an idealised landscape. So we go back to the 17th century and I teach Claude Lorraine, the Dutch landscape painters and I make reference to them. I feel that if students don't understand when landscape was first developed and why, then they fail to understand every landscape that ever came after that. So it is one of things that I really regard as being essential.

Landscape is still part of the great tradition in contemporary art. I went to a Howard Arkley auction the other night and he got $160,000 for an interior and he is known as a landscape painter. Peter Booth is also effectively a landscape painter and my friend Andrew Browne is a landscape painter. I would suggest that landscape is very strong in a contemporary art practice. Peter Graham for example, is a very young artist whose work shows a direct relationship between landscape and the people who inhabit it. So I would think that landscape, portraiture and still-life are great ways to enter art practice. They give students an appreciation of how a simple object can be a poetic composition, whether it be a Claude Lorraine landscape, an impressionist work or a John Glover painting. With John Glover they may learn that he was an artist that arrived in Australia bringing with him a tradition that was 200 years old. It was a tradition that was fairly worn out in the country that he had just left but he was fairly invigorated by the Dutch tradition. These are the sort of links that I hope students will pick up on.

The culture at this school is not an academic one. The students don't have a strong desire to go home and read and then study and apply that information at school. The best learning that we do occurs when I stand out the front of the class and just get really enthusiastic about something. I might show a video and I try to show them how the artist created in his or her time. I use Frida Kahlo as an example because there is a great story to tell about her life. I can talk about her tram accident and how this pole speared her back and came out through her vagina etc. I also talk about her horrendous relationship with Diego Rivera and the fact that she was interested in communism and politics etc. The students can get interested in that and then they can make a choice that they want to read and write about this. But to be honest, in most cases students answer questions from the textbook. Their answers might be also informed by my chalk and talk or from information they have heard from the education staff at the National Gallery of Victoria. On the whole students are reluctant to do theory. They are therefore reluctant to spend time writing too much. They are more interested in just getting on with making some art.

In dealing with contemporary art I don't necessarily consider issues such as gender, culture or class to be only contemporary issues. I think the most important ideas are ageless and different times and different technologies allow artists to express the same ideas in different ways. So if I wanted to teach about feminism or post-colonialism I would go back to Frida Kahlo. I think that I would then point out that she made statements suggesting that she didn't know she was a surrealist until Andre Breton said she was one. This indicates that artists don't always take on board the theory that is associated with them. They don't even sometimes understand theories that critics and historians associate with their work. With most issues I use examples of particular artists. With post-colonialism for example, I might take the notion of John Glover arriving in Australia and look at the way he discussed Aboriginals. I would look at von Guerard's work and issues related to his work. I think you need an appreciation of colonialism to have an appreciation of post-colonialism. Similarly, without ever having an appreciation of Georgia O'Keeffe and the struggles that she may have experienced or the relationship between Lee Krasner and Jackson Pollock, there is little point in addressing contemporary art issues to students in years 7 to 10. So I think for most contemporary issues you can find parallels in art history and I would prefer to go back to those points and start the conversation from these works. Students then have something to draw on. If you don't know what classical is it very difficult to have a conversation about contemporary art.

Contemporary Aboriginal art is something that I get most excited about. I had a conversation with James Mollison when he was director of the National Gallery of Victoria, in which I suggested that it was strange that Trevor Nickolls got a placard next to his work explaining the meaning but Roslyn Piggot's didn't. I wanted to know whether there was some sort of suggestion that Roslyn Piggot's work had no sort of spiritual quality or sense of place to it; didn't she exist inside her particular place and time? Why was it that Trevor Nickolls needed an explanation of his religion or his experience? Did this imply that most people understand the Christian religion? So when I walked in to the European section of the gallery why wasn't here a placard about each of the Christian stories depicted? So there are issues in relation to Aboriginal art. I have always believed that Aboriginal art is best viewed in the same way that you would view a Jackson Pollock or a Rothko. So I have always aligned Aboriginal art to abstract art and I have said that most artists have a sense of spirituality and a sense of place and a sense of their own belonging. And while in Aboriginal art there is that sense of particular stories and locations I think that is also true of the Heidelberg School painters. The question of what it is to be an Australian and what is our relationship to the bush and the land is an overarching issues. Aboriginal art to me is exactly the same as all other forms of contemporary art practice. I don't like to separate things off into art that is essentially feminist or essentially Aboriginal or essentially conceptual. I think there's a common experience that links art and the best element of art is that it is wordless and that you can come to a work and appreciate it without knowing anything about it. And to demand that you actually have to know something to complete the image is something that theorists might apply to artworks rather than artists.

I think the National Gallery of Victoria does a good job of making sure that all cultural groups are hung on a regular basis. We went to the gallery recently and saw works by Shane Cotton etc. And we were able to talk about post-colonialism and Maori culture and then we looked at contemporary Aboriginal artists like Rover Thomas. We then moved to Jenny Watson, Lindy Lee and other artists who have brought in various approaches from different cultural perspectives. But I don't do this in a way that tries to marginalise things. It is always a case of 'these people are fine artists and they happen to come from a particular background'. But it doesn't necessarily always follow that a female might be making a feminist statement which should be seen as one coming from a woman. I really do believe that certain female artists make particular feminist paintings and that they see things through the eye of a woman. I also believe that some female artists make work that no man could make. That is the sort of issue that I like to take up with students. I like to have them debate that particular point. But sometimes you might find that some particularly politically correct people might suggest that that is a very bogus argument and that it isn't appropriate and shouldn't even be spoken about. It is difficult and I am essentially Eurocentric in my approach to art history. I pay little attention to and have little enthusiasm in Asian art. But if there is a good exhibition of Asian ceramics I make sure that we go and see it and I will learn more about it myself and become a little more enthusiastic about it. But I don't pretend that I spend a lot of time in Asian or African art galleries .

Another display that I have in this room sets up relationships between different ideas and how ideas travel across time and tide. This example shows a relationship between Goya's 'The third of May', Picasso's 'Guernica' and Peter Booth's 'Untitled 1982'. What I am attempting to do is to show students that ideas are picked up by other artists, that influence doesn't mean imitation. An idea can be used in many different ways. It can be realistic, semi-abstract or it could be figurative or expressive. I did have little red cotton lines that went from the outstretched hands of the figure about to be executed in Goya's work which linked to the figure on the right hand side in the Guernica. It then linked down to a single hand in the Peter Booth work. So I set up that relationship. We then look at Manet's painting that was based on the Goya work and another painting that Picasso did in 1951 of the war in Korea, which is based on Goya's 'Third of May'. So this display board sets up a relationship that enables students to see how ideas travel through time.

What I am basically trying to do is get my students to appreciate art; to find a way of understanding all forms of art; to open themselves up to experience. I think that 'There is none so blind as those who cannot see' and to me that is what it is all about. I continually use analogies between music and art. I get them to realise that they want to listen to the most contemporary forms of music but in art they want to experience traditional and conservative forms of art. I want them to realise that there are ways to appreciate contemporary art practice by simply opening themselves up to the ideas and the techniques and forms that are being used by contemporary artists. What I want them to do is to realise that there is value in all art practice and in all forms and ideas in art. I use whatever methods I have developed over many years, to get students to appreciate that.

Maybe every art room is postmodern in as much as some of the concepts that I deal with could only be dealt with in a postmodern age. When I attempt to deconstruct 'Shearing the Rams' I know that I couldn't have deconstructed that artwork from a feminist perspective twenty years ago. I don't think I would have had the textbooks. Books such as Michelle Stockley's in which she has made such an obvious attempt to find the great female artists of history and to place them alongside the male artists and address their sorts of concerns and issues are a great leap forward. Most art rooms would also have a computer in them and be linked to the Internet which gives us amazing ability to track down images from all over the world. But in relation to students or teachers being able to communicate what postmodern might mean, I think that would be a misreading.

Chapter 16

Janis Dunkley

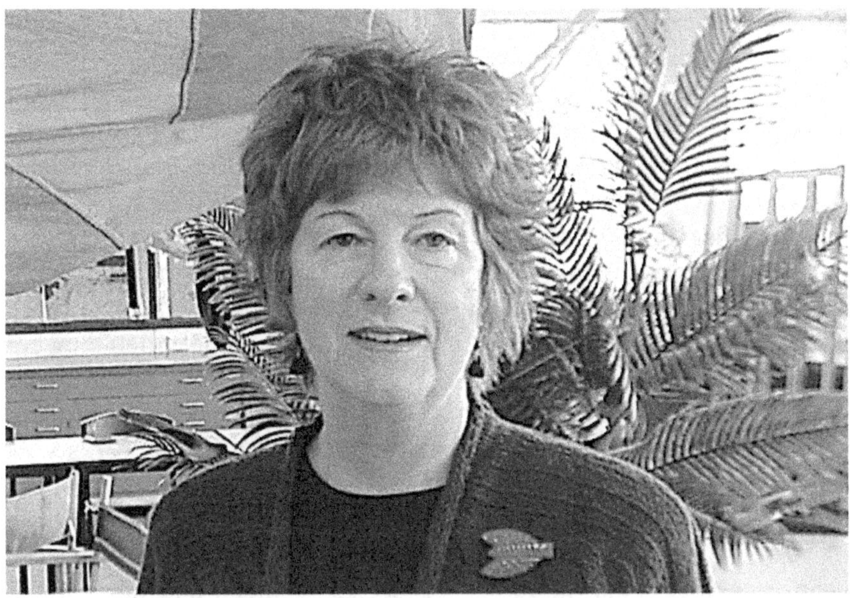

Janis Dunkley is Head of Art at Trinity Grammar Boys' School in Melbourne. The school has a large population of Asian students and a reputation for its discipline and behavioural codes. Janis has been teaching art for 25 years. She taught 8 of those years in London where she became immersed in the British art system which stressed the importance of drawing from observation. As Head of art Janis was responsible for designing the new art wing which comprises several general art rooms, a printmaking room and a room for ceramics and sculpture. The most striking things about these rooms are the large installations of drawing objects set in the middle of the art rooms. Comprising cupboards, costumes, furniture, books, vases, children's toys, piles of magazines, kitchen utensils, rugs, swatches of fabric etc. the installations are usually identifiable by theme, such as colour or material and they are changed two or three times each year. All students in the school carry laptop computers and these are used for graphics and art research. Digital imagery is also being used and this has led Janis to seek artists in this field. (ed.)

One of my aims as an art educator is to ensure that students learn about their own environment through looking. I want them to use their own visual experiences as a starting point for their work. To do this they must be either taken outside to start their work, or we bring visual resources into the studios. These can be small scale, like toys or shoes, but we also build installations from which they select areas for investigation.

At this particular time, the younger boys, years 7 and 8, have been using the collection of toys as subject matter for their linocut prints. Year 7s get really attached to their adopted toys as they first draw from them then design their lino blocks. For such activities we direct them towards knitted and furry toys suitable for their prints.

Our installations are like very large still life installations. We set them up in the centre of the room and have tables or easels arranged so that every boy is confronted by a part of the installation he needs for his work. The installations can be used for skill-based exercises, like drawing. Students can use different areas for different media to build up their drawing skills. They might then proceed to painting or collage. The installation can also be used as a setting for figure drawing or painting. We generally like to set up the installations twice a year so that they can be used for semester work. Very often they are based on a theme and the current one is about 'contained spaces'. Year eleven are developing their folio around this theme and many of them are using the installation as their starting point. But it also works well as a study of the art elements for other boys.

In the past we have worked on a wide variety of themes. A couple of years ago we had four studios set up, loosely based on materials. One room was china, the others wood, glass, metal and fabrics. We have also used rooms as themes, for example, a bedroom, bathroom, and a kitchen theme, which inspired a year 12 boy to paint portraits of himself in the bath.

This method of working is not only an important way to get children to look for themselves but it can be great fun collecting objects and putting them together. People give their discarded household items and it is amazing what can be found on Council collection nights. Our collection of visual resources is now quite large enabling us to treat it as a visual library. If we are working on drawings to develop an understanding of texture, for example, then we can borrow objects from our 'library' to use for students to develop a better understanding and investigate ways of making appropriate marks within that context. Children should not have to rely on memory alone. This generally produces learned images. I firmly believe they achieve more informed, independent results, and are prouder of them, if they look for themselves.

If I had to name three favourite artists I am particularly fond of Howard Hodgkin, and Patrick Heron but then I also like Piero della

Francesca. I mostly like works that are to do with colour. Matisse and the Fauves are wonderful and I thought the best exhibition we have ever had in this city was the Fauve show. I went many times. And I thought it was interesting that the boys liked it so much. It means you can get children to love artworks just because they are sensuous things. We all love rich colours and surfaces.

As a product of the feminist movement I would not deliberately encourage the boys to look at works by women. That would defeat the purpose of equality. We do, however, use the work of Paula Rego as an example of a print maker. She is very open about her work and what has influenced her. There is a splendid video where she tells all. Such artists give us much support in the teaching of the subject. Hodgkin, Heron and Hockney are equally informative. We are very fortunate in our times to have access to artists through this medium.

Paula Rego is a painter and a printmaker and I particularly like her work because she puts into action the concepts I believe in. She makes observations from life and then uses them to express her own emotions and her work reflects her own personal life. She borrows nothing. This piece of work is 'The Grand Old Duke of York' from a collection of nursery rhymes that she illustrated. You can see that there is an influence from other Hispanic artists such as Goya. So she has carried on a tradition that he began. So this is a superb aquatint which the boys at the school bought. It is probably the most valuable print in our collection and we use it a lot to demonstrate aquatinting. She had a tragic life in that her husband, whom she met in London at an art school, died and she moved back to Portugal. But now she works in London. Her work is my idea of how artists ought to be reflecting the world around them. I mean artists don't have to do anything but what I mean is that it suits me to have this work to show the boys. The reason is that not only has she learned the crafts of drawing, painting and printmaking (in that order because drawing is the basis of everything) well, but she uses it to explain ideas. So this is at the imaginative end. You cannot expect children in year 7 to be as imaginative as her because obviously they need to experience life to be imaginative in their work.

One of the qualities that appears in her paintings aside from reflections of her own childhood is the series where she is force feeding or giving medicine to her pets. She admits that this is to do with her relationship with her husband. Her observations about people and things that have happened to her are used imaginatively and that is what we would hope for at the senior level. One would hope that even boys at year 12 would do that once they have learned the crafts. And some of them do have sexual innuendos. I was unable to buy the print that belongs to the National Gallery in London. It was an illustration of a poem and shows children romping on a bed on a Sunday afternoon and the little girl just looks as if she is enjoying it all rather too much. So obviously that wasn't a good one for us to buy, but it was beautiful. Her work is fabulous really. I think it is important to introduce these artists to the boys. I could teach about Fred Williams and Brett Whitely but they can get that information easily if they are interested. It surrounds them. So to alert them to artists they would not normally see is the job of the educator in my view.

I don't know that Paula Rego is really portraying social justice issues. I think she is interesting because she reflects her life. She is not quite autobiographical. She is very good at talking about what she has done, rather like David Hockney. She is a very good educator; open about why she doing certain paintings. In the Melvin Bragg video interview with her she tells you about these paintings. These women, who seem muscular, are simply Portuguese women so she is used to looking at people who look like that. Whereas she is certainly making some statements she is also observing things around her. The work reflects what objects, such as quilts, curtains and shoes, look like. She is a good example of someone who has learned to look at the world around her, make observations and then use them imaginatively and certainly to also make comments. This man is dead and this little girl is bringing him back to life, or trying to. This is for senior boys as I think it's a bit hard for junior boys.

Patrick Herron is also a British artist who was born and bred in England. His father was a clock maker and these beautiful images here were scarves. He is also very open about being influenced by Matisse and you can see this in his use of colour and wonderful flat shapes. The boys get to love him too. He is another artist who will freely talk about his work. That is important and it is really valuable for the boys to know that he is still alive. We can write him a letter. He came to Australia in 1992 and did paintings in Sydney at the botanical gardens. These are beautiful. They are like drawings in colour.

Earlier work certainly reflects Matisse and some of the cubists and develops through several styles. He worked in Cornwall with the St

Ives group and you can see these are all images from there. He has a wonderful relationship with his wife and two daughters and you see them in the pictures all the time. This is just the household. This is good for the boys once again because you can teach them the value of using things that are around them. They don't have to think up really clever things. You can make a wonderful picture of your kitchen or a bowl of fruit.

Children don't have sophistication to think what will I do today. Very often if they go to books they will use a learned image or someone else's image. When I say a learned image, I mean an image that comes from a book, comic or television series or something they have seen and kept in their mind. I discourage that. I want them to feel proud of their own image. I think you must build up their confidence and praise them for the things they have done themselves; try to find something positive. A boy said to me once, 'Miss Dunkley you never say anything bad about your students' work' and I like that.

Patrick Herron is interesting because the striped pictures that he did predate Rothko. So he changes his style a lot and he talks about that. Again there is a wonderful interview with Melvin Bragg. He makes such a good selection of artists to interview.

The VCE requirement that students look at artists post 1970 is interesting because it does restrict the artists you can study. I mean certainly we can use the work of Patrick Herron, Howard Hodgkin and Paula Rego, but what about Frances Bacon? His work is important. What about some Australian artists who are important as well? It seems a shame to have restricted the time frame but I suppose we will just have to cope. You can still teach about what happened before 1970.

Howard Hodgkin is another British painter who is probably in his sixties now because he was evacuated to America during the first world war. He is another artist who is pretty good at talking about his own work and he talks about painting his feelings and the feelings are generally about situations in which he has been. I think you really need to study his work and know what it is about before you can begin to appreciate the content. I think of him like the fauve painters because we all appreciate work that is sensual and the application of paint is of course very sensual. So there are groups of his paintings. There is one collection that I like very much that was done in Venice.

They are all images that I can relate to because I can recognise the shapes of the shutters etc.

His painting 'Waking up in Naples' is a fascinating painting because we can certainly identify the shoulder of the man, and the blue area which could be water through the window etc. He paints on board, generally speaking and sometimes the board is revealed so the wood grain becomes the shoulder and part of the torso of the man waking up in Naples. He also uses the frames. He looks for frames and they are part of the painting or image. Usually the paintings are about episodes in his own life and usually they are about sex, so the older boys like to relate to that. So if you say 'What is this a painting of boys?' they can identify with it. He produces these vibrant rich, rich colours and you can see that there is an image, but you need to know the name before you can understand the image. The distance he creates in these sometimes small 16cm x 20cm paintings is done with fabulous colours; for example wonderful blues with warm colours pushing forward. At an exhibition of his recently in London, I heard a young little girl say to her mother 'Mummy what is behind that painting? and I thought that was a really clever observation for that child to make.

His early images are flat and they are about his relationship with this particular woman with whom he was boarding in America. So he is always painting about his own experiences and situation. But there is always plenty of observation there. So the observation becomes reduced to shapes and he suggests through colour. There is one called 'Lovers' and I sometimes ask the boys what this is about. And some of them really observe the white sheets and the twisting bodies and the frenetic relationship of the red and green. He is a wonderful painter and printmaker. In fact he is probably best known for his prints. There is a big collection of them at the Tate gallery and I used to know the person who framed his work at the Tate.

So they are three artists that I am fond of at the moment. But then there is the Renaissance and where does one start. And then there is Roy de Maistre. I think his work is fabulous too. My favourite Australian artist is Fred Williams. He must be such a wonderful representation of our country and they are beautiful paintings. They are not paintings that everyone understands. They are painters' paintings. I am not a photographer and don't know contemporary photography well.

However like most art teachers I looked at the first digital images and thought 'My God, do we really have to?'. I got so tired of people telling us how wonderful digital art was because very often they are often made by people without any art training. It was not until I went to an exhibition and workshop on digital imaging that was held at this time last year at RMIT. I met Tristan Humphries and got to know him really well. I also know David Harley who is doing beautiful work and that is a wonderful catalogue. These works work with layers and Tristan had a show here last year which was portraits and he talks about shoebox portraits. He gets a shoebox and literally puts things about the person into a shoebox and that is what we are doing with the boys with our experimental digital class. What we are doing is using digital cameras and scanning images in. We then build up layer upon layer of work done in that way. It is very slow to do. Tristan is married to an Australian so they are back and forward from England a lot. One of Tristan's works that I particularly remember is about Japan where they stopped over. All of the images are computer generated and I was so enthusiastic about them all.

These works are not drawn but they still involve looking. You can of course, draw with the computer and we have plates where you can actually draw with the mouse. We get the younger boys to do this and they are still observing. It doesn't matter how they make the image. It doesn't matter whether they draw it or paint it so long as they have a starting point at school where they learn to make images from the world around them, not to borrow images. Our year 12 digital works show that the boys can observe and draw. I can see a relationship between the sort of drawing he is doing and the sort of attention to detail that also appears in the digital imaging. I will certainly see that this drawing goes into his final folio as support work. It does support that kind of layering and textures. There is a strong relationship between the two and he has really learned to look.

I still believe that drawing is the basis of everything because it teaches people to look or it should do. So I am quite happy about the use of digital imaging. There is some very interesting work and certainly when we finish experimenting with this course it will be interesting work. The boys are collecting their shoeboxes and they are going to do a shoebox portrait. They will collect things about themselves and they will either scan them or take digital photos of them and they will build up layers on the screen that becomes their portrait. They are doing exercises in Adobe Photoshop first to learn the tools. We didn't want to teach this class but we were greatly influenced by Tristan's work. Hopefully it will be a successful course. It still relies on looking at things so it still fits in with our basic philosophy.

Alternatively students could use images from magazines but I think that would be wrong. It is better for them to do things that are personal to them. They can take photographs of things that are around them, such as in their bedroom. A photograph of their drawer of socks or things that they value means that they have looked. We tell them to steer away from football and television. We don't want Bart Simpsons. That is someone else's work. We want their work. I think that we build their confidence if we say to them 'Your ideas are important. They are more important for us than the person who designed Bart Simpson'. We are interested in the students' work. This subject is about developing confidence and their belief in themselves.

Sometimes students work together on projects. Hopefully they can bring their own ideas to that. At the VCE level I don't think students can submit work together. We do talk about the unique qualities of the individual and that's what we are working towards. Even in Photoshop although the programmer has made the program, all Photoshop is doing is helping you to make the marks; to use your own image and to manipulate it to make an image that you feel good about. Photoshop is really like a collection of different drawing materials. It is like charcoal in one box, coloured pastels in another and airbrush in another. So all it really is about is tools and materials. When we look at this catalogue of digital images by artists at London Institute we can see that there is great individuality. So it must be possible to be an individual and create digital images. Once you get to know the works you can recognise the artists who created them. We are studying Tristan Humphries as an artist and yet his work was only done a year ago. I don't see why you couldn't group him with an artist like Paula Rego. After all she is doing work about her life, and Tristan Humphries is doing work about his. They are just using different materials and methods. And Patrick Herron is doing oil paintings of his surroundings which happen to be in Cornwall in St Ives.

Individualism is not dead. I took a great range of age groups to the Fauves exhibition. I took the senior year 12 students right down to little boys and although I hadn't prepared them, they loved it. I think it is because all people respond to the sensuous quality that paint and canvas make. It is just a bit like looking at sweets in a sweet shop. They're shiny, they're beautiful, they are luscious. Human beings do respond to those qualities that the Fauve painters had. I suppose the Fauve painters were really very traditional. They were still painting very traditional subject matter. What they were doing might have seemed pretty amazing in their day but we now don't think of them as particularly outrageous. Those students were not used to seeing a mass of work like that and they responded very positively to it. Do people need to understand a work of art in order to respond to it? I think understanding it and learning about it might help them improve their response. I have year 12 boys who respond very positively to the Howard Hodgkin prints I have and to his book.

We had an Aboriginal art exhibition here. It was on a small scale. I think none of us knows nearly enough about Aboriginal art and perhaps that's because for them it is not an art that they want to talk about. That's not the purpose of their picture making. That is how it seems to me. There were one or two quite spectacular paintings in that Koorie exhibition that we all responded to before we knew what they were about. Like 'The man with the scarves' which was a black background with star shapes of fabulous colour and we all responded to that.

Finally I have chosen to discuss one student's work. I am very fond of this drawing by Imran. Imran is a very interesting boy from a mixed religion family as his name suggests. He loves drawing and painting and the visual arts generally. He has the support of his family and this drawing is based on his observation of a part of our existing installation. That installation has a theme of 'contained spaces'. Some times our installations are about themes and some times they are just about visuals. So Imran was looking at a tea chest with some pussy willow branches emerging from it. And then he is looking into an old cupboard with some sort of grill on the side of it, possibly fly wire. Then he is looking at the picture frames that make trapezoid shapes. All of these parts of the picture contain space. The theme was directed at older boys so that they could imaginatively use the still life but Imran is simply learning to make marks and that's what we would want him to do in year 7. We want him to learn to use tools to understand the craft he is using so that he can later on use them imaginatively to make the pictures he wants to make. I love this picture because it shows enormous enthusiasm for the work. It has such energy and he has been very brave. He has mixed up his mediums. He has conte crayon, charcoal and pastels and it just represents his enthusiasm. I still think drawing is the basis of everything. Yes drawing is the basis of it all.

Section 3

Strategies for Interpreting Art in a Postmodern World

This section outlines a range of interpretive frameworks for looking at art in a postmodern world. Seven interpretive frameworks are presented to guide discussion when responding to art. A formalist approach focuses on modernist principles of form and composition while the remaining frameworks are designed to deconstruct artworks to reveal less obvious social and cultural assumptions upon which artworks are based.

Chapter 17

Interpretive Frameworks as Belief Systems

Students making art in a postmodern world

As makers of art in the classroom contemporary students in the western world will embrace all of the nine orientations outlined in the first section of this book. They will explore issues of their own identity within broad societal and cultural frameworks. They will examine issues of gender and class as these issues impact on their lives. They will explore pluralistic art practices which may derive from diverse fields within and beyond the arts. And they will examine ways in which art serves to define traditions, roles and values. Hopefully they will become critical thinkers through art practice. The products they make will be evidence of their capacity to challenge the boundaries of art.

Above all they may use some of the postmodern devices which were not available to students of modernist art classrooms. They may use irony and parody as strategies for commentary and they may appropriate the works of other artists if they think it relevant. They may fuse fine art traditions with popular art forms and they may explore art processes and cultural traditions previously marginalised in modernist art classrooms. They will, at the same time, explore issues surrounding ownership of artworks and consider the roles of gallery directors, art critics, schools of art and art auction houses in the life of an artwork. In making their own art they will come to understand that values about art are not fixed but are continually reconstructed by all those who engage in it.

Students viewing art in a postmodern world

However, while art making is probably the most significant thing that students do in art classes, this final section focuses on art responding rather than art making. While modernist approaches to art making and responding are common in western art classrooms, postmodern artworks tend to confuse if they are examined in modernist ways. This section offers a simplified approach for students as they approach both modernist and postmodern artworks.

Postmodern approaches to art history and criticism have been referred to as the 'new' art criticism (Smuglia, 1991) or the 'new' art history (Harris, 2001). Most contemporary art theorists agree that new approaches to writing about art focus on socio-cultural perspectives rather than addressing the visual style or qualities of an artwork. The focus then is often upon the ideological, economic, political, cultural or social implications of a work. As Smuglia says:

> Instead of viewing the work of art as an expression of individual creativity ….the new art criticism has for the most part focused on the social process and interaction between producer (artist) and consumer (viewer or owner) (Smuglia, p 1).

In other words formalist art criticism, as defined by the art educator Edmund Feldman, involving description, analysis, interpretation and judgement, has given way to new ways of interpreting art from different belief systems. Whereas formalist forms of interpretation were concerned with the analysis of the actual image in terms of its quality, style and compositional structure, new forms of interpretation examine the work to reveal the undisclosed assumptions upon which the work is based. These assumptions may be based on the nine orientations outlined in the first section of this book. These nine orientations form useful categories for examining key differences between modernism and postmodernism. However most of them also form the basic belief systems which underpin postmodern art theory. As such they also become belief systems (or ideologies) which frame the key ways in which postmodernists interpret artworks.

The social construction of art

The most significant factor in understanding postmodern thinking is the acknowledgement that values about art are never neutral. Art is always situated in context and values about it are provisional and indeterminate. This suggests that knowledge about art is dependent upon the ways in which viewers frame their experience of it. Theories of art in a postmodern world are extremely diverse but the key frameworks for viewing art have been primarily developed by those groups previously marginalised by modernist theories. Modernist art theory focused on the formalist properties of the artwork itself (ie. use of art elements, style, composition etc) and privileged the white male western artists who made it. Postmodern theorists however, look at the economic, political, ideological and cultural implications of artworks and give more consideration to the ways in which diverse viewers interpret art. Contemporary art theory has therefore developed from individuals or groups who focus on issues of class (Marxism), gender (feminism and masculinism), and culture (indigenous art and post colonial art). Other theorists have also scrutinised the role of the mind of the individual artist and what his or her artwork says about identity (psychoanalysis).

Postmodernists acknowledge that viewers interpret art differently. They acknowledge that the one artwork may be understood differently by men and women, by white and Aboriginal Australians, by heterosexual and gay people and by individuals of different ages etc. Postmodernists consider that meanings of artworks are never fixed and stable. When students of art talk and write about art it is essential that they first come to realise that they each have unique ways of looking, framed within the context of their own background, beliefs, attitudes and preferences. One way of thinking about this is to imagine how different people watching the same game of football may interpret it. Think of the language and focus of the coach as distinct from the supporters, the media, the families of the players, the ground keeper, tourists from other countries etc. Each frames the experience in relation to individual interests and background and thus the one phenomenon is conceptualised differently by each.

Artists

While modernist art critics and historians think of the artist as an independent person engaged in art as an individualistic pursuit, postmodern thinkers see artists as products of the world they inhabit. Artists are often products of art schools which imbue students with particular values and understanding about art. Many suggest that artists are always influenced by their upbringing and by the art that they have seen. Even though artists seek to make unique contributions to their culture they are aware of the audience which may view their work. Artists may be thought of as cultural agents who make visual products for consumption.

Viewers

Viewers play key roles in constructing meaning of an artwork by talking and writing about it. Some say that artworks are actually orphaned once they are made. In other words the artist cannot control the meaning of a work once it is completed. Viewers bring to the works their own values and understanding. Viewers from differing contexts will see the work in different ways, and writers who interpret artworks do so from their own points of view. Because of this no one interpretation may be seen as neutral and definitive. Perception is always framed by the experiences, beliefs, attitudes and understanding of the viewer.

Society

Art plays different roles in different societies. While in western societies art plays a significant role in defining individual freedom and in the expression of ideas and feelings, in some cultures art is confined to decorative, religious or ceremonial roles. Postmodern theorists suggest that values about art are constructed by all those involved in educating, displaying, writing about and publicising the whole practice of art. Within most western societies various cultural agencies provide education about art, spaces to view art, media commentary on art, and support for artists in the form of grants and awards. The significance of art in any society depends on the way artists, viewers and the broader society functions. The following interpretive frameworks highlight the ways in which societal values frame the way viewers see art.

Seven interpretive frameworks (belief systems)

The following section outlines seven key interpretive frameworks which students may use to examine art works. A selection of artists who explore these issues is then presented:

1. A formalist interpretive framework
2. Deconstruction as an interpretive framework
3. A gender interpretive framework
4. A cultural interpretive framework
5. A semiotic interpretive framework
6. A psychoanalytic interpretive framework
7. A social realist interpretive framework

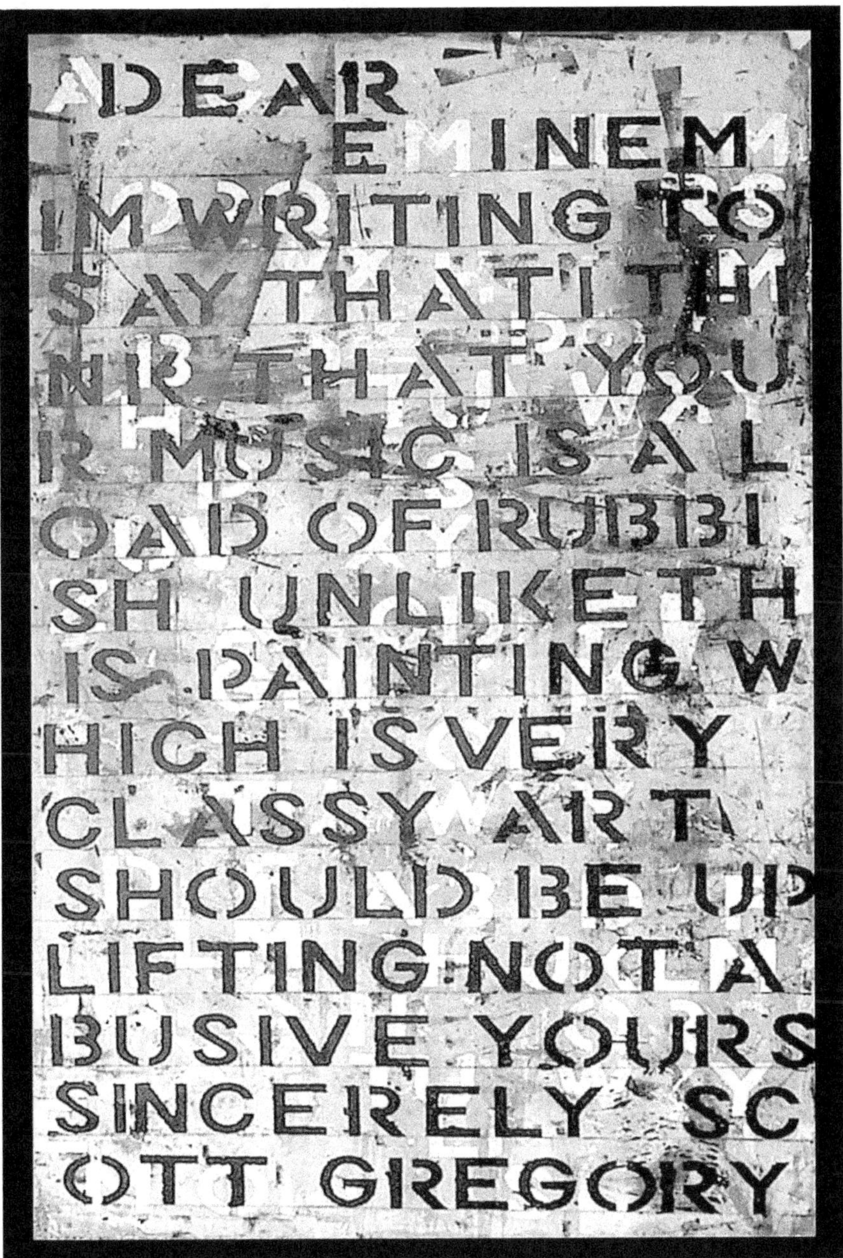

Scott Gregory, Year 12, Camberwell Grammar School, Melbourne

1. A formalist interpretive framework

This framework focuses on the formal organisation and aesthetic qualities of the artwork and was (and is) the general approach used by modernist art critics (such as Clement Greenberg). Formalist commentary on art centres on the particular visual sensibility of the artist and his (rarely her) unique contribution to innovation in art (as a member of the Avant garde). When viewing an artwork in a formalist way attention is drawn to the surface and structure of the work itself; the form of the work being emphasised over the content. While formalist interpretation can be made of artworks from any period, the modernist art movements gave rise to a prolific number of art critics and historians who interpreted the modernist art movements of impressionism, post impressionism, cubism, fauvism, abstract expressionism, surrealism etc using a formalist approach. Such formalist interpretation discussed the aesthetic qualities of art elements (shape, colour, texture etc) and analysed the artist's use of composition (balance, depth, surface and structure). Formalist interpretation of meaning was usually developed from statements by the artist or through knowledge of the life of the artist.

A simple model using the formalist framework was developed by the art educator Edmund Feldman (1970). This simple four step analysis requires students to interpret from direct observation of the artwork. Students are however urged to seek further information about the work to explore the intentionality of the maker.

Key questions for students

Using a formalist interpretive framework

1. Can you **describe** what can be seen eg. the medium used, objects depicted, figures, setting, narrative etc?
2. Can you **analyse** the use of art elements, compositional devices and style?
3. Can you **interpret** the intention of the artist i.e. the purpose or meaning of the work?
4. Can you **evaluate** the innovative significance of the work?

Use the four-stage formalist analysis to comment on works by these artists:

Australian artists

- Clarice Beckett (1887–1935)
- Charles Blackman (b. 1928)
- Arthur Boyd (1920–1999)
- Inge King (b. 1918)
- John Olsen (b. 1928)
- William Robinson (b. 1936)
- Fred Williams (1927–1982)

English artists

- Lucian Freud (b. 1922)
- Andy Goldsworthy (b. 1956)
- Patrick Heron (b. 1920)
- Howard Hodgkin (b. 1932)

Canadian artists

- Emily Carr (1871–1945)

USA artists

- Helen Frankenthaler (b. 1928)
- Jackson Pollock (1912–1956)
- Mark Rothko (1903–1970)

2. Deconstruction as an interpretive framework

Whereas formalist approaches to interpretation focus on the surface structure of artworks, postmodern writers (such as Jacques Derrida) and many contemporary artists (such as Jeff Koons) use deconstruction as a device to reveal the underlying suppositions upon which artworks are based. Deconstruction is used to peel away the layers of meaning of an artwork to expose 'taken for granted' notions implicit in the work, especially in relation to aspects of power and authority. Therefore deconstruction is often used to reveal relationships in respect of gender, class, culture and other social situations where there is a presumed hierarchy (hegemony) of authority. Postmodern art critics may deconstruct art from any era (pre-modern, modern or postmodern) with the purpose of commenting on the established values implicit in the work. Because it is often a form of commentary, deconstruction (in visual and verbal form) often relies on strategies such as irony, parody and pastiche to 'debunk' or 'send up' mythical or iconic values. These values may have previously been considered as serious subject matter or technique in art. In other words deconstruction is a strategy which exposes ‘the rules of the game’; it identifies the codes and practices which determine the aesthetic climate in which artworks have been made or in which they are viewed.

Deconstruction may also be used as a device to show that there are often inconsistencies of interpretation within artworks. The notion that there can be a fixed and stable meaning of an artwork is challenged through deconstruction to reveal that meaning is constantly reconstructed by viewers who bring to the work their own interpretation and use of language. Deconstruction can therefore be used to reveal the sources of influence which have shaped the meaning of an artwork. Postmodern theorists suggest that both artists and viewers are influenced by everything else they have ever seen and read and thus nothing can be original or neutral. This means that artworks are always products which refer to other artworks and other texts. Deconstruction then can be a way of revealing the other texts which have impacted on the artist and the work. This is often referred to as intertextuality; the notion that meaning of one artwork is always constructed in relation to other artworks.

Key questions for students

When deconstructing artworks

1. Does the work reference other works?
2. What social and cultural influences are apparent in the work (is it western, traditional, consistent in style with other artworks, or familiar in any way?)
3. What does the work say about values of the time of making? (or at the time of viewing?)
4. Is the work itself postmodern? What devices have been used eg parody, satire, appropriation, irony etc?
5. What does the work say about power, patterns of authority or marginalisation?

Deconstruct works by these artists:

Australian artists

- Rose Farrell (b. 1949) and George Parkin (b. 1949)
- Les Kossatz (b. 1943)
- Patricia Piccinini (b. 1965)
- Imants Tillers (b. 1950)
- Anne Zahalka (b. 1957)

English artists

- Christine Borland (1965)
- Gavin Turk (b. 1967)

American artists

- Jenny Holzer (b. 1950)
- Barbara Kruger (b. 1945)
- Andres Serrano (b. 1950)

Japanese artist

- Yasumasa Morimura (b. 1950)

3. A gender interpretive framework

While some feminists have attempted to join the modernist movement others have reacted to modernism by developing postmodern views which reject patriarchal art movements. Therefore while some feminist thinkers and artists claim to be part of the established modernist art world others claim that feminist art is quite different to male oriented art. Either way it is useful to examine how art serves to establish and reinforce gender attitudes and roles. When using a gender interpretive framework the focus can be upon identifying the ways in which the artwork seems feminine or masculine. This may involve examining the viewer's own perceptions of such qualities and comparing them with those conveyed in the artwork. If the work contains figures the relationship between the figures can be examined to see how the work conveys stereotypical roles and hegemony (domination and subordination). The work may also be examined to see what it reveals about societal expectations of gender.

The viewer can also view the work through masculinist eyes and examine it as a statement of masculinity. In this way the work may be seen to reinforce stereotypical values about how men should perform or behave. Students can then examine whether their own situation matches that depicted in the artwork. Viewers need to consider whose viewpoint is being advantaged in the work and whether the image suggests aspects of power, domination, subordination or any aspect of inequality.

The following framework for socially critical analysis of artworks by gender has been adapted from a model developed by Annie Reid (Reid, 1985). The model is based on the assumption that students firstly understand that all knowledge about art is socially constructed. This is based on the premise that there is no fixed and determined truth when it comes to the construction of gender social roles or status. These things are subject to change and are continually reconstructed within given societies and cultural settings.

Key questions for students

Using a gender interpretive framework

1. What is the social context of this work in time, place and class?
2. Whose values/beliefs do these social relations reflect?
3. How do these values compare with present day attitudes?
4. What does this work say about social expectation in relation to gender?
5. Does the work convey notions of power, relationships, domination?
6. What was the purpose of art at this time?
7. What have different writers said about this work?
8. What values/beliefs of my own have affected my interpretation?
9. What is the comparison between my own attitudes towards relationships of gender/class with those reflected in this artwork?

How do these artists comment on gender in their work?

Australian artists

- Juan Davila (b. 1946)
- Tracey Moffatt (b.1960)
- Sally Smart (b. 1960)
- Jenny Watson (b. 1951)

English artists

- Sarah Lucas (b. 1962)
- Paula Rego (b. 1935)

French artist

- Louise Bourgeois (b. 1911)

USA artists

- Judy Chicago (b. 1939)
- Georgia O'Keeffe (1887–1986)
- Cindy Sherman (b. 1954)

4. A cultural interpretive framework

One of the key challenges to modernist art is that it was a western set of art movements which served to marginalise and devalue non-western art and traditions. Post-colonial theorists have deconstructed modernist works to reveal the inherent racist attitudes embedded when non-western motifs have been incorporated or non-western people depicted in a subordinate way. Indigenous groups have established a strong voice in the postmodern art world and have established a niche in mainstream art markets. The increasingly multicultural nature of western societies has also forced a rethink about the ways in which predominantly western cultures have been conceived. Postcolonial western artists frequently expose the prejudices and injustices of society pertaining to issues such as land rights, discrimination and marginalisation. Indigenous artists explore similar themes and attempt to reconcile their dual cultural roles as indigenous people living in a western-oriented society. Issues of identity are also questioned relating to migrants and refugees who have attempted to resettle away from their country of origin.

Graham Chalmers (1996) suggests that student need to understand that art serves many different purposes and roles in different cultures and that students need to develop tolerance of a range of art forms. This may involve looking at artworks in diverse ways as non-western works may simply not conform to a western way of thinking about aesthetic values. When using a cultural interpretive framework students need to firstly consider whether the work was made as art or whether it served some other functional or spiritual purpose. The main focus is to establish understanding of the context of making and to recognise the way non-western 'artworks' are different because they are conceived within a different belief system.

When using cultural interpretive frameworks based on indigenous and post-colonial discourses students examine the contextuality of artworks and explore their own cultural positioning.

Key questions for students

Using a cultural interpretive framework

1. What is the purpose of this work?
2. Why was it originally made?
3. Who was supposed to see it?
4. What spiritual significance does it have for its maker and for the culture?
5. Is it displayed as it was intended?
6. Is it being viewed through western eyes?
7. Has it always been labelled as 'art'?

How do these artists comment on cultural issues in their work?

Australian artists

- Gordon Bennett (b. 1955)
- Emily Kame Kngwarreye (1910–1996)
- Trevor Nickolls (b. 1949)
- Lin Onus (1948-1996)
- Ginger Riley (b. 1937)
- Rover Thomas (1926–1998)

English artist

- Chris Ofili ((b. 1968)

Korean artist

- Ik-Joong Kang (b. 1960)

New Zealand artist

- Jacqueline Fraser (b. 1956)

Vietnamese artist

- Vu Dan Tan (b. 1946)

5. A semiotic interpretive framework

When viewers look at artworks they may recognise certain familiar images or objects. However, while objects may be read literally they may also represent ideas which are less literal. For example, a dog may be seen to represent faithfulness or white may represent death etc. The placement, size, materials or colour of objects may also produce meaningful ideas. Viewers need to ask 'What is in this work (objects, arrangement, colours etc.) that indicates some meaning?' Semiotics has become known as the study of sign systems focusing on how different cultures, societies and groups develop signs which may be seen to signify certain ideas. Football clubs, for example, use colours, logos and mascots to represent their club. In similar fashion different religions have symbols to represent ideas, and different people in society are known for their style of clothing, manner of speaking or behaviour. These things may be read as signs which indicate belief systems, codes of meaning or preference. Artworks also contain indicators or signs which often tell viewers how to interpret the work. For example, if an artwork is surrounded by a heavy gilt frame this may signify something about the status and attributed value of the work. If the work is painted on silk and displayed in a scroll format the viewer can determine some meaning from the actual format of the work.

In summary, viewers need to look for signs that indicate what a work might mean? Of course, it may mean many things, so viewers should look for more than one way in which the sign may be interpreted.

When using a semiotic interpretive framework the viewer looks for signs that signify meaning. What might these things symbolise, suggest or evoke? What do they represent?

Key questions for students

Using a semiotic interpretive framework

1. What overall meaning do I get from this work? (mood, ideas, feelings, associations)
2. What is the work saying or referring to?
3. What is familiar in the work? What might these things refer to?
4. Are the objects to be read literally or metaphorically?
5. What does the position of objects or people imply?
6. Are there any signs in this image that convey ideas about gender, class or race?

Explore signs and meanings in the works of these artists

Australian artist

- Stelarc (b. 1946)

Canadian artists

- Bruce Alfred (b. 1950)
- Joe David (b. 1946)

English artists

- Jake Chapman (b. 1966) and Dinos Chapman (b. 1962)
- Susan Hiller (b. 1940)
- Damien Hirst (b. 1965)
- Tim Noble (b. 1966) and Sue Webster (b. 1967)
- Gilbert Proesch (b. 1943) and George Pasmore (b. 1942)
- Rachel Whiteread (b. 1963)

German artist

- Rebecca Horn (b. 1944)

USA artists

- Christo (b. 1935) and Jeanne-Claude ((b. 1935)
- Roni Horn (b. 1955)

6. A psychoanalytic interpretive framework

Art critics and historians are fascinated to know how the mind of an artist works. In particular, art has often been connected with notions of individual identity, self and personality. The psychoanalytic theorist Sigmund Freud suggested that art manifested unconscious drives related to sexuality however later theorists have suggested other theories about the use of art as a manifestation of cognition, feelings and aesthetic disposition (e.g. Gardner, 1983). However while modernist theories gave prominence to individualism, postmodern theories conceive the individual as part of the social order. As such postmodernists would say that individuals are always products of their world, and what they make is always framed within a societal context that approves and values what is made. In other words modernists and postmodernists tend to think about individuality in different ways.

Many other theorists seem unsure whether making art is an act of sanity or madness. Some see it as a reasoned activity involving intellectual capacity while others see it as involving unconscious unfettered and involuntary action. Whatever thought processes are involved in making art, it does seem that viewers tend to believe that art is a window to the mind. This is not always a simple and direct notion and the path from artwork to interpretation of the mind is fraught with inconsistencies. This is especially so when it is understood that artists can manufacture all sorts of fantasies and imagined ideas in their art; ideas that could not possibly be part of their real lives. Computer generated art, for example, enables artists to invent many identities, none of which may be a reflection of their daily grind.

Psychoanalytic theoretical frameworks may be useful if viewers see some connection between the nature of the artwork and the life or beliefs of the artist. However, sometimes psychoanalysis can reveal more about the viewer than the artist as viewers can bring personal fantasies or interests to their interpretation of the work. So it is useful to declare personal interests when using psychoanalytic theory.

Key questions for students

Using a psychoanalytic interpretive framework

1. Is there a link between the life of the artist and the work?
2. Is this work the expression of the feeling and experience of the artist?
3. How does this work affect the viewer?
4. Are there deep-seated human emotions embodied in this work?
5. How do my own values and beliefs affect my interpretation?

Using a psychoanalytic framework explore the works of these artists

Australian artists

- Davida Allen (b. 1951)
- Peter Booth (b. 1940)
- George Gittoes (b. 1949)

English artists

- Tracey Emin (b. 1963)
- Gillian Wearing (b. 1963)

Italian artist

- Maurizio Cattelan (b. 1960)

Mexican artist

- Frida Kahlo (1907–1954)

New Zealand artist

- Colin McCohn (1919–1987)

7. A social realist interpretive framework (Marxist)

Marxist theorists suggest that art can be seen as a manifestation of class. In particular modernist art, by the mid 1960s was considered to have become an elitist activity, spoken about by those who understood the aesthetic language of abstraction and viewed by those who frequented art galleries. Art had come to be known as a western phenomenon which highly valued the fine art traditions of painting and sculpture but which marginalised non-western cultures and art forms such as craft, graphic arts, film and all forms of popular art (such as kitsch). This hierarchy of art forms was also reflected in the choice of subject matter. Still life, portraiture and landscape had become acceptable subject matter whereas images from mass culture were considered as aesthetically of a lower order. This aspect was challenged by Pop artists of the 1960s and artists such as Andy Warhol deliberately represented Campbell's soup cans to show that art could represent images from everyday life and mass culture.

When using a social realist interpretive framework focus is upon the portrayal of issues related to class. Issues of equality become significant as the viewer defines how the artwork represents class and issues of dominance and marginalisation. The viewer can try to define the intended audience of the work to determine how the work communicates certain understanding about social issues.

Key questions for students

Using social realist interpretive framework

1. What does this work say about class and social issues?
2. Whose voice is the work representing?
3. What political views are contested in the work?
4. Does the work comment on elitism, popular culture, the role of the common person etc?
5. Are there global issues involved?

How do works by these issues explore issues of class?

Australian artists

- Howard Arkley (1951-1999)
- Margaret Dodd (b. 1941)
- Elizabeth Gower (b. 1952)
- Maria Kozic (b. 1957)
- Reg Mombassa (b. 1951)

English artists

- Darren Almond (b. 1971)
- Julian Opie (b. 1958)
- Georgina Starr (b. 1968)
- Wolfgang Tillmans (b. 1968)

USA artists

- Keith Haring (1958-1990)
- Jeff Koons (b. 1955)
- Claes Oldenburg (b. 1929)
- Robert Rauschenberg (b. 1925)

Concluding comments

When the Australian digital artist Patricia Piccinini presents an image of a human ear being cloned on a mouse the viewer is confronted with complex signs. The work is immediately compelling because it seemingly belongs in the world of science and genetic engineering. It resonates because of its potential meaning for humanity and all forms of life and it begs us to question the meaning of art divorced from the power of critical social issues. This work is very much in the contemporary postmodern world. Although it has startling aesthetic attraction its aesthetic qualities are far distant from modernist notions of 'art for arts' sake'. By juxtaposing this work with Leonardo da Vinci's 'Mona Lisa' and Matisse's 'Woman with Green Stripe' viewers can use all seven interpretive frameworks to simultaneously focus on the representation of the self, gender, class, authority and culture. By examining signs in each image the viewer can infer differences between pre-modernist, modernist and postmodern artworks.

Teaching art in a postmodern world presents exciting possibilities for teachers and students. It enables art teachers to embrace modernist approaches to certain principles of western art making but also calls for teachers to embrace a wide range of social and cultural approaches. Interpretive frameworks equip students with a varied set of lenses through which to examine artworks. Art teachers in a postmodern world present students with a range of approaches and hope that students see and pursue an ever-expanding world of possibilities.

References

Addison, N. and Burgess, L. 2000, *Learning to Teach Art and Design in the Secondary School*, London, Routledge Falmer.

Aronowitz, S., & Giroux. H.A. 1991, *Postmodern Education: Politics, culture, and social criticism.* Minneapolis, University of Minnesota Press.

Ashley, K., Gilmore, L. & Peters. G. 1994, *Autobiography and Postmodernism*, Boston, University of Massachusetts Press.

Atkinson, R. 1995, *The Gift of Stories*, USA, Bergin and Garvey.

Barthes, R. 1977, 'The Death of the Author', in *Image—music—text*, NY, Hill and Wang

Battin, M. 1989, *Puzzles About Art: an aesthetic casebook,* NY, St Martin's Press.

Baudrillard, J. 1994 'The Masses: The Implosion of the Social in the Media', in *The Polity Reader in Cultural Theory*, Cambridge, Polity Press, (pp. 50–65).

Best, S. and Kellner, D. 1991, *Postmodern Theory: Critical interrogations*, London, Macmillan.

Bookchin, M. 1987, *The Modern Crisis*, Montreal, Black Rose Books.

Boughton, D. & Mason, R. 1999, *Beyond Multicultural Art Education: International Perspectives,* NY, Waxmann.

Bourdieu, P. 1994, 'The Field of Cultural Production', in *The Polity Reader in Cultural Theory*, Cambridge, Polity Press, (pp. 50–65).

Brooker, P. 1992, *Modernism/Postmodernism*, London, Longman.

Buck, L. 2000, *Moving Targets 2: A User's Guide to British Art Now*, London, Tate Publishing.

Caputo, J. 1987, *Radical Hermeneutics: Repetition, Deconstruction, and the Hermaneutic Project,* Bloomington, Indianna University Press.

Chadwick, W. 1992, *Women, Art and Society*, London, Thames and Hudson.

Chalmers, G. 1996, *Celebrating Pluralism: Art, Education and Cultural Diversity,* Los Angles, Getty Institute for the Arts.

Clark, R. 1996, *Art Education: Issues in Postmodern Pedagogy*, Virginia, NAEA.

Collier. P. and Davies. J. 1990, *Modernism and the European Unconscious*, Cambridge, Polity Press.

Danto, A. 1990, *Encounters and Reflections: Art in the Historical Present*, NY, Farrar Straus & Giroux.

Denzin, N. K. 1989, *Interpretive biographies*, USA, Sage.

Derrida, J. 1976, *Of Grammatology*, Baltimore, John Hopkins Press.

Dissanayake, E. 1990, What is Art For? USA, University of Washington.

Docherty, T. 1993, *Postmodernism: A Reader.* Great Britain, Harvester Wheatsheaf.

Efland, A., Freedman. K., and Stuhr. P., 1996, *Postmodern Art Education, An Approach to Curriculum*, Virginia, NAEA.

Efland, A. 1992, 'Curriculum Problems at Century's End: Art Education and Postmodernism', in *Power of Images*, Liisa Piironen (Ed.), Finland, InSEA.

Eisner, E. 1972, *Educating Artistic Vision*, New York, Macmillan.

Fehr, D. 1997, 'Clutching the Lectern, or Shouting from the Back of the Hall: A comparison of Modern and Postmodern Arts Education' in *Arts Education Policy Review,* March 1997, vol. 98: (p. 27).

Feldman, E. 1970, *Becoming Human through Art, Aesthetic Experience in the School*, New Jersey, Prentice-Hall.

Foucault, M. 1970, *The Order of Things: An Archaeology of the Human Sciences*, London, Tavistock.

Foucault, M. 1994, *The Archaeology of Knowledge*, trans. A.M. Sheridan Smith, London, Routledge, first published 1969.
Gablik, S. 1991, *The Reenchantment of Art*, London, Thames and Hudson.
Gardner, H. 1983, *Frames of Mind*, NY, Basic Books.
Gardner, H. 1999, *The Disciplined Mind*, NY, Simon and Schuster.
Giroux, H. & McLaren, P. 1994, *Between borders: Pedagogy and the Politics of Cultural Studies*, London, Routledge.
Giroux, H. 1991, 'Towards a Postmodern Pedagogy' in *From Modernism to Postmodernism: An Anthology*, Cahoone, Lawrence ed. Great Britain, Blackwell, (pp. 687–697).
Gombrich, E. H. 1950, *The Story of Art*, London, Phaidon.
Greenberg, C. 1961, *Art and Culture*, London, Thames and Hudson.
Hall, J. 2000, 'Art Education and Spirituality' in *Art Education 11–18: Meaning, purpose and direction*, R. Hickman, (ed.) London, Continuum, (pp. 133–151).
Harris, J. 2001, The New Art History: A Critical Introduction, NY, Routledge.
Harvey, D. 1989, *The Condition of Postmodernity*, USA, Basil Blackwell.
Hassan, I. 1996, POSTmodernISM: A Paracritical Bibliography' in *From Modernism to Postmodernism: An anthology*, Cahoone, Lawrence ed. Great Britain, Blackwell
Hickman, R. 1999, 'Representational Art and Islam—a case for further study', in *Beyond Multicultural Art Education: International Perspectives,* NY, Waxmann, (pp. 289–301).
Hickman, R. ed. 2000, *Art Education 11–18: Meaning, purpose and direction*, London, Continuum.
Hopwood, G. 1955, *Art Students' Handbook*, Melbourne, Graham Hopwood.
Janson, H. H. 1962, *History of Art*, London, Thames and Hudson.
Jencks, C. 1986, *What is Post-modernism*? NY, St Martin's Press.
Jencks, C. 1987, *Postmodernism—The New Classicism in Art and Architecture*, London, Academy editions.
Langer, S. 1953, *Feeling and form*, NY, Scribner.
Lowenfeld, V. 1950, *Creative and Mental Growth*: Revised Edition, NY, Macmillan.
Lyotard F. 1992, 'Answering the Question: What is Postmodernism?' in P. Brooker, *Modernism/Postmodernism*, London, Longman.
Lyotard, J.F. 1992, *The Postmodern Condition: A Report on Knowledge*, Manchester, Manchester University Press.
Meechan, P. and Sheldon, 2000, *Modern Art: A Critical Introduction*, London, Routledge.
Parker, S. 1997, *Reflective Teaching in the Postmodern World*, England, Open University Press
Read, H. 1943, *Education through Art,* NY, Pantheon.
Reid, A. 1985, 'Deconstruction: A methodology for exploring dominant ideologies and gendered relations in the visual arts', *Australian Art Education*, Vol. 18:2.
Sandler, I. 1996, *Art of the Postmodern Era*, NY, Harper Collins
Smith, R. 1992, 'Problems for a Philosophy of Art Education', *Studies in Art Education*, Vol. 33 4: (pp. 253–266).
Smuglia, H. 1991, *Re-visions: New perspectives of Art Criticism*, NJ., Prentice-Hall.
Taylor, B. 1987, *Modernism, Postmodernism, Realism: a critical perspective for art.* Hampshire, Winchester School of Art Press.
Turkle, S. 1995, *Life on the screen: Identity in the age of the internet*, London, Weidenfeld and Nicolson.
Usher, R. and Edwards, R. 1994, *Postmodernism and Education: cultural diversity*, Los Angles, Getty Education Institute.

Wigram, M. 2000 *Apocalypse: Beauty and Horror in Contemporary Art,* in Introduction to Exhibition Catalogue, Royal Academy of Art, London.
Williams, R. 1981, *Culture*, Great Britain, Fontana.
Wilson, B. & M. 1982 *Teaching Children to Draw*, NJ., Prentice-Hall.
Witkin, R. 1974, *The Intelligence of Feeling*, London, Heinemann.

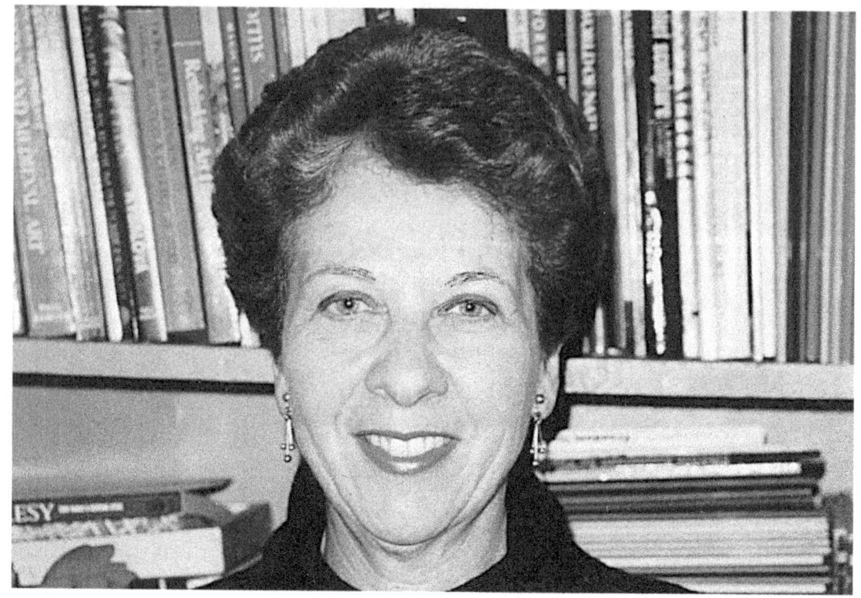

Lee Emery (Ph.D.) is Associate Professor in arts education at The University of Melbourne. She is a past editor of Australian Art Education and an honorary life member of the Australian Institute of Art Education.

www.ingramcontent.com/pod-product-compliance
Lightning Source LLC
LaVergne TN
LVHW020509100826
845148LV00003B/732

* 9 7 8 1 8 6 3 3 5 5 0 1 8 *